The Power of God to Heal

Also by George Garland

SUBJECT GUIDE TO BIBLE STORIES

The Power of God to Heal

All the accounts of healings in the Bible reproduced in their entirety

compiled by

George F. Garland

ROBERT H. SOMMER
PUBLISHER
HARRINGTON PARK, N.J. 07640
1983

LIBRARY OF CONGRESS CATALOG CARD

NUMBER 73-79273

PUBLISHED JUNE 1973

SECOND PRINTING 1983

To Milton Simon,
healer, advisor, friend,
who gave this book its title.

CONTENTS

1 FOREWORD ix

2 NEW TESTAMENT 1

174 selections of healings
and healing thoughts

3 OLD TESTAMENT 101

209 selections of healings
and healing thoughts

4 INDEX 233

Including diseases
reported healed in the Bible

FOREWORD

While mankind seeks healing in many directions, the power of God to heal through prayer is just as available today as it has always been. Though Jeremiah's rhetorical question, "Is anything too hard for God?" may still be asked, each one can find out in this book that to God no problem, physical or mental, is incurable.

In every age some spiritually minded men and women have proved this. As the Bible was being written (orally or by hand) its authors recorded accounts of the power of God to heal themselves and others who were sick, through prayer. How many healings are recorded in the Scriptures? Hundreds of them. You will find them all in this book.

This book begins with the New Testament because its stories are clearer and come nearer to the heart. Jesus, the healer by Gennesaret, was the greatest of all time. His healings are found in the New Testament. But it may surprise you to discover how many incidents of physical healings accomplished by prayerful men who preceded Jesus are recorded in the Old Testament. The healings selected in each Testament follow the order of the books of the Bible.

The King James Version was chosen because there are still more copies of this version in English-speaking homes than of recent translations of the Bible. And more people are familiar with the King James than any other, although the current sale of newer translations is considerable.

The selections in this book include healings of general sickness of the body and healings of discord related to specific parts of the body. They also refer to accidents, loss of the faculties, insanity, deformities—all problems which still face mankind. Narrative accounts are included which describe miracles of transportation, expansion of food quantities, supply during famine, the reversing of the law of the specific gravity of water and the changing of the substances of liquids. Included also are inspirational passages which relate to general health, strength, dominion over the elements; also to the overcoming of hunger, thirst, grief, heredity, poverty, loss, age, and decay.

The repeated inferences, particularly in the Old Testament, that sickness and death are the instruments by which God punishes man have no place in a book on Scriptural healings. These passages have caused a credibility gap and turned many individuals from faith to disbelief. They state the crude but widespread primitive view that plagues were sent by God. Such statements conflict with the more advanced concept of God as Spirit, Truth, and Love articulated by the more inspired Hebrew writers and leaders. Job denies that disease is God's punishment for his spiritual deficiency (Job 37: 23) and Jesus handles the same general point again by denying it (Luke 13: 1-5).

Jesus instructed his disciples to heal the sick. They did. You will see this from the records. Since Jesus prayed not only for his disciples alone but "for those also which shall believe on me through their word" (John 17: 20), his instructions about healing are for us too. His expectations for believers were great: "He that believeth on me, the works that I do shall he do also; and greater works than these shall he do; because I go unto my Father." (John 14: 12). He is talking to us too when he says "with God all things are possible" (Matthew 19: 26). So no physical problem is beyond the power of God to heal. In this book are the Scriptural demonstrations of that power.

This book is a non-sectarian compilation of Scripture. It is a response to increasing interest among the churches in fostering the healing of sickness as well as of sin. Efforts are being made not only to minister to the sick but to heal them just as successfully as sinners have been reformed. This book should promote the accomplishment of physical healing through prayer in all denominations for it presents the sacred healing word of the Bible. Isaiah gave us God's promise concerning His word: "So shall my word be that goeth forth out of my mouth: it shall not return unto me void, but it shall accomplish that which I please, and it shall prosper in the thing whereto I sent it." (Isaiah 55: 11).

New Testament

MATTHEW

Jesus' Healing Ministry

After teaching and preaching Jesus begins to illustrate what he said by healing all manner of sicknesses and diseases

Jesus went about all Galilee, teaching in their synagogues, and preaching the gospel of the kingdom, and healing all manner of sickness and all manner of disease among the people. His fame went throughout all Syria: and they brought unto him all sick people that were taken with divers diseases and torments, and those which were possessed with devils, and those which were lunatick, and those that had the palsy; and he healed them. There followed him great multitudes of people from Galilee, and from Decapolis, and from Jerusalem, and from Judaea, and from beyond Jordan. MAT 4. 23-25

Sermon on the Mount

Jesus lists the mental qualities that heal and make perfect

Seeing the multitudes, he went up into a mountain: and when he was set, his disciples came unto him: and he opened his mouth, and taught them, saying,

"Blessed are the poor in spirit: for theirs is the kingdom of heaven.

Blessed are they that mourn: for they shall be comforted.
Blessed are the meek: for they shall inherit the earth.
Blessed are they which do hunger and thirst after righteousness: for they shall be filled.
Blessed are the merciful: for they shall obtain mercy.
Blessed are the pure in heart: for they shall see God.
Blessed are the peacemakers: for they shall be called the children of God.

Be ye therefore perfect, even as your Father which is in heaven is perfect." MAT 5. 1-9, 48

HEALING PRAYER

Jesus offers his followers a method of prayer, other than public praying, by means of which they can do the works he did

"When thou prayest, enter into thy closet, and when thou hast shut thy door, pray to thy Father which is in secret; and thy Father which seeth in secret shall reward thee openly. But when ye pray, use not vain repetitions, as the heathen do: for they think that they shall be heard for their much speaking. Be not ye therefore like unto them: for your Father knoweth what things ye have need of, before ye ask him. After this manner therefore pray ye:

"Our Father which art in heaven, Hallowed be thy name.
Thy kingdom come.
Thy will be done in earth, as it is in heaven.
Give us this day our daily bread.
And forgive us our debts, as we forgive our debtors.
And lead us not into temptation, but deliver us from evil:
For thine is the kingdom, and the power, and the glory, for ever. Amen.

"The light of the body is the eye: if therefore thine eye be single, thy whole body shall be full of light. But if thine eye be evil, thy whole body shall be full of darkness. If therefore the light that is in thee be darkness, how great is that darkness!

"No man can serve two masters: for either he will hate the one, and love the other; or else he will hold to the one, and despise the other. Ye cannot serve God and mammon. Therefore I say unto you, Take no thought for your life, what ye shall eat, or what ye shall drink; nor yet for your body, what ye shall put on. Is not the life more than meat, and the body than raiment? Behold the fowls of the air: for they sow not, neither do they reap, nor gather into barns; yet your heavenly Father feedeth them. Are ye not much better than they? But seek ye first the kingdom of God, and his righteousness; and all these things shall be added unto you." MAT 6. 6-13, 22-26, 33
LUKE 11. 1-4

PETER'S MOTHER-IN-LAW HAS FEVER

Jesus quickly heals her and she waits on them. After supper he heals townspeople

When Jesus was come into Peter's house, he saw his wife's mother laid, and sick of a fever. He touched her hand, and the fever left her: and she arose, and ministered unto them. When the even was come, they brought unto him many that were possessed with devils: and he cast out the spirits with his word, and healed all that were sick: that it might be fulfilled which was spoken by Esaias the prophet, saying, "Himself took our infirmities, and bare our sicknesses." MAT 8. 14-17
MARK 1. 29-34
LUKE 4. 38-41

TWO BLIND MEN

Disregarding Jesus' instruction not to spread the news, they blaze abroad their healings to the multitude

When Jesus departed thence, two blind men followed him, crying, and saying, "Thou son of David, have mercy on us."

When he was come into the house, the blind men came to him: and Jesus saith unto them, "Believe ye that I am able to do this?" They said unto him, "Yea, Lord." Then touched he their eyes, saying, "According to your faith be it unto you." Their eyes were opened; and Jesus straitly charged them, saying, "See that no man know it." But they, when they were departed, spread abroad his fame in all that country.

MAT 9. 27-31

DUMB MAN SPEAKS

The Pharisees' reaction to Jesus' healings causes them to say that he heals through the devil

As they went out, behold, they brought to him a dumb man possessed with a devil. When the devil was cast out, the dumb spake: and the multitudes marvelled, saying, "It was never so seen in Israel." But the Pharisees said, "He casteth out devils through the prince of the devils." Jesus went about all the cities and villages, teaching in their synagogues, and preaching the gospel of the kingdom, and healing every sickness and every disease among the people. MAT 9. 32-35

MASTER'S COMMAND TO HEAL

He is able to teach the Twelve to preach and heal successfully

When he had called unto him his twelve disciples, he gave them power against unclean spirits, to cast them out, and to heal all manner of sickness and all manner of disease. These twelve Jesus sent forth, and commanded them, saying, "Go not into the way of the Gentiles, and into any city of the Samaritans enter ye not: but go rather to the lost sheep of the house of Israel. As ye go, preach, saying, 'The kingdom of heaven is at hand.' Heal the sick, cleanse the lepers, raise the dead, cast out devils: freely ye have received, freely give."

MAT 10. 1, 5-8

HAIRS ALL NUMBERED
The Father cares in detail for His creation

Are not two sparrows sold for a farthing? and one of them shall not fall on the ground without your Father. But the very hairs of your head are all numbered. Fear ye not therefore, ye are of more value than many sparrows. MAT 10. 29-31

HEALING WORKS PROVE JESUS IS THE CHRIST
John's doubts about Jesus are dispelled by his healings

It came to pass, when Jesus had made an end of commanding his twelve disciples, he departed thence to teach and to preach in their cities. Now when John had heard in the prison the works of Christ, he sent two of his disciples, and said unto him, "Art thou he that should come, or do we look for another?" Jesus answered and said unto them, "Go and shew John again those things which ye do hear and see: the blind receive their sight, and the lame walk, the lepers are cleansed, and the deaf hear, the dead are raised up, and the poor have the gospel preached to them. Blessed is he, whosoever shall not be offended in me.

"Come unto me, all ye that labour and are heavy laden, and I will give you rest. Take my yoke upon you, and learn of me; for I am meek and lowly in heart: and ye shall find rest unto your souls. For my yoke is easy, and my burden is light."

MAT 11. 1-6, 28-30

MULTITUDES HEALED
Jesus fulfills Isaiah's prophecy of the Messiah

Then the Pharisees went out, and held a council against him, how they might destroy him. But when Jesus knew it he withdrew himself from thence: and great multitudes followed him, and he healed them all; and charged them that they should not make him known: that it might be fulfilled which was spoken by Esaias the prophet, saying, "Behold my servant, whom I have chosen; my beloved, in whom my soul is well pleased: I will put my spirit upon him, and he shall shew judgment to the Gentiles. He shall not strive, nor cry; neither shall any man hear his voice in the streets. A bruised reed shall he not break, and smoking flax shall he not quench, till he send forth judgment unto victory. In his name shall the Gentiles trust." MAT 12. 14-21

BLIND AND DUMB

People amazed when man speaks and sees but Pharisees say it's the work of the devil

Then was brought unto him one possessed with a devil, blind, and dumb: and he healed him, insomuch that the blind and dumb both spake and saw. All the people were amazed, and said, "Is not this the son of David?" But when the Pharisees heard it, they said, "This fellow doth not cast out devils, but by Beelzebub the prince of the devils."

Jesus knew their thoughts, and said unto them, "Every kingdom divided against itself is brought to desolation; and every city or house divided against itself shall not stand: If Satan cast out Satan, he is divided against himself; how shall then his kingdom stand? If I by Beelzebub cast out devils, by whom do your children cast them out? therefore they shall be your judges. But if I cast out devils by the Spirit of God, then the kingdom of God is come unto you. Or else how can one enter into a strong man's house, and spoil his goods, except he first bind the strong man? and then he will spoil his house. He that is not with me is against me; and he that gathereth not with me scattereth abroad." MAT 12. 22-30

JESUS OVERCOMES GRAVITY

He saves Peter who tries to walk on the water too

Straightway Jesus constrained his disciples to get into a

ship, and to go before him unto the other side, while he sent the multitudes away. When he had sent the multitudes away, he went up into a mountain apart to pray: and when the evening was come, he was there alone. But the ship was now in the midst of the sea, tossed with waves: for the wind was contrary. In the fourth watch of the night Jesus went unto them, walking on the sea. When the disciples saw him walking on the sea, they were troubled, saying, "It is a spirit," and they cried out for fear. But straightway Jesus spake unto them, saying, "Be of good cheer; it is I; be not afraid."

Peter answered him and said, "Lord, if it be thou, bid me come unto thee on the water." He said, "Come." And when Peter was come down out of the ship, he walked on the water, to go to Jesus. But when he saw the wind boisterous, he was afraid; and beginning to sink, he cried, saying, "Lord, save me." Immediately Jesus stretched forth his hand, and caught him, and said unto him, "O thou of little faith, wherefore didst thou doubt?" When they were come into the ship, the wind ceased. Then they that were in the ship came and worshipped him, saying, "Of a truth thou art the Son of God." MAT 14. 22-33
MARK 6. 45-52

Touching the Hem of the Garment

The approach to Christ heals many diseased

When they were gone over, they came into the land of Gennesaret. When the men of that place had knowledge of him, they sent out into all that country round about, and brought unto him all that were diseased; and besought him that they might only touch the hem of his garment: and as many as touched were made perfectly whole. MAT 14. 34-36

A Mental Case

Jesus rewards a mother's persistence and heals her daughter

Then Jesus went thence, and departed into the coasts of

Tyre and Sidon. And, behold, a woman of Canaan came out of the same coasts and cried unto him, saying, "Have mercy on me, O Lord, thou son of David; my daughter is grievously vexed with a devil." But he answered her not a word. And his disciples came and besought him, saying, "Send her away; for she crieth after us." But he answered and said, "I am not sent but unto the lost sheep of the house of Israel." Then came she and worshipped him, saying, "Lord, help me." But he answered and said, "It is not meet to take the children's bread, and to cast it to dogs." And she said, "Truth, Lord: yet the dogs eat of the crumbs which fall from their masters' table." Then Jesus answered and said unto her, "O woman, great is thy faith: be it unto thee even as thou wilt." And her daughter was made whole from that very hour.

MAT 15. 21-28
MARK 7. 24-30

ANOTHER MULTITUDE HEALED, THEN FED

Lame, blind, dumb, maimed and others restored

Jesus departed from thence, and came nigh unto the sea of Galilee; and went up into a mountain, and sat down there. Great multitudes came unto him, having with them those that were lame, blind, dumb, maimed, and many others, and cast them down at Jesus' feet; and he healed them: insomuch that the multitude wondered, when they saw the dumb to speak, the maimed to be whole, the lame to walk, and the blind to see: and they glorified the God of Israel.

Then Jesus called his disciples unto him, and said, "I have compassion on the multitude, because they continue with me now three days, and have nothing to eat: and I will not send them away fasting, lest they faint in the way." His disciples say unto him, "Whence should we have so much bread in the wilderness, as to fill so great a multitude?" Jesus saith unto them, "How many loaves have ye?" And they said, "Seven, and a few little fishes." He commanded the multitude to sit down on the ground. He took the seven loaves and the fishes, and gave thanks, and brake them, and gave to his disciples, and the disciples to the multitude. They did all eat, and were filled: and they took up of the broken meat that was left seven baskets full. They that did eat were four thousand men, beside **women and children. And he sent away the multitude, and took ship, and came into the coasts of Magdala.** MAT 15. 29-39 MARK 8. 1-10

TAX MONEY FROM FISH

Jesus instructs Peter where to get ample supply

When they were come to Capernaum, they that received tribute money came to Peter, and said, "Doth not your master pay tribute?" He saith, "Yes." And when he was come into the house, Jesus prevented him, saying, "What thinkest thou, Simon? of whom do the kings of the earth take custom or tribute? of their own children, or of strangers?" Peter saith unto him, "Of strangers." Jesus saith unto him, "Then are the children free. Notwithstanding, lest we should offend them, go thou to the sea, and cast an hook, and take up the fish that first cometh up; and when thou hast opened his mouth, thou shalt find a piece of money: that take, and give unto them for me and thee." MAT 17. 24-27

RICH YOUNG MAN FORGOES ETERNAL LIFE

By clinging to his possessions he misses out on companionship with Jesus

It came to pass, that when Jesus had finished these sayings, he departed from Galilee, and came into the coasts of Judaea beyond Jordan; and great multitudes followed him; and he healed them there. Behold, one came and said unto him, "Good Master, what good thing shall I do, that I may have eternal life?" He said unto him, "Why callest thou me good? there is none good but one, that is, God: but if thou wilt enter into life, keep the commandments." He saith unto him, "Which?"

Jesus said, "Thou shalt do no murder, Thou shalt not commit adultery, Thou shalt not steal, Thou shalt not bear false witness, Honour thy father and thy mother: and, Thou shalt love thy neighbour as thyself." The young man saith unto him, "All these things have I kept from my youth up: what lack I yet?" Jesus said unto him, "If thou wilt be perfect, go and sell that thou hast, and give to the poor, and thou shalt have treasure in heaven: and come and follow me." But when the young man heard that saying, he went away sorrowful: for he had great possessions.

Then said Jesus unto his disciples, "Verily I say unto you, That a rich man shall hardly enter into the kingdom of heaven." "Again I say unto you, It is easier for a camel to go through the eye of a needle, than for a rich man to enter into the kingdom of God." When his disciples heard it, they were exceedingly amazed, saying, "Who then can be saved?" But Jesus beheld them, and said unto them, "With men this is impossible; but with God all things are possible."

MAT 19. 1, 2, 16-26
MARK 10. 17-22
LUKE 18. 18-27

FACULTIES REPRODUCED

Two blind men receive their sight

As they departed from Jericho, a great multitude followed him. And, behold, two blind men sitting by the way side, when they heard that Jesus passed by, cried out, saying, "Have mercy on us, O Lord, thou son of David." The multitude rebuked them, because they should hold their peace: but they cried the more, saying, "Have mercy on us, O Lord, thou son of David." Jesus stood still, and called them, and said, "What will ye that I shall do unto you?" They say unto him, "Lord, that our eyes may be opened." So Jesus had compassion on them, and touched their eyes: and immediately their eyes received sight, and they followed him.

MAT 20. 29-34

BLIND AND LAME HEALED
They come to him in the temple after he casts out the money changers

Jesus went into the temple of God, and cast out all them that sold and bought in the temple, and overthrew the tables of the money changers, and the seats of them that sold doves, and said unto them, "It is written, My house shall be called the house of prayer; but ye have made it a den of thieves." The blind and the lame came to him in the temple; and he healed them.

MAT 21. 12-14

FIG TREE WITHERED
Health depends on continual productivity

He left them, and went out of the city into Bethany; and he lodged there. Now in the morning as he returned into the city, he hungered. When he saw a fig tree in the way, he came to it, and found nothing thereon, but leaves only, and said unto it, "Let no fruit grow on thee henceforward for ever." And presently the fig tree withered away. When the disciples saw it, they marvelled, saying, "How soon is the fig tree withered away!" Jesus answered and said unto them, "Verily I say unto you, if ye have faith, and doubt not, ye shall not only do this which is done to the fig tree, but also if ye shall say unto this mountain, 'Be thou removed, and be thou cast into the sea,' it shall be done. All things, whatsoever ye shall ask in prayer, believing, ye shall receive."

MAT 21. 17-22
MARK 11. 12-14, 20-24

CRUCIFIXION
Following death on the cross, Jesus is buried

They crucified him, and parted his garments, casting lots. Jesus, when he had cried again with a loud voice, yielded up the ghost. And, behold, the veil of the temple was rent in twain from the top to the bottom; and the earth did quake, and the rocks rent; and the graves were opened; and many bodies of the saints which slept arose, and came out of the graves after his resurrection, and went into the holy city, and appeared unto many. Now when the centurion, and they that were with him, watching Jesus, saw the earthquake, and those things that were done, they feared greatly, saying, "Truly this was the Son of God." Many women were there beholding afar off, which followed Jesus from Galilee, ministering unto him: among which was Mary Magdalene, and Mary the mother of James and Joses, and the mother of Zebedee's children.

When Joseph had taken the body, he wrapped it in a clean linen cloth, and laid it in his own new tomb, which he had hewn out in the rock: and he rolled a great stone to the door of the sepulchre, and departed. So they went, and made the sepulchre sure, sealing the stone, and setting a watch.

MAT 27. 35, 50-56, 59, 60, 66

RESURRECTION

Jesus exhibits his raised body to disciples and commissions them to teach all nations

In the end of the sabbath, as it began to dawn toward the first day of the week, came Mary Magdalene and the other Mary to see the sepulchre. And, behold, there was a great earthquake: for the angel of the Lord descended from heaven, and came and rolled back the stone from the door, and sat upon it. His countenance was like lightning, and his raiment white as snow: and for fear of him the keepers did shake, and became as dead men. The angel answered and said unto the women, "Fear not ye: for I know that ye seek Jesus, which was crucified. He is not here: for he is risen, as he said. Come, see the place where the Lord lay. Go quickly, and tell his disciples that he is risen from the dead; and, behold, he goeth before you into Galilee; there shall ye see him: lo, I have told you." They departed quickly from the sepulchre with fear and great joy; and did run to bring his disciples word. As they went to tell his disciples, behold, Jesus met them, saying, "All hail." And they came and held him by the feet, and worshipped him. Then said Jesus unto them, "Be not afraid: go tell my brethren that they go into Galilee, and there shall they see me."

Then the eleven disciples went away into Galilee, into a mountain where Jesus had appointed them. When they saw him, they worshipped him: but some doubted. Jesus came and spake unto them, saying, "All power is given unto me in heaven and in earth. Go ye therefore, and teach all nations, baptizing them in the name of the Father, and of the Son, and of the Holy Ghost: Teaching them to observe all things whatsoever I have commanded you: and, lo, I am with you alway, even unto the end of the world. Amen." MAT 28. 1-10, 16-20

MARK

UNCLEAN SPIRIT CAST OUT

After verbally convincing the synogogue of his authority, Jesus then demonstrated his ability to heal a mental case

They went into Capernaum; and straightway on the sabbath day he entered into the synagogue, and taught. They were astonished at his doctrine: for he taught them as one that had authority, and not as the scribes. There was in their synagogue a man with an unclean spirit; and he cried out, saying, "Let us alone; what have we to do with thee, thou Jesus of Nazareth? art thou come to destroy us? I know thee who thou art, the Holy One of God." Jesus rebuked him, saying, "Hold thy peace, and come out of him." When the unclean spirit had torn him, and cried with a loud voice, he came out of him. They were all amazed, insomuch that they questioned among themselves, saying, "What thing is this? what new doctrine is this? for with authority commandeth he even the unclean spirits, and they do obey him." Immediately his fame spread abroad throughout all the region round about Galilee. MARK 1. 21-28 LUKE 4. 33-37

LEPROSY CLEANSED

Jesus shows his immunity to contagion by touching the leper, then heals him

There came a leper to him, beseeching him, and kneeling down to him, and saying unto him, "If thou wilt, thou canst make me clean." Jesus, moved with compassion, put forth his hand, and touched him, and saith unto him, "I will; be thou clean." As soon as he had spoken, immediately the leprosy departed from him, and he was cleansed. He straitly charged him, and forthwith sent him away; and saith unto him, "See thou say nothing to any man: but go thy way, shew thyself to the priest, and offer for thy cleansing those things which Moses commanded, for a testimony unto them." But he went out, and began to publish it much, and to blaze abroad the matter, insomuch that Jesus could no more openly enter into the city, but was without in desert places: and they came to him from every quarter. MARK 1. 40-45 MAT 8. 1-4 LUKE 5. 12-16

PARALYTIC LET DOWN THROUGH THE ROOF

Jesus asserts his authority to forgive sins as well as heal the body

Again he entered into Capernaum after some days; and it was noised that he was in the house. Straightway many were gathered together, insomuch that there was no room to receive them, no, not so much as about the door: and he preached the word unto them. They come unto him, bringing one sick of the palsy, which was borne of four. When they could not come nigh unto him for the press, they uncovered the roof where he was: and when they had broken it up, they let down the bed wherein the sick of the palsy lay. When Jesus saw their faith, he said unto the sick of the palsy, "Son, thy sins be forgiven thee."

But there were certain of the scribes sitting there, and reasoning in their hearts, "Why doth this man thus speak blasphemies? who can forgive sins but God only?" Immediately when Jesus perceived in his spirit that they so reasoned within themselves, he said unto them, "Why reason ye these things in your hearts? Whether is it easier to say to the sick of the palsy, 'Thy sins be forgiven thee,' or to say, 'Arise, and take up thy bed, and walk'? But that ye may know that the Son of man hath power on earth to forgive sins" (he saith to the sick of the palsy,) "I say unto thee, Arise, and take up thy bed, and go thy way into thine house." Immediately he arose, took up the bed, and went forth before them all; insomuch that they were all amazed, and glorified God, saying, "We never saw it on this fashion."

MARK 2. 1-12
MAT 9. 1-8
LUKE 5. 18-26

PLAGUES AND MENTAL ILLNESSES CAST OUT
Multitudes press upon Jesus to touch him

The Pharisees went forth, and straightway took counsel with the Herodians against him, how they might destroy him. But Jesus withdrew himself with his disciples to the sea: and a great multitude from Galilee followed him, and from Judaea, and from Jerusalem, and from Idumaea, and from beyond Jordan; and they about Tyre and Sidon, a great multitude, when they had heard what great things he did, came unto him. He spake to his disciples, that a small ship should wait on him because of the multitude, lest they should throng him. For he had healed many; insomuch that they pressed upon him for to touch him, as many as had plagues. Unclean spirits, when they saw him, fell down before him, and cried, saying, "Thou art the Son of God." He straitly charged them that they should not make him known.

MARK 3. 6-12

Disciples Taught to Heal

Jesus shows them how to heal physical and mental problems but scribes accuse him of Satanic power

He goeth up into a mountain, and calleth unto him whom he would: and they came unto him. He ordained twelve, that they should be with him, and that he might send them forth to preach, and to have power to heal sicknesses, and to cast out devils: and the scribes which came down from Jerusalem said, "He hath Beelzebub, and by the prince of the devils casteth he out devils." He called them unto him, and said unto them in parables, "How can Satan cast out Satan? If a kingdom be divided against itself, that kingdom cannot stand. If a house be divided against itself, that house cannot stand. And if Satan rise up against himself, and be divided, he cannot stand, but hath an end. No man can enter into a strong man's house, and spoil his goods, except he will first bind the strong man; and then he will spoil his house."

MARK 3. 13-15
22-27

Insanity Cured

Violent lunatic restored to his right mind

They came over unto the other side of the sea, into the country of the Gadarenes. When he was come out of the ship, immediately there met him out of the tombs a man with an unclean spirit, who had his dwelling among the tombs; and no man could bind him, no, not with chains: because that he had been often bound with fetters and chains, and the chains had been plucked asunder by him, and the fetters broken in pieces: neither could any man tame him. Always, night and day, he was in the mountains, and in the tombs, crying, and cutting himself with stones. But when he saw Jesus afar off, he ran and worshipped him, and cried with a loud voice, and said, "What have I to do with thee, Jesus, thou Son of the most high God? I adjure thee by God, that thou torment me not." For he said unto him, "Come out of the man, thou unclean spirit." He asked him, "What is thy name?" And he answered, saying, "My name is Legion: for we are many." He besought him much that he would not send them away out of the country.

Now there was there nigh unto the mountains a great herd of swine feeding. All the devils besought him, saying, "Send us into the swine, that we may enter into them." Forthwith Jesus gave them leave. And the unclean spirits went out, and entered into the swine: and the herd ran violently down a steep place into the sea, (they were about two thousand;) and were choked in the sea.

They that fed the swine fled, and told it in the city, and in the country. And they went out to see what it was that was done. They come to Jesus, and see him that was possessed with the devil, and had the legion, sitting, and clothed, and in his right mind: and they were afraid. They that saw it told them how it befell to him that was possessed with the devil, and also concerning the swine. They began to pray him to depart out of their coasts. When he was come into the ship, he that had been possessed with the devil prayed him that he might be with him. Howbeit Jesus suffered him not, but saith unto him, "Go home to thy friends, and tell them how great things the Lord hath done for thee and hath had compassion on thee." He departed, and began to publish in Decapolis how great things Jesus had done for him: and all men did marvel.

MARK 5. 1-20
MAT 8. 28-32
LUKE 8. 26-40

DEAD GIRL REVIVED

Jesus reduces father's fear, asks him to have faith, and restores life to the twelve-year-old

When Jesus was passed over again by ship unto the other side, much people gathered unto him: and he was nigh unto the sea. And, behold, there cometh one of the rulers of the synagogue, Jairus by name; and when he saw him, he fell at his feet, and besought him greatly, saying, "My little daughter lieth at the point of death: I pray thee, come and lay thy hands on her, that she may be healed; and she shall live." Jesus went with him; and much people followed him, and thronged him.

While he yet spake, there came from the ruler of the synagogue's house certain which said, "Thy daughter is dead: why troublest thou the Master any further?" As soon as Jesus heard the word that was spoken, he saith unto the ruler of the synagogue, "Be not afraid, only believe." He suffered no man to follow him, save Peter, and James, and John the brother of James. He cometh to the house of the ruler of the synagogue, and seeth the tumult, and them that wept and wailed greatly. When he was come in, he saith unto them, "Why make ye this ado, and weep? the damsel is not dead, but sleepeth." They laughed him to scorn. But when he had put them all out, he taketh the father and the mother of the damsel, and them that were with him, and entereth in where the damsel was lying. He took the damsel by the hand, and said unto her, "Talitha cumi," which is, being interpreted, "Damsel, I say unto thee, arise." Straightway the damsel arose, and walked; for she was of the age of twelve years. And they were astonished with a great astonishment. He charged them straitly that no man should know it; and commanded that something should be given her to eat.

MARK 5. 21-24, 35-43
MAT 9. 18, 19, 23-26
LUKE 8. 41,42,49-56

HEMORRHAGE DRIED UP

Woman who could not be healed by doctors admits that she was healed when she approached the Christ

A certain woman, which had an issue of blood twelve years, and had suffered many things of many physicians, and had spent all that she had, and was nothing bettered, but rather grew worse, when she had heard of Jesus, came in the press behind, and touched his garment. For she said, "If I may touch but his clothes, I shall be whole." Straightway the fountain of her blood was dried up; and she felt in her body that she was healed of that plague. Jesus, immediately knowing in himself that virtue had gone out of him, turned him about in the press, and said, "Who touched my clothes?" His disciples said unto him, "Thou seest the multitude thronging thee, and sayest thou, 'Who touched me?'" He looked round about to see her that had done this thing. But the woman fearing and trembling, knowing what was done in her, came and fell down before him, and told him all the truth. He said unto her, "Daughter, thy faith hath made thee whole; go in peace, and be whole of thy plague."

MARK 5. 25-34
MAT 9. 20-22
LUKE 8. 43-48

APOSTLES GIVEN POWER TO HEAL

Jesus gives 12 disciples instructions for their healing mission

He called unto him the twelve, and began to send them forth by two and two; and gave them power over unclean spirits; and commanded them that they should take nothing for their journey, save a staff only; no scrip, no bread, no money in their purse: but be shod with sandals; and not put on two coats. He said unto them, "In what place soever ye enter into an house, there abide till ye depart from that place. Whosoever shall not receive you, nor hear you, when ye depart thence, shake off the dust under your feet for a testimony against them. Verily I say unto you, It shall be more tolerable for Sodom and Gomorrha in the day of judgment, than for that city." They went out, and preached that men should repent. They cast out many devils, and anointed with oil many that were sick, and healed them.

MARK 6. 7-13

CHRIST MAKES WHOLE THE SICK

People throng his path and lay the sick in the streets

When they had passed over, they came into the land of Gennesaret, and drew to the shore. When they were come out of the ship, straightway they knew him, and ran through that whole region round about, and began to carry about in beds those that were sick, where they heard he was. Whithersoever he entered, into villages, or cities, or country, they laid the sick in the streets, and besought him that they might touch if it were but the border of his garment: and as many as touched him were made whole. MARK 6. 53-56

DEAF WITH SPEECH IMPEDIMENT

Through sign language and in stages Jesus heals the deaf mute

Again, departing from the coasts of Tyre and Sidon, he came unto the Sea of Galilee, through the midst of the coasts of Decapolis. They bring unto him one that was deaf, and had an impediment in his speech; and they beseech him to put his hand upon him. He took him aside from the multitude, and put his fingers into his ears, and he spit, and touched his tongue; and looking up to heaven, he sighed, and saith unto him, "Ephphatha," that is, "Be opened." Straightway his ears were opened, and the string of his tongue was loosed, and he spake plain. He charged them that they should tell no man: but the more he charged them, so much the more a great deal they published it; and were beyond measure astonished, saying, "He hath done all things well: he maketh both the deaf to hear, and the dumb to speak." MARK 7. 31-37

UNDERSTANDING AS THE BASIS OF ABUNDANCE

Jesus reminds disciples of source of supply

He left them, and entering into the ship again departed to the other side. Now the disciples had forgotten to take bread, neither had they in the ship with them more than one loaf. He charged them, saying, "Take heed, beware of the leaven of the Pharisees, and of the leaven of Herod." They reasoned among themselves, saying, "It is because we have no bread." When Jesus knew it, he saith unto them, "Why reason ye, because ye have no bread? perceive ye not yet, neither understand? have ye your heart yet hardened? Having eyes, see ye not? and having ears, hear ye not? and do ye not remember? When I brake the five loaves among five thousand, how many baskets full of fragments took ye up?" They say unto him, "Twelve." "When the seven among four thousand, how many baskets full of fragments took ye up?" And they said, "Seven." And he said unto them, "How is it that ye do not understand?"

MARK 8. 13-21

BLIND MAN RECEIVES PARTIAL SIGHT, THEN FULL

Jesus cures him in two treatments

And he cometh to Bethsaida; and they bring a blind man unto him, and besought him to touch him. He took the blind man by the hand, and led him out of the town; and when he had spit on his eyes, and put his hands upon him, he asked him if he saw ought. He looked up, and said, "I see men as trees, walking." After that he put his hands again upon his eyes, and made him look up: and he was restored, and saw every man clearly. And he sent him away to his house, saying, "Neither go into the town, nor tell it to any in the town."

MARK 8. 22-26

BREAKING THE TIME BARRIER

Jesus talks with past prophets, Moses and Elijah

After six days Jesus taketh with him Peter, and James, and John, and leadeth them up into an high mountain apart by themselves: and he was transfigured before them. His raiment became shining, exceeding white as snow; so as no fuller on earth can white them. There appeared unto them Elias with Moses: and they were talking with Jesus. Peter answered and said to Jesus, "Master, it is good for us to be here: and let us make three tabernacles; one for thee, and one for Moses, and one for Elias." For he wist not what to say; for they were sore afraid. There was a cloud that overshadowed them: and a voice came out of the cloud, saying, "This is my beloved Son: hear him." Suddenly, when they had looked round about, they saw no man any more, save Jesus only with themselves.

As they came down from the mountain, he charged them that they should tell no man what things they had seen, till the Son of man were risen from the dead. They kept that saying with themselves, questioning one with another what the rising from the dead should mean. They asked him, saying, "Why say the scribes that Elias must first come?" He answered and told them, "Elias verily cometh first, and restoreth all things; and how it is written of the Son of man, that he must suffer many things, and be set at nought. But I say unto you, That Elias is indeed come, and they have done unto him whatsoever they listed, as it is written of him." MARK 9. 2-13

EPILEPTIC FITS CURED

When disciples fail, Jesus heals boy and explains that greater healing power comes from prayer and fasting

When he came to his disciples, he saw a great multitude about them, and the scribes questioning with them. Straightway all the people, when they beheld him, were greatly amazed, and running to him saluted him. He asked the scribes, "What question ye with them?" One of the multitude answered and said, "Master, I have brought unto thee my son, which hath a dumb spirit; and wheresoever he taketh him, he teareth him: and he foameth, and gnasheth with his teeth, and pineth away: and I spake to thy disciples that they should cast him out; and they could not." He answereth him, and saith, "O faithless generation, how long shall I be with you? how long shall I suffer you? bring him unto me." They brought him unto him: and when he saw him, straightway the spirit tare him; and he fell on the ground, and wallowed foaming.

He asked his father, "How long is it ago since this came unto him?" And he said, "Of a child. And ofttimes it hath cast him into the fire, and into the waters, to destroy him: but if thou canst do any thing, have compassion on us, and help us." Jesus said unto him, "If thou canst believe, all things are possible to him that believeth." Straightway the father of the child cried out, and said with tears, "Lord, I believe; help thou mine unbelief." When Jesus saw that the people came running together, he rebuked the foul spirit, saying unto him, "Thou dumb and deaf spirit, I charge thee, come out of him, and enter no more into him." The spirit cried, and rent him sore, and came out of him: and he was as one dead; insomuch that many said, He is dead. But Jesus took him by the hand, and lifted him up; and he arose.

When he was come into the house, his disciples asked him privately, "Why could not we cast him out?" And he said unto them, "This kind can come forth by nothing, but by prayer and fasting." They departed thence, and passed through Galilee; and he would not that any man should know it.

MARK 9. 14-30
MAT 17. 14-23
LUKE 9. 37-43

BLIND BARTIMAEUS

His persistent crying out was rewarded by Jesus' gift of sight

They came to Jericho: and as he went out of Jericho with his disciples and a great number of people, blind Bartimaeus, the son of Timaeus, sat by the highway side begging. When he heard that it was Jesus of Nazareth, he began to cry out, and say, "Jesus, thou son of David, have mercy on me." Many charged him that he should hold his peace: but he cried the more a great deal, "Thou son of David, have mercy on me." Jesus stood still, and commanded him to be called. And they call the blind man, saying unto him, "Be of good comfort, rise; he calleth thee." He, casting away his garment, rose, and came to Jesus. Jesus answered and said unto him, "What wilt thou that I should do unto thee?" The blind man said unto him, "Lord, that I might receive my sight." And Jesus said unto him, "Go thy way; thy faith hath made thee whole." And immediately he received his sight, and followed Jesus in the way. MARK 10. 46-52 LUKE 18. 35-43

To Receive You Must Believe

Mountains of obstructions are removed

Verily I say unto you, That whosoever shall say unto this mountain, "Be thou removed, and be thou cast into the sea," and shall not doubt in his heart, but shall believe that those things which he saith shall come to pass; he shall have whatsoever he saith. Therefore I say unto you, What things soever ye desire, when ye pray, believe that ye receive them, and ye shall have them. MARK 11. 23, 24

Body in Sepulchre

Stone rolled to block entrance

It was the third hour, and they crucified him. Jesus cried with a loud voice and gave up the ghost. Joseph of Arimathaea, an honourable counsellor, which also waited for the kingdom of God, came, and went in boldly unto Pilate, and craved the body of Jesus. Pilate marvelled if he were already dead: and calling unto him the centurion, he asked him whether he had been any while dead. When he knew it of the centurion, he gave the body to Joseph. He bought fine linen, and took him down, and wrapped him in the linen, and laid him in a sepulchre which was hewn out of a rock, and rolled a stone unto the door of the sepulchre. MARK 15. 25, 37, 43-46

Risen!

The Magdalene reports seeing the resurrected Jesus

When the sabbath was past, Mary Magdalene, and Mary the mother of James, and Salome, had brought sweet spices, that they might come and anoint him. Very early in the morning the first day of the week, they came unto the sepulchre at the rising of the sun. They said among themselves, "Who shall roll us away the stone from the door of the sepulchre?" When they looked, they saw that the stone was rolled away: for it was very great. Entering into the sepulchre, they saw a young man sitting on the right side, clothed in a long white garment; and they were affrighted. He saith unto them, "Be not affrighted: ye seek Jesus of Nazareth, which was crucified: he is risen; he is not here: behold the place where they laid him. But go your way, tell his disciples and Peter that he goeth before you into Galilee: there shall ye see him, as he said unto you." They went out quickly, and fled from the sepulchre; for they trembled and were amazed: neither said they any thing to any man; for they were afraid.

Now when Jesus was risen early the first day of the week, he appeared first to Mary Magdalene, out of whom he had cast seven devils. She went and told them that had been with him, as they mourned and wept. They, when they had heard that he was alive, and had been seen of her, believed not.

MARK 16. 1-11

PERIOD BEFORE ASCENSION

Risen Jesus assures disciples signs of healing will result from faith

After that he appeared in another form unto two of them, as they walked, and went into the country. And they went and told it unto the residue: neither believed they them. Afterward he appeared unto the eleven as they sat at meat, and upbraided them with their unbelief and hardness of heart, because they believed not them which had seen him after he was risen. And he said unto them, "Go ye into all the world, and preach the gospel to every creature. He that believeth and is baptized shall be saved; but he that believeth not shall be damned. These signs shall follow them that believe; in my name shall they cast out devils; they shall speak with new tongues;

they shall take up serpents; and if they drink any deadly thing, it shall not hurt them; they shall lay hands on the sick, and they shall recover."

So then after the Lord had spoken unto them, he was received up into heaven, and sat on the right hand of God. And they went forth, and preached every where, the Lord working with them, and confirming the word with signs following.

MARK 16. 12-20

LUKE

MIRACULOUS CONCEPTION AND BIRTH

John the Baptist born to elderly barren woman.
Her husband, struck dumb by the news of the conception, recovers his voice after the birth

There was in the days of Herod, the king of Judaea, a certain priest named Zacharias, of the course of Abia: and his wife was of the daughters of Aaron, and her name was Elisabeth. They were both righteous before God, walking in all the commandments and ordinances of the Lord blameless. They had no child, because that Elisabeth was barren, and they both were now well stricken in years. It came to pass, that while he executed the priest's office before God in the order of his course, there appeared unto him an angel of the Lord standing on the right side of the altar of incense. When Zacharias saw him, he was troubled, and fear fell upon him. But the angel said unto him, "Fear not, Zacharias: for thy prayer is heard; and thy wife Elisabeth shall bear thee a son, and thou shalt call his name John." Zacharias said unto the angel, "Whereby shall I know this? for I am an old man, and my wife well stricken in years." And the angel answering said unto him, "I am Gabriel, that stand in the presence of God; and am sent to speak unto thee, and to shew thee these glad tidings. Behold, thou shalt be dumb, and not able to speak, until the day that these things shall be performed, because thou believest not my words, which shall be fulfilled in their season." The people waited for Zacharias, and marvelled that he tarried so long in the temple. When he came out, he could not speak unto them.

After those days his wife Elisabeth conceived, and hid herself five months, saying, "Thus hath the Lord dealt with me in the days wherein he looked on me, to take away my reproach among men." Now Elisabeth's full time came that she should be delivered; and she brought forth a son. Her neighbours and her cousins heard how the Lord had shewed great mercy upon her; and they rejoiced with her.

It came to pass, that on the eighth day they came to circumcise the child; and they called him Zacharias, after the name of his father. His mother answered and said, "Not so; but he shall be called John." They said unto her, "There is none of thy kindred that is called by this name. And they made signs to his father, how he would have him called. He asked for a writing table, and wrote, saying, "His name is John." And they marvelled all. His mouth was opened immediately, and his tongue loosed, and he spake, and praised God. Fear came on all that dwelt round about them: and all these sayings were noised abroad throughout all the hill country of Judaea. All they that heard them laid them up in their hearts, saying, "What manner of child shall this be!" And the hand of the Lord was with him.

His father Zacharias was filled with the Holy Ghost, and prophesied, saying, "Blessed be the Lord God of Israel; for he hath visited and redeemed his people, and hath raised up an horn of salvation for us in the house of his servant David; as he spake by the mouth of his holy prophets, which have been since the world began: that we should be saved from our enemies, and from the hand of all that hate us; to perform the mercy promised to our fathers, and to remember his holy covenant; the oath which he sware to our father Abraham, that he would grant unto us, that we being delivered out of the hand of our enemies might serve him without fear, in holiness and righteousness before him, all the days of our life. Thou, child, shalt be called the prophet of the Highest: for thou shalt go before the face of the Lord to prepare his ways; to give knowledge of salvation unto his people by the remission of their sins, through the tender mercy of our God; whereby the dayspring from on high hath visited us, to give light to them that sit in darkness and in the shadow of death, to guide our feet into the way of peace." The child grew, and waxed strong in spirit, and was in the deserts till the day of his shewing unto Israel.

LUKE 1. 5-8
11-13, 18-22
24, 25, 57-80

SALVATION PROPHESIED

John preaches that repentance prepares the way for the Messiah

The word of God came unto John the son of Zacharias in the wilderness. He came into all the country about Jordan, preaching the baptism of repentance for the remission of sins; as it is written in the book of the words of Esaias the prophet, saying, "The voice of one crying in the wilderness, Prepare ye the way of the Lord, make his paths straight. Every valley shall be filled, and every mountain and hill shall be brought low; and the crooked shall be made straight, and the rough ways shall be made smooth; and all flesh shall see the salvation of God."

LUKE 3. 2-6

SPIRIT ANOINTS JESUS TO HEAL

Jesus reads and quotes Scripture about himself and escapes assassination attempt

Jesus returned in the power of the Spirit into Galilee: and there went out a fame of him through all the region round about. He taught in their synagogues, being glorified of all. He came to Nazareth, where he had been brought up: and, as his custom was, he went into the synagogue on the sabbath day, and stood up for to read. There was delivered unto him the book of the prophet Esaias. And when he had opened the book, he found the place where it was written, "The Spirit of the Lord is upon me, because he hath anointed me to preach the gospel to the poor; he hath sent me to heal the broken-hearted, to preach deliverance to the captives, and recovering of sight to the blind, to set at liberty them that are bruised, to preach the acceptable year of the Lord." And he closed the book, and he gave it again to the minister, and sat down. And the eyes of all them that were in the synagogue were fastened on him.

He began to say unto them, "This day is this scripture fulfilled in your ears." All bare him witness, and wondered at the gracious words which proceeded out of his mouth. And they said, "Is not this Joseph's son?" He said unto them, "Ye will surely say unto me this proverb, 'Physician, heal thyself: whatsoever we have heard done in Capernaum, do also here in thy country.'" And he said, "Verily I say unto you, No prophet is accepted in his own country. But I tell you of a truth, many widows were in Israel in the days of Elias, when the heaven was shut up three years and six months, when great famine was throughout all the land; but unto none of them was Elias sent, save unto Sarepta, a city of Sidon, unto a woman that was a widow. Many lepers were in Israel in the time of Eliseus the prophet; and none of them was cleansed, saving Naaman the Syrian." All they in the synagogue, when they heard these things, were filled with wrath, and rose up, and thrust him out of the city, and led him unto the brow of the hill whereon their city was built, that they might cast him down headlong. But he passing through the midst of them went his way, and came down to Capernaum, a city of Galilee, and taught them on the sabbath days. They were astonished at his doctrine: for his word was with power. LUKE 4. 14-32

GREAT HAUL OF FISH

Disciples, convinced when Jesus overcomes lack, leave their former trade to "catch men"

It came to pass, that, as the people pressed upon him to hear the word of God, he stood by the lake of Gennesaret, and saw two ships standing by the lake: but the fishermen were gone out of them, and were washing their nets. He entered into one of the ships, which was Simon's, and prayed him that he would thrust out a little from the land. And he sat down, and taught the people out of the ship. Now when he had left speaking, he said unto Simon, "Launch out into the deep, and let down your nets for a draught." Simon answering said unto him, "Master, we have toiled all the night, and have taken nothing: nevertheless at thy word I will let down the net." When they had this done, they inclosed a great multitude of fishes: and their net brake. They beckoned unto their partners, which were in the other ship, that they should come and help them. And they came, and filled both the ships, so that they began to sink. When Simon Peter saw it, he fell down at Jesus' knees, saying, "Depart from me; for I am a sinful man, O Lord." For he was astonished, and all that were with him, at the draught of the fishes which they had taken: and so was also James, and John, the sons of Zebedee, which were partners with Simon. And Jesus said unto Simon, "Fear not; from henceforth thou shalt catch men." And when they had brought their ships to land, they forsook all and followed him.

LUKE 5. 1-11

POWER OF GOD TO HEAL

Jesus cures sick in the presence of clerical and legal opposition

He withdrew himself into the wilderness, and prayed. And it came to pass on a certain day, as he was teaching, that there were Pharisees and doctors of the law sitting by, which were come out of every town of Galilee, and Judaea, and Jerusalem: and the power of the Lord was present to heal them.

LUKE 5. 16, 17

WITHERED HAND STRETCHED FORTH

Deformed hand restored and Pharisees incensed. But healing of multitudes continues

It came to pass also on another sabbath, that he entered into the synagogue and taught; and there was a man whose right hand was withered. The scribes and Pharisees watched him, whether he would heal on the sabbath day; that they might find an accusation against him. But he knew their thoughts, and said to the man which had the withered hand, "Rise up, and stand forth in the midst." And he arose and stood forth. Then said Jesus unto them, "I will ask you one thing; Is it lawful on the sabbath days to do good, or to do evil? to save life, or to destroy it?" And looking round about upon them all, he said unto the man, "Stretch forth thy hand." And he did so: and his hand was restored whole as the other. They were filled with madness; and communed one with another what they might do to Jesus.

It came to pass in those days, that he went out into a mountain to pray, and continued all night in prayer to God. When day broke he called his disciples to him. He came down with them, and stood in the plain, and the company of his disciples, and a great multitude of people out of all Judaea and Jerusalem, and from the sea coast of Tyre and Sidon, which came to hear him, and to be healed of their diseases; and they that were vexed with unclean spirits: and they were healed. The whole multitude sought to touch him: for there went virtue out of him, and healed them all.

LUKE 6. 6-12, 13
17-19
MAT 12. 9-13
MARK 3. 1-5

FRIENDLY CENTURION'S SERVANT ON DEATH-BED

Soldier acknowledges Jesus' authority to heal even when not present with the patient.

Now when he had ended all his sayings in the audience of the people, he entered into Capernaum. A certain centurion's servant, who was dear unto him, was sick, and ready to die.

When he heard of Jesus, he sent unto him the elders of the Jews, beseeching him that he would come and heal his servant. When they came to Jesus, they besought him instantly, saying, that he was worthy for whom he should do this: "For he loveth our nation, and he hath built us a synagogue." Then Jesus went with them. And when he was now not far from the house, the centurion sent friends to him, saying unto him, "Lord, trouble not thyself: for I am not worthy that thou shouldest enter under my roof: wherefore neither thought I myself worthy to come unto thee: but say in a word, and my servant shall be healed. For I also am a man set under authority, having under me soldiers, and I say unto one, Go, and he goeth; and to another, Come, and he cometh; and to my servant, Do this, and he doeth it." When Jesus heard these things, he marvelled at him, and turned him about, and said unto the people that followed him, "I say unto you, I have not found so great faith, no, not in Israel." And they that were sent, returning to the house, found the servant whole that had been sick.

LUKE 7. 1-10
MAT 8. 5-10, 13

DEAD MAN RESTORED

Jesus has compassion on a widow and raises her son

It came to pass the day after, that he went into a city called Nain; and many of his disciples went with him, and much people. Now when he came nigh to the gate of the city, behold, there was a dead man carried out, the only son of his mother, and she was a widow: and much people of the city was with her. And when the Lord saw her, he had compassion on her, and said unto her, "Weep not." He came and touched the bier: and they that bare him stood still. And he said, "Young man, I say unto thee, Arise." He that was dead sat up, and began to speak. And he delivered him to his mother. There came a fear on all: and they glorified God, saying, "A great prophet is risen up among us" and "God hath visited his people." And this rumour of him went forth throughout all Judaea, and throughout all the region round about.

LUKE 7. 11-17

HEALING, THE PROOF OF CHRIST

John the Baptist is convinced that Jesus is the Messiah when Jesus demonstrates the power of God to heal

The disciples of John shewed him of all these things. John calling unto him two of his disciples sent them to Jesus, saying, "Art thou he that should come? or look we for another?" When the men were come unto him, they said, "John Baptist hath sent us unto thee, saying, Art thou he that should come? or look we for another?" In that same hour he cured many of their infirmities and plagues, and of evil spirits; and unto many that were blind he gave sight. Then Jesus answering said unto them, "Go your way, and tell John what things ye have seen and heard; how that the blind see, the lame walk, the lepers are cleansed, the deaf hear, the dead are raised, to the poor the gospel is preached. And blessed is he, whosoever shall not be offended in me." When the messengers of John were departed, he began to speak unto the people concerning John, "What went ye out into the wilderness for to see? A reed shaken with the wind?"

LUKE 7. 18-24

INCLEMENT WEATHER CONTROLLED

Jesus calms disciples' fear of shipwreck, rebukes tempest

Now it came to pass on a certain day, that he went into a ship with his disciples: and he said unto them, "Let us go over unto the other side of the lake." And they launched forth. But as they sailed he fell asleep: and there came down a storm of wind on the lake; and they were filled with water, and were in jeopardy. And they came to him, and awoke him, saying, "Master, master, we perish." Then he arose, and rebuked the wind and the raging of the water: and they ceased, and there was a calm. And he said unto them, "Where is your faith?" And they being afraid wondered, saying one to another, "What manner of man is this! for he commandeth even the winds and water, and they obey him."

LUKE 8. 22-25
MAT 8. 23-27
MARK 4. 35-41

Twelve Taught to Heal

Jesus proves he can teach others to use the power of God to heal

Then he called his twelve disciples together, and gave them power and authority over all devils, and to cure diseases. He sent them to preach the kingdom of God, and to heal the sick. And he said unto them, "Take nothing for your journey, neither staves, nor scrip, neither bread, neither money; neither have two coats apiece. Whatsoever house ye enter into, there abide, and thence depart. Whosoever will not receive you, when ye go out of that city, shake off the very dust from your feet for a testimony against them." They departed, and went through the towns, preaching the gospel, and healing every where. LUKE 9. 1-6

Those that Need Healing

Jesus relates the kingdom of God to healing

The people, when they knew it, followed him: and he received them, and spake unto them of the kingdom of God, and healed them that had need of healing. LUKE 9. 11

Retaliation by Disciples Not Permitted

Jesus will not harm village that forbad him to enter. He says he came to save, not destroy

They went, and entered into a village of the Samaritans, to make ready for him. And they did not receive him, because his face was as though he would go to Jerusalem. When his disciples James and John saw this, they said, "Lord, wilt thou that we command fire to come down from heaven, and consume them, even as Elias did?" But he turned, and rebuked them, and said, "Ye know not what manner of spirit ye are of. For the Son of man is not come to destroy men's lives, but to save them." And they went to another village. LUKE 9. 52-56

SEVENTY INSTRUCTED FOR HEALING MISSION

He commands them to heal in every city they enter

After these things the Lord appointed other seventy also, and sent them two and two before his face into every city and place, whither he himself would come. Therefore said he unto them, "The harvest truly is great, but the labourers are few: pray ye therefore the Lord of the harvest, that he would send forth labourers into his harvest. Go your ways: behold, I send you forth as lambs among wolves. Carry neither purse, nor scrip, nor shoes: and salute no man by the way. And into whatsoever house ye enter, first say, 'Peace be to this house.' And if the son of peace be there, your peace shall rest upon it: if not, it shall turn to you again. And in the same house remain, eating and drinking such things as they give: for the labourer is worthy of his hire. Go not from house to house. Into whatsoever city ye enter, and they receive you, eat such things as are set before you: and heal the sick that are therein, and say unto them, 'The kingdom of God is come nigh unto you.' "

LUKE 10. 1-9

ARE SIN AND DEATH RELATED?

Not necessarily, says Jesus, but unless you repent you shall perish

There were present at that season some that told him of the Galilaeans, whose blood Pilate had mingled with their sacrifices. And Jesus answering said unto them, "Suppose ye that these Galilaeans were sinners above all the Galilaeans, because they suffered such things? I tell you, Nay: but, except ye repent, ye shall all likewise perish. Or those eighteen, upon whom the tower in Siloam fell, and slew them, think ye that they were sinners above all men that dwelt in Jerusalem? I tell you, Nay: but, except ye repent, ye shall all likewise perish."

LUKE 13. 1-5

SPINAL DEFORMITY 18 YEARS

Woman instantly released and made straight on the Sabbath

And he was teaching in one of the synagogues on the sabbath. And, behold, there was a woman which had a spirit of infirmity eighteen years, and was bowed together, and could in no wise lift up herself. And when Jesus saw her, he called her to him, and said unto her, "Woman, thou art loosed from thine infirmity." And he laid his hands on her: and immediately she was made straight, and glorified God. And the ruler of the synagogue answered with indignation, because that Jesus had healed on the sabbath day, and said unto the people, "There are six days in which men ought to work: in them therefore come and be healed, and not on the sabbath day." The Lord then answered him, and said, "Thou hypocrite, doth not each one of you on the sabbath loose his ox or his ass from the stall, and lead him away to watering? And ought not this woman, being a daughter of Abraham, whom Satan hath bound, lo, these eighteen years, be loosed from this bond on the sabbath day?" When he had said these things, all his adversaries were ashamed: and all the people rejoiced for all the glorious things that were done by him. LUKE 13. 10-17

DROPSY HEALED

Unlawful healing on Sabbath observed by the power structure

It came to pass, as he went into the house of one of the chief Pharisees to eat bread on the sabbath day, that they watched him. And, behold, there was a certain man before him which had the dropsy. Jesus answering spake unto the lawyers and Pharisees, saying, "Is it lawful to heal on the sabbath day?" And they held their peace. And he took him, and healed him, and let him go; and answered them, saying, "Which of you shall have an ass or an ox fallen into a pit, and will not straightway pull him out on the sabbath day?" And they could not answer him again to these things. LUKE 14. 1-6

SUSTENANCE CONTINUOUS

Ever-presence reassures man

He said unto him, "Son, thou art ever with me, and all that I have is thine." LUKE 15. 31

TEN LEPERS HEALED AT ONCE

One returns to thank Jesus

It came to pass, as he went to Jerusalem, that he passed through the midst of Samaria and Galilee. As he entered into a certain village, there met him ten men that were lepers, which stood afar off: They lifted up their voices, and said, "Jesus, Master, have mercy on us. When he saw them, he said unto them, "Go shew yourselves unto the priests." And it came to pass, that, as they went, they were cleansed. One of them, when he saw that he was healed, turned back, and with a loud voice glorified God, and fell down on his face at his feet, giving him thanks: and he was a Samaritan. And Jesus answering said, "Were there not ten cleansed? but where are the nine? There are not found that returned to give glory to God, save this stranger." And he said unto him, "Arise, go thy way: thy faith hath made thee whole." LUKE 17. 11-19

AMPUTATED EAR REPLACED

While they are arresting him, Jesus heals the servant of the high priest

One of them smote the servant of the high priest, and cut off his right ear. And Jesus answered and said, "Suffer ye thus far." And he touched his ear, and healed him. LUKE 22. 50, 51

JESUS' BODY INTERRED WITH CARE

Placed in stone sepulchre by a just man

When Jesus had cried with a loud voice, he said, "Father, into thy hands I commend my spirit," and having said thus, he gave up the ghost. Now when the centurion saw what was done, he glorified God, saying, "Certainly this was a righteous man." And all the people that came together to that sight, beholding the things which were done, smote their breasts, and returned. And all his acquaintance, and the women that followed him from Galilee, stood afar off, beholding these things. And, behold, there was a man named Joseph, a counsellor; and he was a good man, and a just: (the same had not consented to the counsel and deed of them;) he was of Arimathaea, a city of the Jews: who also himself waited for the kingdom of God. This man went unto Pilate, and begged the body of Jesus. He took it down, and wrapped it in linen, and laid it in a sepulchre that was hewn in stone, wherein never man before was laid. LUKE 23. 46-53

JESUS' BODY DISAPPEARS
Stone rolled away and rumor spreads that he is risen

Now upon the first day of the week, very early in the morning, they came unto the sepulchre, bringing the spices which they had prepared, and certain others with them. They found the stone rolled away from the sepulchre. They entered in, and found not the body of the Lord Jesus. It came to pass, as they were much perplexed thereabout, behold, two men stood by them in shining garments: and as they were afraid, and bowed down their faces to the earth, they said unto them, "Why seek ye the living among the dead? He is not here, but is risen: remember how he spake unto you when he was yet in Galilee, saying, 'The Son of man must be delivered into the hands of sinful men, and be crucified, and the third day rise again.'" They remembered his words, and returned from the sepulchre, and told all these things unto the eleven, and to all the rest. It was Mary Magdalene, and Joanna, and Mary the mother of James, and other women that were with them, which told these things unto the apostles. Their words seemed to them as idle tales, and they believed them not. Then arose Peter, and ran unto the sepulchre; and stooping down, he beheld the linen clothes laid by themselves, and departed, wondering in himself at that which was come to pass. LUKE 24. 1-12

He Appears to Two Disciples

Spends the day and eats dinner with them. Then he visits with the eleven, eats in front of them and promises pentecostal power

Behold, two of them went that same day to a village called Emmaus, which was from Jerusalem about threescore furlongs. They talked together of all these things which had happened. And it came to pass, that, while they communed together and reasoned, Jesus himself drew near, and went with them. But their eyes were holden that they should not know him. He said unto them, "What manner of communications are these that ye have one to another, as ye walk, and are sad?" The one of them, whose name was Cleopas, answering said unto him, "Art thou only a stranger in Jerusalem, and hast not known the things which are come to pass there in these days?" And he said unto them, "What things?" And they said unto him, "Concerning Jesus of Nazareth, which was a prophet mighty in deed and word before God and all the people: and how the chief priests and our rulers delivered him to be condemned to death, and have crucified him. But we trusted that it had been he which should have redeemed Israel: and beside all this, today is the third day since these things were done. Yea, and certain women also of our company made us astonished, which were early at the sepulchre; and when they found not his body, they came, saying, that they had also seen a vision of angels, which said that he was alive. Certain of them which were with us went to the sepulchre, and found it even so as the women had said: but him they saw not."

Then he said unto them, "O fools, and slow of heart to believe all that the prophets have spoken: ought not Christ to have suffered these things, and to enter into his glory?" Beginning at Moses and all the prophets, he expounded unto them in all the scriptures the things concerning himself. They drew nigh unto the village, whither they went: and he made as though he would have gone further. But they constrained him, saying, "Abide with us: for it is toward evening, and the day is far spent." And he went in to tarry with them. It came to pass, as he sat at meat with them, he took bread, and blessed it, and brake, and gave to them. And their eyes were opened, and they knew him; and he vanished out of their sight. They said one to another, "Did not our heart burn within us, while he talked with us by the way, and while he opened to us the scriptures?"

They rose up the same hour, and returned to Jerusalem, and found the eleven gathered together, and them that were with them, saying, "The Lord is risen indeed, and hath appeared to Simon." And they told what things were done in the way, and how he was known of them in breaking of bread. As they thus spake, Jesus himself stood in the midst of them, and saith unto them, "Peace be unto you." But they were terrified and affrighted, and supposed that they had seen a spirit. And he said unto them, "Why are ye troubled? and why do thoughts arise in your hearts? Behold my hands and my feet, that it is I myself: handle me, and see; for a spirit hath not flesh and bones, as ye see me have." When he had thus spoken, he shewed them his hands and his feet. While they yet believed not for joy, and wondered, he said unto them, "Have ye here any meat?" They gave him a piece of a broiled fish, and of an honeycomb. He took it, and did eat before them.

He said unto them, "These are the words which I spake unto you, while I was yet with you, that all things must be fulfilled, which were written in the law of Moses, and in the prophets, and in the psalms, concerning me." Then opened he their understanding, that they might understand the scriptures, and said unto them, "Thus it is written, and thus it behoved

Christ to suffer, and to rise from the dead the third day: and that repentance and remission of sins should be preached in his name among all nations, beginning at Jerusalem. Ye are witnesses of these things. And, behold, I send the promise of my Father upon you: but tarry ye in the city of Jerusalem, until ye be endued with power from on high." LUKE 24. 13-49

Ascension

Disciples return to Jerusalem with joy

And he led them out as far as to Bethany, and he lifted up his hands, and blessed them. And it came to pass, while he blessed them, he was parted from them, and carried up into heaven. And they worshipped him, and returned to Jerusalem with great joy: and were continually in the temple, praising and blessing God. Amen. LUKE 24. 50-53

JOHN

All Things Made by the Word of God

Without Him nothing was made.

In the beginning was the Word, and the Word was with God, and the Word was God. The same was in the beginning with God. All things were made by him; and without him was not any thing made that was made. In him was life; and the life was the light of men. The light shineth in darkness; and the darkness comprehended it not. JOHN 1. 1-5

Water Turned into Wine

The Christ furnishes a wedding with inspiration

The third day there was a marriage in Cana of Galilee; and the mother of Jesus was there: and both Jesus was called, and his disciples, to the marriage. When they wanted wine, the mother of Jesus saith unto him, "They have no wine." Jesus saith unto her, "Woman, what have I to do with thee? mine hour is not yet come." His mother saith unto the servants, "Whatsoever he saith unto you, do it." There were set there six waterpots of stone, after the manner of the purifying of the Jews, containing two or three firkins apiece. Jesus saith unto them, "Fill the waterpots with water." And they filled them up to the brim. He saith unto them, "Draw out now, and bear unto the governor of the feast." And they bare it.

When the ruler of the feast had tasted the water that was made wine, and knew not whence it was: (but the servants which drew the water knew;) the governor of the feast called the bridegroom, and saith unto him, "Every man at the beginning doth set forth good wine; and when men have well drunk, then that which is worse: but thou hast kept the good wine until now." This beginning of miracles did Jesus in Cana of Galilee, and manifested forth his glory; and his disciples believed on him. JOHN 2. 1-11

THE TEMPLE OF THE BODY

Jesus prophesies that the raising of his body will take three days

Then answered the Jews and said unto him, "What sign shewest thou unto us, seeing that thou doest these things?" Jesus answered and said unto them, "Destroy this temple, and in three days I will raise it up." Then said the Jews, "Forty and six years was this temple in building, and wilt thou rear it up in three days?" But he spake of the temple of his body. When therefore he was risen from the dead, his disciples remembered that he had said this unto them; and they believed the scripture, and the word which Jesus had said.

JOHN 2. 18-22

HOW TO HAVE ETERNAL LIFE

By lifting up the son of man

As Moses lifted up the serpent in the wilderness, even so must the Son of man be lifted up: that whosoever believeth in him should not perish, but have eternal life. JOHN 3. 14, 15

PROSPECT OF EVERLASTING LIFE

Just believe on the son

The Father loveth the Son, and hath given all things into his hand. He that believeth on the Son hath everlasting life: and he that believeth not the Son shall not see life.

JOHN 3. 35, 36

THE NOBLEMAN'S SON AT THE POINT OF DEATH

When a father comes and pleads for his child, Jesus heals the boy who is at home in a distant city

So Jesus came again into Cana of Galilee, where he made the water wine. And there was a certain nobleman, whose son was sick at Capernaum. When he heard that Jesus was come out of Judaea into Galilee, he went unto him, and besought him that he would come down, and heal his son: for he was at the point of death. Then said Jesus unto him, "Except ye see signs and wonders, ye will not believe." The nobleman saith unto him, "Sir, come down ere my child die." Jesus saith unto him, "Go thy way, thy son liveth." And the man believed the word that Jesus had spoken unto him, and he went his way. As he was now going down, his servants met him, and told him, saying, "Thy son liveth." Then enquired he of them the hour when he began to amend. And they said unto him, "Yesterday at the seventh hour the fever left him." So the father knew that it was at the same hour, in the which Jesus said unto him, "Thy son liveth," and himself believed, and his whole house. This is again the second miracle that Jesus did, when he was come out of Judaea into Galilee. JOHN 4. 46-54

HOPELESS INVALID AT MEDICINAL POOL
Healed by Jesus of infirmity and sin

After this there was a feast of the Jews; and Jesus went up to Jerusalem. Now there is at Jerusalem by the sheep market a pool, which is called in the Hebrew tongue Bethesda, having five porches. In these lay a great multitude of impotent folk, of blind, halt, withered, waiting for the moving of the water. For an angel went down at a certain season into the pool, and troubled the water: whosoever then first after the troubling of the water stepped in was made whole of whatsoever disease he had. A certain man was there, which had an infirmity thirty and eight years. When Jesus saw him lie, and knew that he had been now a long time in that case, he saith unto him, "Wilt thou be made whole?" The impotent man answered him, "Sir, I have no man, when the water is troubled, to put me into the pool: but while I am coming, another steppeth down before me." Jesus saith unto him, "Rise, take up thy bed, and walk." Immediately the man was made whole, and took up his bed, and walked: and on the same day was the sabbath.

The Jews therefore said unto him that was cured, "It is the sabbath day: it is not lawful for thee to carry thy bed." He answered them, "He that made me whole, the same said unto me, 'Take up thy bed, and walk.'" Then asked they him, "What man is that which said unto thee, 'Take up thy bed, and walk'?" And he that was healed wist not who it was: for Jesus had conveyed himself away, a multitude being in that place. Afterward Jesus findeth him in the temple, and said unto him, "Behold, thou art made whole: sin no more, lest a worse thing come unto thee." The man departed, and told the Jews that it was Jesus, which had made him whole. Therefore did the Jews persecute Jesus, and sought to slay him, because he had done these things on the sabbath day. JOHN 5. 1-16

JESUS CREDITS THE FATHER

He explains the source of his works and proclaims the overcoming of death

Jesus answered them, "My Father worketh hitherto, and I work." Therefore the Jews sought the more to kill him, because he not only had broken the sabbath, but said also that God was his Father, making himself equal with God. Then answered Jesus and said unto them, "Verily, verily, I say unto you, the Son can do nothing of himself, but what he seeth the Father do: for what things soever he doeth, these also doeth the Son likewise. For the Father loveth the Son, and sheweth him all things that himself doeth: and he will shew him greater works than these, that ye may marvel. For as the Father raiseth up the dead, and quickeneth them; even so the Son quickeneth whom he will. For the Father judgeth no man, but hath committed all judgment unto the Son: that all men should honour the Son, even as they honour the Father. He that honoureth not the Son honoureth not the Father which hath sent him.

"Verily, verily, I say unto you, He that heareth my word, and believeth on him that sent me, hath everlasting life, and shall not come into condemnation; but is passed from death unto life. Verily, verily, I say unto you, the hour is coming, and now is, when the dead shall hear the voice of the Son of God: and they that hear shall live. For as the Father hath life in himself; so hath he given to the Son to have life in himself; and hath given him authority to execute judgment also, because he is the Son of man. Marvel not at this: for the hour is coming, in the which all that are in the graves shall hear his voice, and shall come forth; they that have done good, unto the resurrection of life; and they that have done evil, unto the resurrection of damnation.

"I can of mine own self do nothing: as I hear, I judge: and my judgment is just; because I seek not mine own will, but the will of the Father which hath sent me. If I bear witness of myself, my witness is not true. There is another that beareth witness of me; and I know that the witness which he witnesseth of me is true. Ye sent unto John, and he bare witness unto the truth. But I receive not testimony from man: but these things I say, that ye might be saved. He was a burning and a shining light: and ye were willing for a season to rejoice in his light. But I have greater witness than that of John: for the works which the Father hath given me to finish, the same works that I do, bear witness of me, that the Father hath sent me. And the Father himself, which hath sent me, hath borne witness of me." JOHN 5. 17-37

SUPPLYING THE WANTS OF THOUSANDS

Jesus illustrates God's power to multiply resources

When Jesus then lifted up his eyes, and saw a great company come unto him, he saith unto Philip, "Whence shall we buy bread, that these may eat?" And this he said to prove him: for he himself knew what he would do. Philip answered him, "Two hundred pennyworth of bread is not sufficient for them, that every one of them may take a little." One of his disciples, Andrew, Simon Peter's brother, saith unto him, "There is a lad here, which hath five barley loaves, and two small fishes: but what are they among so many?" And Jesus said, "Make the men sit down." Now there was much grass in the place. So the men sat down, in number about five thousand. And Jesus took the loaves; and when he had given thanks, he distributed to the disciples, and the disciples to them that were set down; and likewise of the fishes as much as they would. When they were filled, he said unto his disciples, "Gather up the fragments that remain, that nothing be lost." Therefore they gathered them together, and filled twelve baskets with the fragments of the five barley loaves, which remained over and above unto them that had eaten. Then those men, when they had seen the miracle that Jesus did, said, "This is of a truth that prophet that should come into the world."

JOHN 6. 5-14
MAT 14. 14-21
MARK 6. 30-44
LUKE 9. 12-17

THE WALK ON THE SEA IN HIGH WIND

Jesus walks three miles from the shore to the ship crossing the lake

When Jesus therefore perceived that they would come and take him by force, to make him a king, he departed again into a mountain himself alone. When even was now come, his disciples went down unto the sea, and entered into a ship, and went over the sea toward Capernaum. And it was now dark, and Jesus was not come to them. The sea arose by reason of a great wind that blew. So when they had rowed about five and twenty or thirty furlongs, they see Jesus walking on the sea, and drawing nigh unto the ship: and they were afraid. But he saith unto them, "It is I; be not afraid." JOHN 6. 15-20

INSTANT TRANSPORTATION

Ship with disciples completes crossing to port at once

Then they willingly received him into the ship: and immediately the ship was at the land whither they went. JOHN 6. 21

THE BREAD OF LIFE

Jesus expands on the meaning of the loaves and fishes, explains that the spirit, not the flesh, gives life

When they had found him on the other side of the sea, they said unto him, "Rabbi, when camest thou hither?" Jesus answered them and said, "Verily, verily, I say unto you, ye seek me, not because ye saw the miracles, but because ye did eat of the loaves, and were filled. Labour not for the meat which perisheth, but for that meat which endureth unto everlasting life, which the Son of man shall give unto you: for him hath God the Father sealed."

Then said they unto him, "What shall we do, that we might work the works of God?" Jesus answered and said unto them, "This is the work of God, that ye believe on him whom he hath sent." They said therefore unto him, "What sign shewest thou then, that we may see, and believe thee? what dost thou work? Our fathers did eat manna in the desert; as it is written, 'He gave them bread from heaven to eat.' " Then Jesus said unto them, "Verily, verily, I say unto you, Moses gave you not that bread from heaven; but my Father giveth you the true bread from heaven. For the bread of God is he which cometh down from heaven, and giveth life unto the world." Then said they unto him, "Lord, evermore give us this bread." And Jesus said unto them, "I am the bread of life: he that cometh to me shall never hunger; and he that believeth on me shall never thirst.

"This is the Father's will which hath sent me, that of all which he hath given me I should lose nothing, but should raise it up again at the last day. This is the will of him that sent me, that every one which seeth the Son, and believeth on him, may have everlasting life: and I will raise him up at the last day. Verily, verily, I say unto you, he that believeth on me hath everlasting life. I am that bread of life. This is the bread which cometh down from heaven, that a man may eat thereof, and not die. I am the living bread which came down from heaven: if any man eat of this bread, he shall live for ever." Then Jesus said unto them, "Verily, verily, I say unto you, except ye eat the flesh of the Son of man, and drink his blood, ye have no life in you. Whoso eateth my flesh, and drinketh my blood, hath eternal life; and I will raise him up at the last day. For my flesh is meat indeed, and my blood is drink indeed. He that eateth my flesh, and drinketh my blood, dwelleth in me, and I in him. As the living Father hath sent me, and I live by the Father: so he that eateth me, even he shall live by me. This is that bread which came down from heaven: not as your fathers did eat manna, and are dead: he that eateth of this bread shall live for ever." These things said he in the synagogue, as he taught in Capernaum. "It is the spirit that quickeneth; the flesh profiteth nothing: the words that I speak unto you, they are spirit, and they are life."

From that time many of his disciples went back, and walked no more with him. Then said Jesus unto the twelve, "Will ye also go away?" Then Simon Peter answered him. "Lord, to whom shall we go? thou hast the words of eternal life."

JOHN 6. 25-35
39, 40, 47, 48
50, 51, 53-59
63, 66-68

HOW TO KNOW THE TRUTH THAT FREES
By persisting in Jesus' word

Then said Jesus to those Jews which believed on him, "If ye continue in my word, then are ye my disciples indeed; and ye shall know the truth, and the truth shall make you free. Verily, verily, I say unto you, if a man keep my saying, he shall never see death."

JOHN 8. 31, 32, 51

THE MAN BORN BLIND
Jesus rejects sin or heredity as the cause, declares the blindness is an opportunity to demonstrate the power of God to heal. Then two facts are established: genuine blindness and genuine cure

As Jesus passed by, he saw a man which was blind from his birth. His disciples asked him, saying, "Master, who did sin, this man, or his parents, that he was born blind?" Jesus answered, "Neither hath this man sinned, nor his parents: but that the works of God should be made manifest in him. I must work the works of him that sent me while it is day: the night cometh, when no man can work. As long as I am in the world I am the light of the world." When he had thus spoken, he spat on the ground, and made clay of the spittle, and he anointed the eyes of the blind man with the clay, and said unto him, "Go, wash in the pool of Siloam," (which is by interpretation, Sent). He went his way therefore, and washed, and came seeing. The neighbours therefore, and they which before had seen him that he was blind, said, "Is not this he that sat and begged?" Some said, "This is he," others said, "He is like him," but he said, "I am he." Therefore said they unto him, "How were thine eyes opened?" He answered and said, "A man that is called Jesus made clay, and anointed mine eyes, and said unto me, 'Go to the pool of Siloam, and wash,' and I went and washed, and I received sight." Then said they unto him, "Where is he?" He said, "I know not."

They brought to the Pharisees him that aforetime was blind. It was the sabbath day when Jesus made the clay, and opened his eyes. Then again the Pharisees also asked him how he had received his sight. He said unto them, "He put clay upon mine eyes, and I washed, and do see." Therefore said some of the Pharisees, "This man is not of God, because he keepeth not the sabbath day." Others said, "How can a man that is a sinner do such miracles?" And there was a division among them. They say unto the blind man again, "What sayest thou of him, that **he hath opened thine eyes?" He said, "He is a prophet."**

But the Jews did not believe concerning him, that he had been blind, and received his sight, until they called the parents of him that had received his sight. And they asked them, saying, "Is this your son, who ye say was born blind? how then doth he now see?" His parents answered them and said, "We know that this is our son, and that he was born blind: but by what means he now seeth, we know not; or who hath opened his eyes, we know not: he is of age; ask him: he shall speak for himself." These words spake his parents, because they feared the Jews: for the Jews had agreed already, that if any man did confess that he was Christ, he should be put out of the synagogue. Therefore said his parents, "He is of age; ask him."

Then again called they the man that was blind, and said unto him, "Give God the praise: we know that this man is a sinner." He answered and said, "Whether he be a sinner or no, I know not: one thing I know, that, whereas I was blind, now I see." Then said they to him again, "What did he to thee? how opened he thine eyes?" He answered them, "I have told you already, and ye did not hear: wherefore would ye hear it again? will ye also be his disciples?" Then they reviled him, and said, "Thou art his disciple; but we are Moses' disciples. We know that God spake unto Moses: as for this fellow, we know not from whence he is." The man answered and said unto them, "Why herein is a marvellous thing, that ye know not from whence he is, and yet he hath opened mine eyes. Now we know that God heareth not sinners: but if any man be a worshipper of God, and doeth his will, him he heareth. Since the world began was it not heard that any man opened the eyes of one that was born blind. If this man were not of God, he could do nothing." They answered and said unto him, "Thou wast altogether born in sins, and dost thou teach us?" And they cast him out.

Jesus heard that they had cast him out; and when he had found him, he said unto him, "Dost thou believe on the Son of God?" He answered and said, "Who is he, Lord, that I might believe on him?" And Jesus said unto him, "Thou hast both seen him, and it is he that talketh with thee." And he said, "Lord, I believe." And he worshipped him. Jesus said, "For judgment I am come into this world, that they which see not might see; and that they which see might be made blind." Some of the Pharisees which were with him heard these words, and said unto him, "Are we blind also?" Jesus said unto them, "If ye were blind, ye should have no sin: but now ye say, 'We see,' therefore your sin remaineth." JOHN 9. 1-41

JESUS' FOLLOWERS GIVEN ETERNAL LIFE

Due to the oneness of Jesus and God

My sheep hear my voice, and I know them, and they follow me: and I give unto them eternal life; and they shall never perish, neither shall any man pluck them out of my hand. My Father, which gave them me, is greater than all; and no man is able to pluck them out of my Father's hand. I and my Father are one. JOHN 10. 27-30

RESURRECTION OF LAZARUS

Although his friend had been buried four days ago Jesus reassures the doubts and fears of the dead man's sister. Then he thanks the Father in advance and calls Lazarus to life again.

Now a certain man was sick, named Lazarus, of Bethany, the town of Mary and her sister Martha. (It was that Mary which anointed the Lord with ointment, and wiped his feet with her hair, whose brother Lazarus was sick.) Therefore his sisters sent unto him, saying, "Lord, behold, he whom thou lovest is sick." When Jesus heard that, he said, "This sickness is not unto death, but for the glory of God, that the Son of God might be glorified thereby." Now Jesus loved Martha, and her sister, and Lazarus. When he had heard therefore that he was sick, he abode two days still in the same place where he was. Then after that saith he to his disciples, "Let us go into Judaea again." His disciples say unto him, "Master, the Jews of late sought to stone thee; and goest thou thither again?" Jesus answered, "Are there not twelve hours in the day? If any man walk in the day, he stumbleth not, because he seeth the light of this world. But if a man walk in the night, he stumbleth, because there is no light in him."

These things said he: and after that he saith unto them, "Our friend Lazarus sleepeth; but I go, that I may awake him out of sleep." Then said his disciples, "Lord, if he sleep, he shall do well." Howbeit Jesus spake of his death: but they thought that he had spoken of taking of rest in sleep. Then said Jesus unto them plainly, "Lazarus is dead. I am glad for your sakes that I was not there, to the intent ye may believe; nevertheless let us go unto him." Then said Thomas, which is called Didymus, unto his fellow disciples, "Let us also go, that we may die with him." Then when Jesus came, he found that he had lain in the grave four days already. Now Bethany was nigh unto Jerusalem, about fifteen furlongs off: and many of the Jews came to Martha and Mary, to comfort them concerning their brother. Then Martha, as soon as she heard that

Jesus was coming, went and met him: but Mary sat still in the house.

Then said Martha unto Jesus, "Lord, if thou hadst been here, my brother had not died. But I know, that even now, whatsoever thou wilt ask of God, God will give it thee." Jesus saith unto her, "Thy brother shall rise again." Martha saith unto him, "I know that he shall rise again in the resurrection at the last day." Jesus said unto her, "I am the resurrection, and the life: he that believeth in me, though he were dead, **yet shall he live: and whosoever liveth and believeth in me** shall never die. Believest thou this?" She saith unto him, "Yea, Lord: I believe that thou art the Christ, the Son of God, which should come into the world."

When she had so said, she went her way, and called Mary her sister secretly, saying, "The Master is come, and calleth for thee." As soon as she heard that, she arose quickly, and came unto him. Now Jesus was not yet come into the town, but was in that place where Martha met him. The Jews then which were with her in the house, and comforted her, when they saw Mary, that she rose up hastily and went out, followed her, saying, "She goeth unto the grave to weep there." Then when Mary was come where Jesus was, and saw him, she fell down at his feet, saying unto him, "Lord, if thou hadst been here, my brother had not died." When Jesus therefore saw her weeping, and the Jews also weeping which came with her, he groaned in the spirit, and was troubled, and said, "Where have ye laid him?" They said unto him, "Lord, come and see." Jesus wept. Then said the Jews, "Behold how he loved him!" Some of them said, "Could not this man, which opened the eyes of the blind, have caused that even this man should not have died?"

Jesus therefore again groaning in himself cometh to the grave. It was a cave, and a stone lay upon it. Jesus said, "Take ye away the stone." Martha, the sister of him that was dead, saith unto him, "Lord, by this time he stinketh: for he hath been dead four days." Jesus saith unto her, "Said I not unto thee, that, if thou wouldest believe, thou shouldest see the glory of God?" Then they took away the stone from the place where the dead was laid. And Jesus lifted up his eyes, and said, "Father, I thank thee that thou hast heard me. And I knew that thou hearest me always: but because of the people which stand by I said it, that they may believe that thou hast sent me." And when he thus had spoken, he cried with a loud voice, "Lazarus, come forth." And he that was dead came forth, bound hand and foot with graveclothes: and his face was bound about with a napkin. Jesus saith unto them, "Loose him, and let him go." Then many of the Jews which came to Mary, and had seen the things which Jesus did, believed on him. But some of them went their ways to the Pharisees, and told them what things Jesus had done. JOHN 11. 1-46

LAZARUS AT DINNER

Proof of his being raised by Jesus

Then Jesus six days before the passover came to Bethany, where Lazarus was which had been dead, whom he raised from the dead. There they made him a supper; and Martha served: but Lazarus was one of them that sat at the table with him. But the chief priests consulted that they might put Lazarus also to death; because that by reason of him many of the Jews went away, and believed on Jesus. JOHN 12. 1, 2, 10, 11

JESUS' WORKS SHOULD BE DUPLICATED

Others can because the Father is the source of the Son's works. The Holy Spirit will teach one how

Thomas saith unto him, "Lord, we know not whither thou goest; and how can we know the way?" Jesus saith unto him, "I am the way, the truth, and the life: no man cometh unto the Father, but by me. If ye had known me, ye should have known my Father also: and from henceforth ye know him, and have seen him." Philip saith unto him, "Lord, shew us the Father, and it sufficeth us." Jesus saith unto him, "Have I been so long time with you, and yet hast thou not known me, Philip? he that hath seen me hath seen the Father; and how sayest thou then, 'Shew us the Father?' Believest thou not that I am in the Father, and the Father in me? the words that I speak unto you I speak not of myself: but the Father that dwelleth in me, he doeth the works. Believe me that I am in the Father, and the Father in me: or else believe me for the very works' sake. Verily, verily, I say unto you, He that believeth on me, the works that I do shall he do also; and greater works than these shall he do; because I go unto my Father. Whatsoever ye shall ask in my name, that will I do, that the Father may be glorified in the Son. If ye shall ask any thing in my name, I will do it.

"If ye love me, keep my commandments. I will pray the Father, and he shall give you another Comforter, that he may abide with you for ever; even the Spirit of truth; whom the world cannot receive, because it seeth him not, neither knoweth him: but ye know him; for he dwelleth with you, and shall be in you. I will not leave you comfortless: I will come to you. Yet a little while, and the world seeth me no more; but ye see me: because I live, ye shall live also. At that day ye shall know that I am in my Father, and ye in me, and I in you. He that hath my commandments, and keepeth them, he it is that loveth me: and he that loveth me shall be loved of my Father, and I will love him, and will manifest myself to him."

Judas saith unto him, not Iscariot, "Lord, how is it that thou wilt manifest thyself unto us, and not unto the world?" Jesus answered and said unto him, "If a man love me, he will keep my words: and my Father will love him, and we will come unto him, and make our abode with him. He that loveth me not keepeth not my sayings: and the word which ye hear is not mine, but the Father's which sent me. These things have

I spoken unto you, being yet present with you. But the Comforter, which is the Holy Ghost, whom the Father will send in my name, he shall teach you all things, and bring all things to your remembrance, whatsoever I have said unto you. Peace I leave with you, my peace I give unto you: not as the world giveth, give I unto you. Let not your heart be troubled, neither let it be afraid." JOHN 14. 5-27

WHATEVER YOU ASK SHALL BE DONE

If you dwell in Christ

If ye abide in me, and my words abide in you, ye shall ask what ye will, and it shall be done unto you. JOHN 15. 7

WHAT ETERNAL LIFE IS

A knowledge of God and Christ

These words spake Jesus, and lifted up his eyes to heaven, and said, "Father, the hour is come; glorify thy Son, that thy Son also may glorify thee: as thou hast given him power over all flesh, that he should give eternal life to as many as thou hast given him. And this is life eternal, that they might know thee the only true God, and Jesus Christ, whom thou hast sent." JOHN 17. 1-3

GOD'S PROTECTING POWER

Officers sent to arrest Jesus fall backward

Jesus therefore, knowing all things that should come upon him, went forth, and said unto them, "Whom seek ye?" They answered him, "Jesus of Nazareth." Jesus saith unto them, "I am he." And Judas also, which betrayed him, stood with them. As soon then as he had said unto them, "I am he," they went backward, and fell to the ground. JOHN 18. 4-6

BURIAL OF BODY

Prior to the resurrection the dead Jesus was laid in new sepulchre

Then took they the body of Jesus, and wound it in linen clothes with the spices, as the manner of the Jews is to bury. Now in the place where he was crucified there was a garden; and in the garden a new sepulchre, wherein was never man yet laid. There laid they Jesus therefore because of the Jews' preparation day; for the sepulchre was nigh at hand.

JOHN 19. 40-42

DISCIPLES DISCOVER BODY MISSING FROM TOMB

At last they begin to believe the predicted resurrection

The first day of the week cometh Mary Magdalene early, when it was yet dark, unto the sepulchre, and seeth the stone taken away from the sepulchre. Then she runneth, and cometh to Simon Peter, and to the other disciple, whom Jesus loved, and saith unto them, "They have taken away the Lord out of the sepulchre, and we know not where they have laid him." Peter therefore went forth, and that other disciple, and came to the sepulchre. So they ran both together: and the other disciple did outrun Peter, and came first to the sepulchre. And he stooping down, and looking in, saw the linen clothes lying; yet went he not in. Then cometh Simon Peter following him, and went into the sepulchre, and seeth the linen clothes lie, and the napkin, that was about his head, not lying with the linen clothes, but wrapped together in a place by itself. Then went in also that other disciple, which came first to the sepulchre, and he saw, and believed. For as yet they knew not the scripture, that he must rise again from the dead. Then the disciples went away again unto their own home.

JOHN 20. 1-10

APPEARANCE TO MARY

In the garden Mary finally recognizes the Master

Mary stood without at the sepulchre weeping: and as she wept, she stooped down, and looked into the sepulchre, and seeth two angels in white sitting, the one at the head, and the other at the feet, where the body of Jesus had lain. And they say unto her, "Woman, why weepest thou?" She saith unto them, "Because they have taken away my Lord, and I know not where they have laid him." And when she had thus said, she turned herself back, and saw Jesus standing, and knew not that it was Jesus. Jesus saith unto her, "Woman, why weepest thou? whom seekest thou?" She, supposing him to be the gardener, saith unto him, "Sir, if thou have borne him hence, tell me where thou hast laid him, and I will take him away." Jesus saith unto her, "Mary." She turned herself, and saith unto him, "Rabboni," which is to say, "Master." Jesus saith unto her, "Touch me not; for I am not yet ascended to my Father: but go to my brethren, and say unto them, I ascend unto my Father, and your Father; and to my God, and your God." Mary Magdalene came and told the disciples that she had seen the Lord, and that he had spoken these things unto her. JOHN 20. 11-18

THOMAS CONVINCED
Jesus' body handled by disciples

Then the same day at evening, being the first day of the week, when the doors were shut where the disciples were assembled for fear of the Jews, came Jesus and stood in the midst, and saith unto them, "Peace be unto you." And when he had so said, he shewed unto them his hands and his side. Then were the disciples glad, when they saw the Lord. Then said Jesus to them again, "Peace be unto you: as my Father hath sent me, even so send I you." And when he had said this, he breathed on them, and saith unto them, "Receive ye the Holy Ghost: whose soever sins ye remit, they are remitted unto them; and whose soever sins ye retain, they are retained. But Thomas, one of the twelve, called Didymus, was not with them when Jesus came. The other disciples therefore said unto him, "We have seen the Lord." But he said unto them, "Except I shall see in his hands the print of the nails, and put my finger into the print of the nails, and thrust my hand into his side, I will not believe."

And after eight days again his disciples were within, and Thomas with them: then came Jesus, the doors being shut, and stood in the midst, and said, "Peace be unto you." Then saith he to Thomas, "Reach hither thy finger, and behold my hands; and reach hither thy hand, and thrust it into my side: and be not faithless, but believing." Thomas answered and said unto him, "My Lord and my God." Jesus saith unto him, "Thomas, because thou hast seen me, thou hast believed: blessed are they that have not seen, and yet have believed."

JOHN 20. 19-29

MIRACULOUS HAUL OF FISH

Jesus breakfasts on the shore with disciples

After these things Jesus shewed himself again to the disciples at the sea of Tiberias; and on this wise shewed he himself. There were together Simon Peter, and Thomas called Didymus, and Nathanael of Cana in Galilee, and the sons of Zebedee, and two other of his disciples. Simon Peter saith unto them, "I go a-fishing." They say unto him, "We also go with thee." They went forth, and entered into a ship immediately; and that night they caught nothing. But when the morning was now come, Jesus stood on the shore: but the disciples knew not that it was Jesus. Then Jesus saith unto them, "Children, have ye any meat?" They answered him, "No." And he said unto them, "Cast the net on the right side of the ship, and ye shall find." They cast therefore, and now they were not able to draw it for the multitude of fishes. Therefore that disciple whom Jesus loved saith unto Peter, "It is the Lord." Now when Simon Peter heard that it was the Lord, he girt his fisher's coat unto him, (for he was naked,) and did cast himself into the sea. And the other disciples came in a little ship; (for they were not far from land, but as it were two hundred cubits,) dragging the net with fishes.

As soon then as they were come to land, they saw a fire of coals there, and fish laid thereon, and bread. Jesus saith unto them, "Bring of the fish which ye have now caught." Simon Peter went up, and drew the net to land full of great fishes, an hundred and fifty and three: and for all there were so many, yet was not the net broken. Jesus saith unto them, "Come and dine." And none of the disciples durst ask him, "Who art thou?" knowing that it was the Lord. Jesus then cometh, and taketh bread, and giveth them, and fish likewise. This is now the third time that Jesus shewed himself to his disciples, after that he was risen from the dead. JOHN 21. 1-14

ACTS

JESUS ALIVE AFTER HIS DEATH

He showed himself by many infallible proofs

The former treatise have I made, O Theophilus, of all that Jesus began both to do and teach, until the day in which he was taken up, after that he through the Holy Ghost had given commandments unto the apostles whom he had chosen: to whom also he shewed himself alive after his passion by many infallible proofs, being seen of them forty days, and speaking of the things pertaining to the kingdom of God: and when he had spoken these things, while they beheld, he was taken up; and a cloud received him out of their sight.

ACTS 1. 1-3, 9

SALVATION BY CALLING ON GOD

We are all witnesses to the resurrection

And it shall come to pass, that whosoever shall call on the name of the Lord shall be saved. Therefore did my heart rejoice, and my tongue was glad; moreover also my flesh shall rest in hope: because thou wilt not leave my soul in hell, neither wilt thou suffer thine Holy One to see corruption. Thou hast made known to me the ways of life; thou shalt make me full of joy with thy countenance. This Jesus hath God raised up, whereof we all are witnesses. ACTS 2. 21, 26-28, 32

THE LAME BEGGAR AT THE GATE

Peter and John's treatment of the man enables him to walk

Now Peter and John went up together into the temple at the hour of prayer, being the ninth hour. And a certain man lame from his mother's womb was carried, whom they laid daily at the gate of the temple which is called Beautiful, to ask alms of them that entered into the temple; who seeing Peter and John about to go into the temple asked an alms. Peter, fastening his eyes upon him with John, said, "Look on us." And he gave heed unto them, expecting to receive something of them. Then Peter said, "Silver and gold have I none; but such as I have give I thee: in the name of Jesus Christ of Nazareth rise up and walk." He took him by the right hand, and lifted him up: and immediately his feet and ankle bones received strength. He leaping up stood, and walked, and entered with them into the temple, walking, and leaping, and praising God. All the people saw him walking and praising God: and they knew that it was he which sat for alms at the Beautiful gate of the temple: and they were filled with wonder and amazement at that which had happened unto him.

As the lame man which was healed held Peter and John, all the people ran together unto them in the porch that is called Solomon's, greatly wondering. When Peter saw it, he answered unto the people, "Ye men of Israel, why marvel ye at this or why look ye so earnestly on us, as though by our own power or holiness we had made this man to walk? The God of Abraham, and of Isaac, and of Jacob, the God of our fathers, hath glorified his Son Jesus; whom ye delivered up, and denied him in the presence of Pilate, when he was determined to let him go. But ye denied the Holy One and the

Just, and desired a murderer to be granted unto you; and killed the Prince of life, whom God hath raised from the dead; whereof we are witnesses. His name through faith in his name hath made this man strong, whom ye see and know: yea, the faith which is by him hath given him this perfect soundness in the presence of you all." ACTS 3. 1-16

SIGNS AND WONDERS AS JESUS PROMISED

Disciples speak boldly, encouraged by the proof they could heal

"Be it known unto you all, and to all the people of Israel, that by the name of Jesus Christ of Nazareth, whom ye crucified, whom God raised from the dead, even by him doth this man stand here before you whole. This is the stone which was set at nought of you builders, which is become the head of the corner. Neither is there salvation in any other: for there is none other name under heaven given among men, whereby we must be saved."

Now when they saw the boldness of Peter and John, and perceived that they were unlearned and ignorant men, they marvelled; and they took knowledge of them, that they had been with Jesus. Beholding the man which was healed standing with them, they could say nothing against it. But when they had commanded them to go aside out of the council, they conferred among themselves, saying, "What shall we do to these men? for that indeed a notable miracle hath been done by them is manifest to all them that dwell in Jerusalem; and we cannot deny it." All men glorified God for that which was done for the man was above forty years old, on whom this miracle of healing was shewed.

"Now, Lord, grant unto thy servants, that with all boldness they may speak thy word, by stretching forth thine hand to heal; and that signs and wonders may be done by the name of thy holy child Jesus." When they had prayed, the place was shaken where they were assembled together; and they were all filled with the Holy Ghost, and they spake the word of God with boldness. The multitude of them that believed were of one heart and of one soul: and with great power gave the apostles witness of the resurrection of the Lord Jesus: and great grace was upon them all. Neither was there any among them that lacked: for as many as were possessors of lands or houses sold them, and brought the prices of the things that were sold, and laid them down at the apostles' feet. ACTS 4. 10-16 21, 22, 29-35

DISCIPLES HEAL MANY

Sick laid in the streets where Peter passed

By the hands of the apostles were many signs and wonders wrought among the people; (and they were all with one accord in Solomon's porch. And of the rest durst no man join himself to them: but the people magnified them. And believers were the more added to the Lord, multitudes both of men and women.) Insomuch that they brought forth the sick into the streets, and laid them on beds and couches, that at the least the shadow of Peter passing by might overshadow some of them. There came also a multitude out of the cities round about unto Jerusalem, bringing sick folks, and them which were vexed with unclean spirits: and they were healed every one.

ACTS 5. 12-16

THE INSANE, PARALYZED, LAME HEALED

The works of Philip in Samaria

Then Philip went down to the city of Samaria, and preached Christ unto them. And the people with one accord gave heed unto those things which Philip spake, hearing and seeing the miracles which he did. For unclean spirits, crying with loud voice, came out of many that were possessed with them: and many taken with palsies, and that were lame, were healed. And there was great joy in that city. ACTS 8. 5-8

PAUL STRUCK BLIND

Ananias heals enemy of the Christians

Saul, yet breathing out threatenings and slaughter against the disciples of the Lord, went unto the high priest, and desired of him letters to Damascus to the synagogues, that if he found any of this way, whether they were men or women, he might bring them bound unto Jerusalem. As he journeyed, he came near Damascus: and suddenly there shined round about him a light from heaven: and he fell to the earth, and heard a voice saying unto him, "Saul, Saul, why persecutest thou me?" And he said, "Who art thou, Lord?" And the Lord said, "I am Jesus whom thou persecutest: it is hard for thee to kick against the pricks." He trembling and astonished said, "Lord, what wilt thou have me to do?" And the Lord said unto him, "Arise, and go into the city, and it shall be told thee what thou must do." The men which journeyed with him stood speechless, hearing a voice, but seeing no man. Saul arose from the earth; and when his eyes were opened, he saw no man: but they led him by the hand, and brought him into Damascus.

He was three days without sight, and neither did eat nor drink. There was a certain disciple at Damascus, named Ananias; and to him said the Lord in a vision, "Ananias." And he said, "Behold, I am here, Lord." The Lord said unto him, "Arise, and go into the street which is called Straight, and enquire in the house of Judas for one called Saul, of Tarsus: for, behold, he prayeth, and hath seen in a vision a man named Ananias coming in, and putting his hand on him, that he might receive his sight." Then Ananias answered, "Lord, I have heard by many of this man, how much evil he hath done to thy saints at Jerusalem: and here he hath authority from the chief priests to bind all that call on thy name." But the Lord said unto him, "Go thy way: for he is a chosen vessel unto me, to bear my name before the Gentiles, and kings, and the children of Israel: for I will shew him how great things he must suffer for my name's sake." Ananias went his way, and entered into the house; and putting his hands on him said, "Brother Saul, the Lord, even Jesus, that appeared unto thee in the way as thou camest, hath sent me, that thou mightest receive thy sight, and be filled with the Holy Ghost." Immediately there fell from his eyes as it had been scales: and he received sight forthwith, and arose, and was baptized.

When he had received meat, he was strengthened. Then was Saul certain days with the disciples which were at Damascus. Straightway he preached Christ in the synagogues, that he is the Son of God. But all that heard him were amazed, and said, "Is not this he that destroyed them which called on this name in Jerusalem, and came hither for that intent, that he might bring them bound unto the chief priests?" But Saul increased the more in strength, and confounded the Jews which dwelt at Damascus, proving that this is very Christ.

ACTS 9. 1-22
ACTS 22. 1-13
ACTS 26. 1, 9-21

PAUL ESCAPES ASSASSINATION

He is let down over wall in a basket

After that many days were fulfilled, the Jews took counsel to kill him: but their laying await was known of Saul. And they watched the gates day and night to kill him. Then the disciples took him by night, and let him down by the wall in a basket. When Saul was come to Jerusalem, he assayed to join himself to the disciples: but they were all afraid of him, and believed not that he was a disciple. But Barnabas took him, and brought him to the apostles, and declared unto them how he had seen the Lord in the way, and that he had spoken to him, and how he had preached boldly at Damascus in the name of Jesus. He was with them coming in and going out at Jerusalem. He spake boldly in the name of the Lord Jesus, and disputed against the Grecians: but they went about to slay him. Which when the brethren knew, they brought him down to Caesarea, and sent him forth to Tarsus. Then had the churches rest throughout all Judaea and Galilee and Samaria, and were edified; and walking in the fear of the Lord, and in the comfort of the Holy Ghost, were multiplied.

ACTS 9. 23-31

PARALYZED EIGHT YEARS
Peter heals Aeneas

It came to pass, as Peter passed throughout all quarters, he came down also to the saints which dwelt at Lydda. And there he found a certain man named Aeneas, which had kept his bed eight years, and was sick of the palsy. And Peter said unto him, "Aeneas, Jesus Christ maketh thee whole: arise, and make thy bed." And he arose immediately. And all that dwelt at Lydda and Saron saw him, and turned to the Lord.

ACTS 9. 32-35

DEAD RAISED
Peter presents Tabitha alive to mourners

Now there was at Joppa a certain disciple named Tabitha, which by interpretation is called Dorcas: this woman was full of good works and alms-deeds which she did. It came to pass in those days, that she was sick, and died: whom when they had washed, they laid her in an upper chamber. Forasmuch as Lydda was nigh to Joppa, and the disciples had heard that Peter was there, they sent unto him two men, desiring him that he would not delay to come to them. Then Peter arose and went with them. When he was come, they brought him into the upper chamber: and all the widows stood by him weeping, and shewing the coats and garments which Dorcas made, while she was with them. But Peter put them all forth, and kneeled down, and prayed; and turning him to the body said, "Tabitha, arise." And she opened her eyes: and when she saw Peter, she sat up. He gave her his hand, and lifted her up, and when he had called the saints and widows, presented her alive. And it was known throughout all Joppa; and many believed in the Lord.

ACTS 9. 36-42

ESCAPE FROM PRISON AGAIN

Angel leads Peter out to street

Now about that time Herod the king stretched forth his hands to vex certain of the church. Peter therefore was kept in prison: but prayer was made without ceasing of the church unto God for him. When Herod would have brought him forth, the same night Peter was sleeping between two soldiers, bound with two chains: and the keepers before the door kept the prison. And, behold, the angel of the Lord came upon him, and a light shined in the prison: and he smote Peter on the side, and raised him up, saying, "Arise up quickly." And his chains fell off from his hands. And the angel said unto him, "Gird thyself, and bind on thy sandals." And so he did. And he saith unto him, "Cast thy garment about thee, and follow me." And he went out, and followed him; and wist not that it was true which was done by the angel; but thought he saw a vision. When they were past the first and the second ward, they came unto the iron gate that leadeth unto the city; which opened to them of his own accord: and they went out, and passed on through one street; and forthwith the angel departed from him.

When Peter was come to himself, he said, "Now I know of a surety, that the Lord hath sent his angel, and hath delivered me out of the hand of Herod, and from all the expectation of the people of the Jews." When he had considered the thing, he came to the house of Mary the mother of John, whose surname was Mark; where many were gathered together praying. As Peter knocked at the door of the gate, a damsel came to hearken, named Rhoda. When she knew Peter's voice, she opened not the gate for gladness, but ran in, and told how Peter stood before the gate. They said unto her, "Thou art mad." But she constantly affirmed that it was even so. Then said they, "It is his angel." But Peter continued knocking: and when they had opened the door, and saw him, they were astonished. But he, beckoning unto them with the hand to hold their peace, declared unto them how the Lord had brought him out of the prison. ACTS 12. 1, 5-17

Cripple Who Never Had Walked
Healed as he listens to Paul's sermon

There sat a certain man at Lystra, impotent in his feet, being a cripple from his mother's womb, who never had walked. The same heard Paul speak: who stedfastly beholding him, and perceiving that he had faith to be healed, said with a loud voice, "Stand upright on thy feet." And he leaped and walked. When the people saw what Paul had done, they lifted up their voices, saying in the speech of Lycaonia, "The gods are come down to us in the likeness of men." They called Barnabas, Jupiter; and Paul, Mercurius, because he was the chief speaker. Then the priest of Jupiter, which was before their city, brought oxen and garlands unto the gates, and would have done sacrifice with the people. Which when the apostles, Barnabas and Paul, heard of, they rent their clothes, and ran in among the people, crying out, and saying, "Sirs, why do ye these things? We also are men of like passions with you, and preach unto you that ye should turn from these vanities unto the living God, which made heaven, and earth, and the sea, and all things that are therein: who in times past suffered all nations to walk in their own ways. Nevertheless he left not himself without witness, in that he did good, and gave us rain from heaven, and fruitful seasons, filling our hearts with food and gladness." With these sayings scarce restrained they the people, that they had not done sacrifice unto them. ACTS 14. 8-18

Later Paul Stoned Till Unconscious
Disciples revive him

There came thither certain Jews from Antioch and Iconium, who persuaded the people, and, having stoned Paul, drew him out of the city, supposing he had been dead. Howbeit, as the disciples stood round about him, he rose up, and came into the city: and the next day he departed with Barnabas to Derbe.

ACTS 14. 19, 20

MIRACLES REPORTED
Paul tells the wonders God worked among the Gentiles

We believe that through the grace of the Lord Jesus Christ we shall be saved. Then all the multitude kept silence, and gave audience to Barnabas and Paul, declaring what miracles and wonders God had wrought among the Gentiles by them.

ACTS 15. 11, 12

POSSESSED FORTUNE TELLER CURED
Paul heals with a command

It came to pass, as we went to prayer, a certain damsel possessed with a spirit of divination met us, which brought her masters much gain by soothsaying. The same followed Paul and us, and cried, saying, "These men are the servants of the most high God, which shew unto us the way of salvation." This did she many days. But Paul, being grieved, turned and said to the spirit, "I command thee in the name of Jesus Christ to come out of her." And he came out the same hour.

ACTS 16. 16-18

PAUL AND SILAS IMPRISONED BECAUSE OF THIS HEALING
An earthquake frees them and they convert the jailor

When her masters saw that the hope of their gains was gone, they caught Paul and Silas, and drew them into the marketplace unto the rulers, and brought them to the magistrates, saying, "These men, being Jews, do exceedingly trouble our city, and teach customs, which are not lawful for us to receive, neither to observe, being Romans." The multitude rose up together against them: and the magistrates rent off their clothes, and commanded to beat them. When they had laid many stripes upon them, they cast them into prison, charging the jailor to keep them safely: who, having received such a charge, thrust them into the inner prison, and made their feet fast in the stocks.

At midnight Paul and Silas prayed, and sang praises unto God: and the prisoners heard them. Suddenly there was a great earthquake, so that the foundations of the prison were shaken: and immediately all the doors were opened, and every one's bands were loosed. The keeper of the prison awaking out of his sleep, and seeing the prison doors open, he drew out his sword, and would have killed himself, supposing that the prisoners had been fled. But Paul cried with a loud voice, saying, "Do thyself no harm: for we are all here." Then he called for a light, and sprang in, and came trembling, and fell down before Paul and Silas, and brought them out, and said, "Sirs, what must I do to be saved?" They said, "Believe on the Lord Jesus Christ, and thou shalt be saved, and thy house." They spake unto him the word of the Lord, and to all that were in his house. He took them the same hour of the night, and washed their stripes; and was baptized, he and all his, straightway. When he had brought them into his house, he set meat before them, and rejoiced, believing in God with all his house.

When it was day, the magistrates sent the serjeants, saying, "Let those men go." The keeper of the prison told this saying to Paul, "The magistrates have sent to let you go: now therefore depart, and go in peace." But Paul said unto them, "They have beaten us openly uncondemned, being Romans, and have cast us into prison; and now do they thrust us out privily? nay verily; but let them come themselves and fetch us out." The serjeants told these words unto the magistrates: and they feared, when they heard that they were Romans. They came and besought them, and brought them out, and desired them to depart out of the city. They went out of the prison, and entered into the house of Lydia: and when they had seen the brethren, they comforted them and departed. ACTS 16. 19-40

FALSE CHRISTIANS UNSUCCESSFUL IN HEALING

Exorcists who imitate Paul's healings are attacked by demoniac

And God wrought special miracles by the hands of Paul: so that from his body were brought unto the sick handkerchiefs or aprons, and the diseases departed from them, and the evil spirits went out of them.

Then certain of the vagabond Jews, exorcists, took upon them to call over them which had evil spirits the name of the Lord Jesus, saying, "We adjure you by Jesus whom Paul preacheth." There were seven sons of one Sceva, a Jew, and chief of the priests, which did so. The evil spirit answered and said, "Jesus I know, and Paul I know; but who are ye?" The man in whom the evil spirit was leaped on them, and overcame them, and prevailed against them, so that they fled out of that house naked and wounded. This was known to all the Jews and Greeks also dwelling at Ephesus; and fear fell on them all, and the name of the Lord Jesus was magnified. Many that believed came, and confessed, and shewed their deeds. Many of them also which used curious arts brought their books together, and burned them before all men: and they counted the price of them, and found it fifty thousand pieces of silver. So mightily grew the word of God and prevailed. ACTS 19. 11-20

DEATH FROM ACCIDENT

Fall from third story kills young man but Paul raises him

Upon the first day of the week, when the disciples came together to break bread, Paul preached unto them, ready to depart on the morrow; and continued his speech until midnight. There were many lights in the upper chamber, where they were gathered together. There sat in a window a certain young man named Eutychus, being fallen into a deep sleep: and as Paul was long preaching, he sunk down with sleep, and fell down from the third loft, and was taken up dead. And Paul went down, and fell on him, and embracing him said, "Trouble not yourselves; for his life is in him." When he therefore was come up again, and had broken bread, and eaten, and talked a long while, even till break of day, so he departed. They brought the young man alive, and were not a little comforted.

ACTS 20. 7-12

Raising the Dead

Paul challenges King Agrippa's incredulity regarding resurrection

Why should it be thought a thing incredible with you, that God should raise the dead? ACTS 26. 8

Safety During Tempest and Shipwreck

Paul's prophecy about no loss of life comes true

When it was determined that we should sail into Italy, they delivered Paul and certain other prisoners unto one named Julius, a centurion of Augustus' band. Entering into a ship of Adramyttium, we launched, meaning to sail by the coasts of Asia. And we being exceedingly tossed with a tempest, the next day they lightened the ship; and the third day we cast out with our own hands the tackling of the ship. When neither sun nor stars in many days appeared, and no small tempest lay on us, all hope that we should be saved was then taken away. But after long abstinence Paul stood forth in the midst of them, and said, "Sirs, ye should have hearkened unto me, and not have loosed from Crete, and to have gained this harm and loss. Now I exhort you to be of good cheer: for there shall be no loss of any man's life among you, but of the ship. When he had thus spoken, he took bread, and gave thanks to God in presence of them all: and when he had broken it, he began to eat. Then were they all of good cheer, and they also took some meat. We were in all in the ship two hundred threescore and sixteen souls. When they had eaten enough, they lightened the ship, and cast out the wheat into the sea.

When it was day, they knew not the land: but they discovered a certain creek with a shore, into the which they were minded, if it were possible, to thrust in the ship. When they had taken up the anchors, they committed themselves unto the sea, and loosed the rudder bands, and hoisted up the mainsail to the wind, and made toward shore. Falling into a place where two seas met, they ran the ship aground; and the forepart stuck fast, and remained unmoveable, but the hinder part was broken with the violence of the waves. The soldiers' counsel was to kill the prisoners, lest any of them should swim out, and escape. But the centurion, willing to save Paul, kept them from their purpose; and commanded that they which could swim should cast themselves first into the sea, and get to land: and the rest, some on boards, and some on broken pieces of the ship. And so it came to pass, that they escaped all safe to land.

ACTS 27. 1, 2
18-22, 35-44

VIPER STING HARMLESS

Paul protected from the effects of poison

When they were escaped, then they knew that the island was called Melita. And the barbarous people shewed us no little kindness: for they kindled a fire, and received us every one, because of the present rain, and because of the cold. When Paul had gathered a bundle of sticks, and laid them on the fire, there came a viper out of the heat, and fastened on his hand. When the barbarians saw the venomous beast hang on his hand, they said among themselves, "No doubt this man is a murderer, whom though he hath escaped the sea, yet vengeance suffereth not to live." He shook off the beast into the fire, and felt no harm. Howbeit they looked when he should have swollen, or fallen down dead suddenly: but after they had looked a great while, and saw no harm come to him, they changed their minds, and said that he was a god. ACTS 28. 1-6

FEVER AND HEMORRHAGE HEALED

Paul cures friendly islander

In the same quarters were possessions of the chief man of the island, whose name was Publius; who received us, and lodged us three days courteously. It came to pass, that the father of Publius lay sick of a fever and of a bloody flux: to whom Paul entered in, and prayed, and laid his hands on him, and healed him. So when this was done, others also, which had diseases in the island, came, and were healed: who also honoured us with many honours; and when we departed, they laded us with such things as were necessary. ACTS 28. 7-10

ROMANS

THE GIFT OF ETERNAL LIFE

It is given us by God

Now if we be dead with Christ, we believe that we shall also live with him: knowing that Christ being raised from the dead dieth no more; death hath no more dominion over him. For in that he died, he died unto sin once: but in that he liveth, he liveth unto God. But now being made free from sin, and become servants to God, ye have your fruit unto holiness, and the end everlasting life. For the wages of sin is death; but the gift of God is eternal life through Jesus Christ our Lord.

RO 6. 8-10, 22-23

DELIVERED FROM DEATH

The law of right thinking saves from the law of sin

For I delight in the law of God after the inward man: but I see another law in my members, warring against the law of my mind, and bringing me into captivity to the law of sin which is in my members. O wretched man that I am! who shall deliver me from the body of this death? I thank God through Jesus Christ our Lord. RO 7. 22-25

LIFE AND PEACE VERSUS DEATH

The life-giving Spirit frees from the power of sin and death

There is therefore now no condemnation to them which are in Christ Jesus, who walk not after the flesh, but after the Spirit. For the law of the Spirit of life in Christ Jesus hath made me free from the law of sin and death. For to be carnally minded is death; but to be spiritually minded is life and peace.

RO 8. 1, 2, 6

CHILDREN OF GOD ARE THE HEIRS OF GOD

Nothing can separate them from the love of God

Therefore, brethren, we are debtors, not to the flesh, to live after the flesh. For if ye live after the flesh, ye shall die: but if ye through the Spirit do mortify the deeds of the body, ye shall live. For as many as are led by the Spirit of God, they are the sons of God. For ye have not received the spirit of bondage again to fear; but ye have received the Spirit of adoption, whereby we cry, "Abba, Father." The Spirit itself beareth witness with our spirit, that we are the children of God: and if children, then heirs; heirs of God, and joint-heirs with Christ; if so be that we suffer with him, that we may be also glorified together.

For I reckon that the sufferings of this present time are not worthy to be compared with the glory which shall be revealed in us. For the earnest expectation of the creature waiteth for the manifestation of the sons of God. For the creature was made subject to vanity, not willingly, but by reason of him who hath subjected the same in hope, because the creature itself also shall be delivered from the bondage of corruption into the glorious liberty of the children of God. For we know that the whole creation groaneth and travaileth in pain together until now. Not only they, but ourselves also, which have the firstfruits of the Spirit, even we ourselves groan within ourselves, waiting for the adoption, to wit, the redemption of our body. For we are saved by hope: but hope that is seen is not hope: for what a man seeth, why doth he yet hope for? But if we hope for that we see not, then do we with patience wait for it. Likewise the Spirit also helpeth our infirmities: for we know not what we should pray for as we ought: but the Spirit itself maketh intercession for us with groanings which cannot be uttered. He that searcheth the hearts knoweth what is the mind of the Spirit, because he maketh intercession for the saints according to the will of God.

We know that all things work together for good to them that love God, to them who are the called according to his purpose. For whom he did foreknow, he also did predestinate to be conformed to the image of his Son. Who shall separate us from the love of Christ? shall tribulation, or distress, or persecution, or famine, or nakedness, or peril, or sword? Nay, in all these things we are more than conquerors through him that loved us. For I am persuaded, that neither death, nor life, nor angels, nor principalities, nor powers, nor things present, nor things to come, nor height, nor depth, nor any other creature, shall be able to separate us from the love of God, which is in Christ Jesus our Lord. RO 8. 12-29, 35, 37-39

GOD THE SOURCE, GUIDE, GOAL
All things created to praise Him

For of him, and through him, and to him, are all things: to whom be glory for ever. Amen. RO 11. 36

TRANSFORMED TO PURITY AND HEALTH
It comes by a change of thinking

Be ye transformed by the renewing of your mind. RO 12. 2

Love is the Basic Need
All laws are obeyed when you love

Love is the fulfilling of the law. RO 13. 10

1st CORINTHIANS

The Gift of Healing
It comes from the one Spirit

Now there are diversities of gifts, but the same Spirit. And there are differences of administrations, but the same Lord. And there are diversities of operations, but it is the same God which worketh all in all. But the manifestation of the Spirit is given to every man to profit withal. For to one is given by the Spirit the word of wisdom; to another the word of knowledge by the same Spirit; to another faith by the same Spirit; to another the gifts of healing by the same Spirit; to another the working of miracles; to another prophecy. 1st COR 12. 4-10

God Assigns Healers and Other Offices
Aim at the highest

Now ye are the body of Christ, and members in particular. God hath set some in the church, first apostles, secondarily prophets, thirdly teachers, after that miracles, then gifts of healings, helps, governments, diversities of tongues. Are all apostles? are all prophets? are all teachers? are all workers of miracles? Have all the gifts of healing? do all speak with tongues? do all interpret? But covet earnestly the best gifts.

1st COR 12. 27-31

IN ADAM ALL DIE, IN CHRIST ALL LIVE

The first man is material, the second spiritual. This concept gives us the victory over death

Now if Christ be preached that he rose from the dead, how say some among you that there is no resurrection of the dead? But if there be no resurrection of the dead, then is Christ not risen: and if Christ be not risen, then is our preaching vain, and your faith is also vain. Yea, and we are found false witnesses of God; because we have testified of God that he raised up Christ: whom he raised not up, if so be that the dead rise not. For if the dead rise not, then is not Christ raised: and if Christ be not raised, your faith is vain; ye are yet in your sins. Then they also which are fallen asleep in Christ are perished. If in this life only we have hope in Christ, we are of all men most miserable. But now is Christ risen from the dead, and become the firstfruits of them that slept. For since by man came death, by man came also the resurrection of the dead. For as in Adam all die, even so in Christ shall all be made alive. But every man in his own order: Christ the firstfruits; afterward they that are Christ's at his coming.

So also is the resurrection of the dead. It is sown in corruption; it is raised in incorruption: it is sown in dishonour; it is raised in glory: it is sown in weakness; it is raised in power: it is sown a natural body; it is raised a spiritual body. There is a natural body, and there is a spiritual body. And so it is written, "The first man Adam was made a living soul; the last Adam was made a quickening spirit." Howbeit that was not first which is spiritual, but that which is natural; and afterward that which is spiritual. The first man is of the earth, earthy: the second man is the Lord from heaven. As is the earthy, such are they also that are earthy: and as is the heavenly, such are they also that are heavenly. And as we have borne the image of the earthy, we shall also bear the image of the heavenly.

Now this I say, brethren, that flesh and blood cannot inherit the kingdom of God; neither doth corruption inherit incorruption. Behold, I shew you a mystery; we shall not all sleep, but we shall all be changed, in a moment, in the twinkling of an eye, at the last trump: for the trumpet shall sound, and the dead shall be raised incorruptible, and we shall be changed. For this corruptible must put on incorruption, and this mortal must put on immortality. So when this corruptible shall have put on incorruption, and this mortal shall have put on immortality, then shall be brought to pass the saying that is written, "Death is swallowed up in victory." O death, where is thy sting? O grave, where is thy victory? The sting of death is sin; and the strength of sin is the law. But thanks be to God, which giveth us the victory through our Lord Jesus Christ. Therefore, my beloved brethren, be ye stedfast, unmoveable, always abounding in the work of the Lord, forasmuch as ye know that your labour is not in vain in the Lord.

1st COR 15. 12-23, 42-58

2nd CORINTHIANS

GOD DELIVERS US FROM DEATH-SENTENCE

This is the comfort with which Christ blesses us

Blessed be God, even the Father of our Lord Jesus Christ, the Father of mercies, and the God of all comfort; who comforteth us in all our tribulation, that we may be able to comfort them which are in any trouble, by the comfort wherewith we ourselves are comforted of God. For as the sufferings of Christ abound in us, so our consolation also aboundeth by Christ. And whether we be afflicted, it is for your consolation and salvation, which is effectual in the enduring of the same sufferings which we also suffer: or whether we be comforted, it is for your consolation and salvation. Our hope of you is stedfast, knowing, that as ye are partakers of the sufferings, so shall ye be also of the consolation. For we would not, brethren, have you ignorant of our trouble which came to us in Asia, that we were pressed out of measure, above strength, insomuch that we despaired even of life: but we had the sentence of death in ourselves, that we should not trust in ourselves, but in God which raiseth the dead: who delivered us from so great a death, and doth deliver: in whom we trust that he will yet deliver us.

2nd COR 1. 3-10

ABILITY COMES FROM GOD

It is the Spirit of the Word that gives life

Such trust have we through Christ to God-ward: not that we are sufficient of ourselves to think any thing as of ourselves; but our sufficiency is of God; who also hath made us able ministers of the new testament; not of the letter, but of the spirit: for the letter killeth, but the spirit giveth life.

2nd COR 3. 4-6

TROUBLES ARE TEMPORARY

The outward man suffers but the inward man is renewed

We having the same spirit of faith, according as it is written, I believed, and therefore have I spoken; we also believe, and therefore speak; knowing that he which raised up the Lord Jesus shall raise up us also by Jesus, and shall present us with you. For all things are for your sakes, that the abundant grace might through the thanksgiving of many redound to the glory of God. For which cause we faint not; but though our outward man perish, yet the inward man is renewed day by day. For our light affiction, which is but for a moment, worketh for us a far more exceeding and eternal weight of glory; while we look not at the things which are seen, but at the things which are not seen: for the things which are seen are temporal; but the things which are not seen are eternal.

2nd COR 4. 13-18

TURN FROM THE BODY TO THE PRESENCE OF THE LORD

If we are in Christ, a new life is begun

For we know that if our earthly house of this tabernacle were dissolved, we have a building of God, an house not made with hands, eternal in the heavens. For in this we groan, earnestly desiring to be clothed upon with our house which is from heaven: if so be that being clothed we shall not be found naked. For we that are in this tabernacle do groan, being burdened: not for that we would be unclothed, but clothed upon, that mortality might be swallowed up of life. Now he that hath wrought us for the selfsame thing is God, who also hath given unto us the earnest of the Spirit. Therefore we are always confident, knowing that, whilst we are at home in the body, we are absent from the Lord: (for we walk by faith, not by sight:) we are confident, I say, and willing rather to be absent from the body, and to be present with the Lord. Wherefore henceforth know we no man after the flesh: yea, though we have known Christ after the flesh, yet now henceforth know we him no more. Therefore if any man be in Christ, he is a new creature: old things are passed away; behold, all things are become new. All things are of God, who hath reconciled us to himself by Jesus Christ, and hath given to us the ministry of reconciliation.

2nd COR 5. 1-8, 16-18

THE DAY OF DELIVERANCE IS TODAY

God comes to our aid

For he saith, I have heard thee in a time accepted, and in the day of salvation have I succoured thee: behold, now is the accepted time; behold, now is the day of salvation.

2nd COR 6. 2

SEEKING RELIEF FOR THE BODY

God comforts us

When we were come into Macedonia, our flesh had no rest,

but we were troubled on every side; without were fightings, within were fears. Nevertheless God, that comforteth those that are cast down, comforted us. 2nd COR 7. 5, 6

LEARNING TO REJOICE IN PAIN

Power develops even in weakness

Lest I should be exalted above measure through the abundance of the revelations, there was given to me a thorn in the flesh, the messenger of Satan to buffet me, lest I should be exalted above measure. For this thing I besought the Lord thrice, that it might depart from me. He said unto me, "My grace is sufficient for thee: for my strength is made perfect in weakness." Most gladly therefore will I rather glory in my infirmities, that the power of Christ may rest upon me. Therefore I take pleasure in infirmities, in reproaches, in necessities, in persecutions, in distresses for Christ's sake: for when I am weak, then am I strong. 2nd COR 12. 7-10

LIFE THROUGH THE POWER OF GOD

Because Christ lives, we live

Though he was crucified through weakness, yet he liveth by the power of God. For we also are weak in him, but we shall live with him by the power of God toward you. Be perfect, be of good comfort, be of one mind, live in peace; and the God of love and peace shall be with you. 2nd COR 13. 4, 11

GALATIANS

RESCUED FROM EVIL WORLD
Jesus Christ gave himself for this

Grace be to you and peace from God the Father, and from our Lord Jesus Christ, who gave himself for our sins that he might deliver us from this present evil world. GAL 1. 3, 4

THE LIFE LIVED IN THE FLESH
Is lived by faith in divine sonship

I am crucified with Christ: nevertheless I live; yet not I, but Christ liveth in me: and the life which I now live in the flesh I live by the faith of the Son of God, who loved me, and gave himself for me. GAL 2. 20

LIFE BY FAITH
By their trust shall the just live

The just shall live by faith. GAL 3. 11

CHRIST SETS US FREE
Walk in the Spirit and be free of the flesh

Stand fast therefore in the liberty wherewith Christ hath made us free, and be not entangled again with the yoke of bondage. This I say then, walk in the Spirit, and ye shall not fulfil the lust of the flesh. For the flesh lusteth against the Spirit, and the Spirit against the flesh: and these are contrary the one to the other: so that ye cannot do the things that ye would. But if ye be led of the Spirit, ye are not under the law. If we live in the Spirit, let us also walk in the Spirit.

GAL 5. 1, 16-18, 25

EPHESIANS

CREATED TO DO GOOD DEEDS
By God's grace man is saved

By grace are ye saved through faith; and that not of yourselves: it is the gift of God. For we are his workmanship, created in Christ Jesus unto good works, which God hath before ordained that we should walk in them. EP 2. 8, 10

STRENGTHENED BY HIS SPIRIT
To grasp the power of Christ's love

For this cause I bow my knees unto the Father of our Lord Jesus Christ, of whom the whole family in heaven and earth is named, that he would grant you, according to the riches of his glory, to be strengthened with might by his Spirit in the inner man; that Christ may dwell in your hearts by faith; that ye, being rooted and grounded in love, may be able to comprehend with all saints what is the breadth, and length, and depth, and height; and to know the love of Christ, which passeth knowledge, that ye might be filled with all the fulness of God. Now unto him that is able to do exceeding abundantly above all that we ask or think, according to the power that worketh in us, unto him be glory in the church by Christ Jesus throughout all ages, world without end. Amen. EP 3. 14-21

SPEAK THE TRUTH THROUGH LOVE
Until the body is whole

He gave some, apostles; and some, prophets; and some, evangelists; and some, pastors and teachers; for the perfecting of the saints, for the work of the ministry, for the edifying of the body of Christ: till we all come in the unity of the faith, and of the knowledge of the Son of God, unto a perfect man, unto the measure of the stature of the fulness of Christ: that we henceforth be no more children, tossed to and fro, and carried about with every wind of doctrine, by the sleight of men, and cunning craftiness, whereby they lie in wait to deceive; but speaking the truth in love, may grow up into him in all things, which is the head, even Christ: from whom the whole body fitly joined together and compacted by that which every joint supplieth, according to the effectual working in the measure of every part, maketh increase of the body unto the edifying of itself in love.

EP 4. 11-16

CHRIST SAVES THE BODY AND THE CHURCH
Awake and rise from the dead

Wherefore he saith, "Awake thou that sleepest, and arise from the dead, and Christ shall give thee light." Christ is the head of the church: and he is the saviour of the body.

EP 5. 14, 23

THE WHOLE ARMOR OF GOD PROTECTS FROM THE DEVIL
The sword of the Spirit is the Word of God

Put on the whole armour of God, that ye may be able to stand against the wiles of the devil. For we wrestle not against flesh and blood, but against principalities, against powers, against the rulers of the darkness of this world, against spiritual wickedness in high places. Wherefore take unto you the whole armour of God, that ye may be able to withstand in the evil day, and having done all, to stand. Stand therefore, having your loins girt about with truth, and having on the breastplate of righteousness; and your feet shod with the preparation of the gospel of peace; above all, taking the shield of faith, wherewith ye shall be able to quench all the fiery darts of the wicked. And take the helmet of salvation, and the sword of the Spirit, which is the word of God.

EP 6. 11-17

PHILIPPIANS

PAUL'S COMPANION HEALED

Let the mind that was in Christ be in you also

Let this mind be in you, which was also in Christ Jesus: wherefore, my beloved, as ye have always obeyed, not as in my presence only, but now much more in my absence, work out your own salvation with fear and trembling. Yet I supposed it necessary to send to you Epaphroditus, my brother, and companion in labour, and fellow soldier, but your messenger, and he that ministered to my wants. For he longed after you all, and was full of heaviness, because that ye had heard that he had been sick. For indeed he was sick nigh unto death: but God had mercy on him; and not on him only, but on me also, lest I should have sorrow upon sorrow. I sent him therefore the more carefully, that, when ye see him again, ye may rejoice.

PHIL 2. 5, 12, 25-28

PAUL PRESSES TOWARD THE MARK

Which will change his body to more glorious one

Brethren, I count not myself to have apprehended: but this one thing I do, forgetting those things which are behind, and reaching forth unto those things which are before, I press toward the mark for the prize of the high calling of God in Christ Jesus. For our conversation is in heaven; from whence also we look for the Saviour, the Lord Jesus Christ: who shall change our vile body, that it may be fashioned like unto his glorious body, according to the working whereby he is able even to subdue all things unto himself.

PHIL 3. 13, 14 20, 21

STAND FIRM IN THE LORD

Peace of heart and mind comes through Christ

My brethren dearly beloved and longed for, my joy and

crown, so stand fast in the Lord, my dearly beloved. And the peace of God, which passeth all understanding, shall keep your hearts and minds through Christ Jesus. PHIL 4. 1, 7

COLOSSIANS

RESCUED FROM THE POWER OF DARKNESS
The Father translates us into Christ's kingdom

Be filled with the knowledge of His will in all wisdom and spiritual understanding, giving thanks unto the Father, which hath made us meet to be partakers of the inheritance of the saints in light: who hath delivered us from the power of darkness, and hath translated us into the kingdom of his dear Son.

COL 1. 9, 12, 13

LIFE HID WITH CHRIST IN GOD
When Christ appears we shall appear with him

If ye then be risen with Christ, seek those things which are above, where Christ sitteth on the right hand of God. Set your affection on things above, not on things on the earth. For ye are dead, and your life is hid with Christ in God. When Christ, who is our life, shall appear, then shall ye also appear with him in glory. COL 3. 1-4

THESSALONIANS

COMFORT IN DISTRESS
We live if we stand firm

Therefore, brethren, we were comforted over you in all our affliction and distress by your faith: for now we live, if ye stand fast in the Lord. I THES 3. 7, 8

FORTIFIED IN GOOD WORK

Chosen for salvation through belief in the truth

We are bound to give thanks alway to God for you, brethren beloved of the Lord, because God hath from the beginning chosen you to salvation through sanctification of the Spirit and belief of the truth: whereunto he called you by our gospel, to the obtaining of the glory of our Lord Jesus Christ. Therefore, brethren, stand fast, and hold the traditions which ye have been taught, whether by word, or our epistle. Now our Lord Jesus Christ himself, and God, even our Father, which hath loved us, and hath given us everlasting consolation and good hope through grace, comfort your hearts, and stablish you in every good word and work. II THES 2. 13-17

TIMOTHY

NEVER FEAR

God gives us power, love, and self-control to overcome death

God hath not given us the spirit of fear; but of power, and of love, and of a sound mind. Be not thou therefore ashamed of the testimony of our Lord, nor of me his prisoner: but be thou partaker of the afflictions of the gospel according to the power of God; who hath saved us, and called us with an holy calling, not according to our works, but according to his own purpose and grace, which was given us in Christ Jesus before the world began, but is now made manifest by the appearing of our Saviour Jesus Christ, who hath abolished death, and hath brought life and immortality to light through the gospel.

II TIM 1. 7-10

RESCUED FROM EVERY EVIL

Paul is preserved by God

Notwithstanding the Lord stood with me, and strengthened

me; . . . and I was delivered out of the mouth of the lion. The Lord shall deliver me from every evil work, and will preserve me unto his heavenly kingdom: to whom be glory for ever and ever. Amen. II TIM 4. 17, 18

TITUS

SAVED BY RENEWING POWER OF THE HOLY SPIRIT

By His mercy we are heirs of eternal life

Not by works of righteousness which we have done, but according to his mercy he saved us. That being justified by his grace, we should be made heirs according to the hope of eternal life. TIT. 3. 5, 7

HEBREWS

MINISTERING ANGELS OF SALVATION

God has anointed with the oil of gladness

Thou hast loved righteousness, and hated iniquity; therefore God, even thy God, hath anointed thee with the oil of gladness above thy fellows. To which of the angels said he at any time, "Sit on my right hand?" Are they not all ministering spirits, sent forth to minister for them who shall be heirs of salvation? HE 1. 9, 13, 14

THOSE SUBJECT TO BONDAGE OF FLESH AND BLOOD

Delivered from fear of death

Forasmuch then as the children are partakers of flesh and blood, he also himself likewise took part of the same; that through death he might destroy him that had the power of death, that is, the devil; and deliver them who through fear of death were all their lifetime subject to bondage. HE 2. 14, 15

THE HEALING WORD OF GOD

It helps in time of need

There remaineth therefore a rest to the people of God. For the word of God is quick, and powerful, and sharper than any twoedged sword, piercing even to the dividing asunder of soul and spirit, and of the joints and marrow, and is a discerner of the thoughts and intents of the heart. Let us therefore come boldly unto the throne of grace, that we may obtain mercy, and find grace to help in time of need. HE 4. 9, 12, 16

GOD'S COVENANT WITH MEN AND WOMEN

My laws will be in their hearts and minds

This is the covenant that I will make with them after those days, saith the Lord, "I will put my laws into their hearts, and in their minds will I write them." HE 10. 16

SARA RECEIVES STRENGTH TO GIVE BIRTH

Other Old Testament characters triumph by faith

Through faith also Sara herself received strength to conceive seed, and was delivered of a child when she was past age, because she judged him faithful who had promised. And what shall I more say? for the time would fail me to tell of Gedeon, and of Barak, and of Samson, and of Jephthae; of David also, and Samuel, and of the prophets; who through faith subdued kingdoms, wrought righteousness, obtained promises, stopped the mouths of lions, quenched violence of fire, escaped the edge of the sword, out of weakness were made strong, waxed valiant in fight, turned to flight the armies of the aliens. Women received their dead raised to life again. HE 11. 11, 32-35

God Makes Perfect

He raised Jesus from the dead

Now the God of peace, that brought again from the dead our Lord Jesus, that great shepherd of the sheep, through the blood of the everlasting covenant, make you perfect in every good work to do his will, working in you that which is well-pleasing in his sight, through Jesus Christ; to whom be glory for ever and ever. Amen. HE 13. 20, 21

JAMES

Being Perfect Is the Crown of Life

When tested your fortitude increases

My brethren, count it all joy when ye fall into divers temptations; knowing this, that the trying of your faith worketh patience. But let patience have her perfect work, that ye may be perfect and entire, wanting nothing. If any of you lack wisdom, let him ask of God, that giveth to all men liberally, and upbraideth not; and it shall be given him. But let him ask in faith, nothing wavering. For he that wavereth is like a wave of the sea driven with the wind and tossed. Blessed is the man that endureth temptation: for when he is tried, he shall receive the crown of life, which the Lord hath promised to them that love him. JAMES 1. 2-6, 12

Prayer Heals the Sick

The afflicted can turn to the elders of the church

Is any among you afflicted? let him pray. Is any merry? let him sing psalms. Is any sick among you? let him call for the elders of the church; and let them pray over him, anointing him with oil in the name of the Lord: and the prayer of faith shall save the sick, and the Lord shall raise him up; and if he have committed sins, they shall be forgiven him. Confess your faults one to another, and pray one for another, that ye may be healed. The effectual fervent prayer of a righteous man availeth much. JAMES 5. 13-16

ELIJAH PRAYS FOR RAIN

Weather responds. Crops grow again

Elias was a man subject to like passions as we are, and he prayed earnestly that it might not rain: and it rained not on the earth by the space of three years and six months. He prayed again, and the heaven gave rain, and the earth brought forth her fruit. JAMES 5. 17, 18

PETER

THE TRIAL OF YOUR FAITH

Results in salvation of your soul

Blessed be the God and Father of our Lord Jesus Christ, which according to his abundant mercy hath begotten us again unto a lively hope by the resurrection of Jesus Christ from the dead. That the trial of your faith, being much more precious than of gold that perisheth, though it be tried with fire, might be found unto praise and honour and glory at the appearing of Jesus Christ: whom having not seen, ye love; in whom, though now ye see him not, yet believing, ye rejoice with joy unspeakable and full of glory: receiving the end of your faith, even the salvation of your souls. Of which salvation the prophets have enquired and searched diligently, who prophesied of the grace that should come unto you. I PE 1. 3, 7-10

HEALED BY CHRIST'S STRIPES
Because he suffered for us

Even hereunto were ye called: because Christ also suffered for us, leaving us an example, that ye should follow his steps. By whose stripes ye were healed. I PE 2. 21, 24

GOD PERFECTS, ESTABLISHES, AND STRENGTHENS
If you remain steadfast in faith

Be sober, be vigilant; because your adversary the devil, as a roaring lion, walketh about, seeking whom he may devour: whom resist stedfast in the faith, knowing that the same afflictions are accomplished in your brethren that are in the world. But the God of all grace, who hath called us unto his eternal glory by Christ Jesus, after that ye have suffered a while, make you perfect, stablish, strengthen, settle you. To him be glory and dominion for ever and ever. Amen. I PE 5. 8-11

I JOHN

ETERNAL LIFE
Promised by Jesus

And this is the promise that he hath promised us, even eternal life. I JN 2. 25

THE SONS OF GOD NOW
Every one with the hope to be like God is purified

Behold, what manner of love the Father hath bestowed upon us, that we should be called the sons of God: therefore the world knoweth us not, because it knew him not. Beloved, now are we the sons of God, and it doth not yet appear what we shall be: but we know that, when he shall appear, we shall be like him; for we shall see him as he is. And every man that hath this hope in him purifieth himself, even as he is pure.

I JN 3. 1-3

NO FEAR IN LOVE

Divine Love casts out fear

There is no fear in love; but perfect love casteth out fear: because fear hath torment. He that feareth is not made perfect in love. I JN 4. 18

LIFE IS IN THE SON

He that has the Son has life

This is the record, that God hath given to us eternal life, and this life is in his Son. He that hath the Son hath life; and he that hath not the Son of God hath not life.

I JN 5. 11, 12

PETITION GOD WITH CONFIDENCE

We get the things we ask for

These things have I written unto you that believe on the name of the Son of God; that ye may know that ye have eternal life, and that ye may believe on the name of the Son of God. And this is the confidence that we have in him, that, if we ask any thing according to his will, he heareth us: and if we know that he hear us, whatsoever we ask, we know that we have the petitions that we desired of him. I JN 5. 13-15

III JOHN

Live by the Truth

You will be healthy and all will go well with you

Beloved, I wish above all things that thou mayest prosper and be in health, even as thy soul prospereth. For I rejoiced greatly, when the brethren came and testified of the truth that is in thee, even as thou walkest in the truth. I have no greater joy than to hear that my children walk in truth. III JN 2-4

REVELATION

Fear Not

Christ is all in all

He laid his right hand upon me, saying unto me, "Fear not; I am the first and the last." REV 1. 17

The Tree of Life

He that overcomes shall not be hurt by the second death

He that hath an ear, let him hear what the Spirit saith unto the churches. To him that overcometh will I give to eat of the tree of life, which is in the midst of the paradise of God. Be thou faithful unto death, and I will give thee a crown of life. He that hath an ear, let him hear what the Spirit saith unto the churches. He that overcometh shall not be hurt of the second death. REV 2. 7, 10, 11

Out of Tribulation

God will wipe away all tears

One of the elders answered, saying unto me, "What are these

which are arrayed in white robes? and whence came they?" And I said unto him, "Sir, thou knowest." And he said to me, "These are they which came out of great tribulation, and have washed their robes, and made them white in the blood of the Lamb. Therefore are they before the throne of God, and serve him day and night in his temple: and he that sitteth on the throne shall dwell among them. They shall hunger no more, neither thirst any more; neither shall the sun light on them, nor any heat. For the Lamb which is in the midst of the throne shall feed them, and shall lead them unto living fountains of waters: and God shall wipe away all tears from their eyes."

REV 7. 13-17

NOW COMES THE VICTORY

For the accuser is overthrown

Now is come salvation, and strength, and the kingdom of our God, and the power of his Christ: for the accuser of our brethren is cast down, which accused them before our God day and night. And when the dragon saw that he was cast unto the earth, he persecuted the woman which brought forth the man child. And the earth helped the woman, and the earth opened her mouth and swallowed up the flood which the dragon cast out of his mouth. REV 12. 10, 13, 16

NO MORE PAIN

God makes all things new

God shall wipe away all tears from their eyes; and there shall be no more death, neither sorrow, nor crying, neither shall there be any more pain: for the former things are passed away. He that sat upon the throne said, "Behold, I make all things new." And he said unto me, "Write: for these words are true and faithful." And he said unto me, "It is done. I am Alpha and Omega, the beginning and the end. I will give unto him that is athirst of the fountain of the water of life freely. He that overcometh shall inherit all things; and I will be his God, and he shall be my son."

He that talked with me had a golden reed to measure the city, and the gates thereof, and the wall thereof. The city had no need of the sun, neither of the moon, to shine in it: for the glory of God did lighten it, and the Lamb is the light thereof. And the nations of them which are saved shall walk in the light of it.

REV 21. 4-7
15, 23, 24

THE RIVER OF THE WATER OF LIFE

On both sides a tree whose leaves serve for healing

He shewed me a pure river of water of life, clear as crystal, proceeding out of the throne of God and of the Lamb. In the midst of the street of it, and on either side of the river, was there the tree of life, which bare twelve manner of fruits, and yielded her fruit every month: and the leaves of the tree were for the healing of the nations. And there shall be no more curse: but the throne of God and of the Lamb shall be in it; and his servants shall serve him.

REV 22. 1-3

Old Testament

GENESIS

Nothing Too Hard for God

A son is promised

He lift up his eyes and looked, and lo, three men stood by him . . . They said unto him, "Where is Sarah thy wife?" And he said, "Behold, in the tent." He said, "I will certainly return unto thee according to the time of life; and, lo, Sarah thy wife shall have a son." And Sarah heard it in the tent door, which was behind him. Now Abraham and Sarah were old and well stricken in age; and it ceased to be with Sarah after the manner of women. Therefore Sarah laughed within herself, saying, "After I am waxed old shall I have pleasure, my lord being old also?" The Lord said unto Abraham, "Wherefore did Sarah laugh, saying, 'Shall I of a surety bear a child, which am old?' Is any thing too hard for the Lord? At the time appointed I will return unto thee, according to the time of life, and Sarah shall have a son." GEN 18. 2, 9-14

Another Family Healed of Barrenness

Abraham's prayer for his friend answered

Abimelech said, "Behold, my land is before thee: dwell where it pleaseth thee." Unto Sarah he said, "Behold, I have given thy brother a thousand pieces of silver: behold, he is to thee a covering of the eyes, unto all that are with thee, and with all other:" thus she was reproved. So Abraham prayed unto God: and God healed Abimelech, and his wife, and his maidservants; and they bare children. For the Lord had fast closed up all the wombs of the house of Abimelech, because of Sarah Abraham's wife. GEN 20. 15-18

SON BORN IN OLD AGE

Isaac the child of promise

The Lord visited Sarah as he had said, and the Lord did unto Sarah as he had spoken. For Sarah conceived, and bare Abraham a son in his old age, at the set time of which God had spoken to him. Abraham called the name of his son that was born unto him, whom Sarah bare to him, Isaac. Abraham circumcised his son Isaac being eight days old, as God had commanded him. Abraham was an hundred years old, when his son Isaac was born unto him. Sarah said, "God hath made me to laugh, so that all that hear will laugh with me." And she said, "Who would have said unto Abraham, that Sarah should have given children suck? for I have born him a son in his old age." GEN 21. 1-7

SURVIVAL IN WILDERNESS

God preserves mother and child

Sarah saw the son of Hagar the Egyptian, which she had born unto Abraham, mocking. Wherefore she said unto Abraham, "Cast out this bondwoman and her son: for the son of this bondwoman shall not be heir with my son, even with Isaac." And the thing was very grievous in Abraham's sight because of his son. God said unto Abraham, "Let it not be grievous in thy sight because of the lad, and because of thy bondwoman; in all that Sarah hath said unto thee, hearken unto her voice; for in Isaac shall thy seed be called. Also of the son of the bondwoman will I make a nation, because he is thy seed." Abraham rose up early in the morning, and took bread, and a bottle of water, and gave it unto Hagar, putting it on her shoulder, and the child, and sent her away: and she departed, and wandered in the wilderness of Beersheba.

The water was spent in the bottle, and she cast the child under one of the shrubs. She went, and sat her down over against him a good way off, as it were a bowshot: for she said, "Let me not see the death of the child." And she sat over against him, and lift up her voice, and wept. God heard the voice of the lad; and the angel of God called to Hagar out of heaven, and said unto her, "What aileth thee, Hagar? fear not; for God hath heard the voice of the lad where he is. Arise, lift up the lad, and hold him in thine hand; for I will make him a great nation." God opened her eyes, and she saw a well of water; and she went, and filled the bottle with water, and gave the lad drink. God was with the lad; and he grew, and dwelt in the wilderness, and became an archer. GEN 21. 9-20

DISLOCATED THIGH

Jacob healed by change of name and nature

Jacob was left alone; and there wrestled a man with him until the breaking of the day. When he saw that he prevailed not against him, he touched the hollow of his thigh; and the hollow of Jacob's thigh was out of joint as he wrestled with him. He said, "Let me go, for the day breaketh." And he said, "I will not let thee go, except thou bless me." He said unto him, "What is thy name?" And he said, "Jacob." He said, "Thy name shall be called no more Jacob, but Israel: for as a prince hast thou power with God and with men, and hast prevailed." Jacob asked him, and said, "Tell me, I pray thee, thy name." And he said, "Wherefore is it that thou dost ask after my name?" And he blessed him there.

Jacob called the name of the place Peniel: for I have seen God face to face, and my life is preserved. GEN 32. 24-30

FAMILY HOSTILITY RECONCILED

Jacob sees his brother's face as the reflection of God

Jacob lifted up his eyes, and looked, and, behold, Esau came, and with him four hundred men. And he divided the children unto Leah, and unto Rachel, and unto the two handmaids. He put the handmaids and their children foremost, and Leah and her children after, and Rachel and Joseph hindermost. He passed over before them, and bowed himself to the ground seven times until he came near to his brother. Esau ran to meet him, and embraced him, and fell on his neck, and kissed him: and they wept. He lifted up his eyes, and saw the women and the children; and said, "Who are those with thee?" And he said, "The children which God hath graciously given thy servant." Then the handmaidens came near, they and their children, and they bowed themselves. And Leah also with her children came near, and bowed themselves: and after came Joseph near and Rachel, and they bowed themselves. And he said, "What meanest thou by all this drove which I met?" And he said, "These are to find grace in the sight of my lord." And Esau said, "I have enough, my brother; keep that thou hast unto thyself." And Jacob said, "Nay, I pray thee, if now I have found grace in thy sight, then receive my present at my hand: for therefore I have seen thy face, as though I had seen the face of God, and thou wast pleased with me. Take, I pray thee, my blessing that is brought to thee; because God hath dealt graciously with me, and because I have enough." And he urged him, and he took it. GEN 33. 1-11

PROSPERITY IN SLAVERY

Joseph blesses his master

Joseph was brought down to Egypt; and Potiphar, an officer of Pharaoh, captain of the guard, an Egyptian, bought him of the hands of the Ishmeelites, which had brought him down thither. The Lord was with Joseph, and he was a prosperous man; and he was in the house of his master the Egyptian. His master saw that the Lord was with him, and that the Lord made all that he did to prosper in his hand. GEN 39. 1-3

GOD INTERPRETS MYSTERIES

Joseph solves the king's problem

Then Pharaoh sent and called Joseph, and they brought him hastily out of the dungeon: and he shaved himself, and changed his raiment, and came in unto Pharaoh. Pharaoh said unto Joseph, "I have dreamed a dream, and there is none that can interpret it: and I have heard say of thee, that thou canst understand a dream to interpret it." And Joseph answered Pharaoh, saying, "It is not in me: God shall give Pharaoh an answer of peace." GEN 41. 14-16

GOD GIVES STRENGTH IN BATTLE OF LIFE

The source of Joseph's problem-solving ability

Joseph is a fruitful bough, even a fruitful bough by a well; whose branches run over the wall. The archers have sorely grieved him, and shot at him, and hated him: but his bow abode in strength, and the arms of his hands were made strong by the hands of the mighty God of Jacob. GEN 49. 22-24

FAMILY REUNITES

Brothers' antagonism forgiven by Joseph

Joseph said unto them, "Fear not: for am I in the place of God? But as for you, ye thought evil against me; but God meant it unto good, to bring to pass, as it is this day, to save much people alive. Now therefore fear ye not: I will nourish you, and your little ones." And he comforted them, and spake kindly unto them. GEN 50. 19-21

EXODUS

INFERIORITY COMPLEX

God promises He will be with Moses

Moses said, "I will now turn aside, and see this great sight, why the bush is not burnt." When the Lord saw that he turned aside to see, God called unto him out of the midst of the bush, and said, "Moses, Moses." And he said, "Here am I." He said, "Draw not nigh hither: put off thy shoes from off thy feet, for the place whereon thou standest is holy ground." Moses said unto God, "Who am I, that I should go unto Pharaoh, and that I should bring forth the children of Israel out of Egypt?" He said, "Certainly I will be with thee; and this shall be a token unto thee, that I have sent thee: when thou hast brought forth the people out of Egypt, ye shall serve God upon this mountain."

EX 3. 3-5, 11-12

FEAR AND DISEASE CONTROLLED

Serpent proved harmless and leprosy disappears

Moses answered and said, "But, behold, they will not believe me, nor hearken unto my voice: for they will say, 'The Lord hath not appeared unto thee.' " The Lord said unto him, "What is that in thine hand?" And he said, "A rod." He said, "Cast it on the ground." He cast it on the ground, and it became a serpent; and Moses fled from before it. The Lord said unto Moses, "Put forth thine hand, and take it by the tail." And he put forth his hand, and caught it, and it became a rod in his hand: that they may believe that the Lord God of their fathers, the God of Abraham, the God of Isaac, and the God of Jacob, hath appeared unto thee.

The Lord said furthermore unto him, "Put now thine hand into thy bosom." And he put his hand into his bosom: and when he took it out, behold, his hand was leprous as snow. And he said, "Put thine hand into thy bosom again." And he put his hand into his bosom again; and plucked it out of his bosom, and, behold, it was turned again as his other flesh. "It shall come to pass, if they will not believe thee, neither hearken to the voice of the first sign, that they will believe the voice of the latter sign." EX 4. 1-8

A GIFT OF ELOQUENCE
God is the source of the faculties

Moses said unto the Lord, "O my Lord, I am not eloquent, neither heretofore, nor since thou hast spoken unto thy servant: but I am slow of speech, and of a slow tongue." And the Lord said unto him, "Who hath made man's mouth? or who maketh the dumb, or deaf, or the seeing, or the blind? have not I the Lord? Now therefore go, and I will be with thy mouth, and teach thee what thou shalt say." EX 4. 10-12

GOSHEN UNTOUCHED BY PLAGUES
God protects land where His children live

The Lord said unto Moses, "Rise up early in the morning, and stand before Pharaoh; lo, he cometh forth to the water; and say unto him, 'Thus saith the Lord, Let my people go, that they may serve me. Else, if thou wilt not let my people go, behold, I will send swarms of flies upon thee, and upon thy servants, and upon thy people, and into thy houses and the houses of the Egyptians shall be full of swarms of flies, and also the ground whereon they are. And I will sever in that day the land of Goshen, in which my people dwell, that no swarms of flies shall be there; to the end thou mayest know that I am the Lord in the midst of the earth.' " EX 8. 20-22

PROTECTION FOR GOD'S PEOPLE
Their livestock unharmed by epidemics

Behold, the hand of the Lord is upon thy cattle which is

in the field, upon the horses, upon the asses, upon the camels, upon the oxen, and upon the sheep: there shall be a very grievous murrain. The Lord shall sever between the cattle of Israel and the cattle of Egypt: and there shall nothing die of all that is the children's of Israel. The Lord appointed a set time, saying, "Tomorrow the Lord shall do this thing in the land." The Lord did that thing on the morrow, and all the cattle of Egypt died: but of the cattle of the children of Israel died not one. EX 9. 3-6

THE FIRST PASSOVER

Hebrew first-born preserved from death

"Speak ye unto all the congregation of Israel, saying, 'In the tenth day of this month they shall take to them every man a lamb, according to the house of their fathers, a lamb for an house. They shall take of the blood, and strike it on the two side posts and on the upper door post of the houses, wherein they shall eat it.' For I will pass through the land of Egypt this night, and will smite all the firstborn in the land of Egypt, both man and beast; and against all the gods of Egypt I will execute judgment: I am the Lord. And the blood shall be to you for a token upon the houses where ye are: and when I see the blood, I will pass over you, and the plague shall not be upon you to destroy you, when I smite the land of Egypt." It came to pass, that at midnight the Lord smote all the firstborn in the land of Egypt, from the firstborn of Pharaoh that sat on his throne unto the firstborn of the captive that was in the dungeon; and all the firstborn of cattle. Pharaoh rose up in the night, he, and all his servants, and all the Egyptians; and there was a great cry in Egypt; for there was not a house where there was not one dead. He called for Moses and Aaron by night, and said, "Rise up, and get you forth from among my people, both ye and the children of Israel; and go, serve the Lord, as ye have said. Also take your flocks and your herds, as ye have said, and be gone; and bless me also." And the Egyptians were urgent upon the people, that they might send them out of the land in haste.

EX 12. 3, 7, 12, 13, 29-33

THE PILLAR OF CLOUD LEADS THE WAY
God guides out of slavery

It came to pass, when Pharaoh had let the people go, that God led them not through the way of the land of the Philistines, although that was near; for God said, "Lest peradventure the people repent when they see war, and they return to Egypt." But God led the people about, through the way of the wilderness of the Red sea: and the children of Israel went up harnessed out of the land of Egypt. The Lord went before them by day in a pillar of a cloud, to lead them the way; and by night in a pillar of fire, to give them light; to go by day and night. He took not away the pillar of the cloud by day, nor the pillar of fire by night, from before the people.

EX 13. 17, 18, 21, 22

SAVED AT RED SEA
Fearlessly looking to God for deliverance

The Lord hardened the heart of Pharaoh king of Egypt, and he pursued after the children of Israel: and the children of Israel went out with an high hand. But the Egyptians pursued after them, all the horses and chariots of Pharaoh, and his horsemen, and his army, and overtook them encamping by the sea, beside Pi-hahiroth, before Baal-zephon. When Pharaoh drew nigh, the children of Israel lifted up their eyes, and, behold, the Egyptians marched after them; and they were sore afraid: and the children of Israel cried out unto the Lord. They said unto Moses, "Because there were no graves in Egypt, hast thou taken us away to die in the wilderness? wherefore hast thou dealt thus with us, to carry us forth out of Egypt? Is not this the word that we did tell thee in Egypt, saying,

'Let us alone, that we may serve the Egyptians?' For it had been better for us to serve the Egyptians, than that we should die in the wilderness." Moses said unto the people, "Fear ye not, stand still, and see the salvation of the Lord, which he will shew to you today: for the Egyptians whom ye have seen today, ye shall see them again no more forever. The Lord shall fight for you, and ye shall hold your peace." And Moses stretched out his hand over the sea; and the Lord caused the sea to go back by a strong east wind all that night, and made the sea dry land, and the waters were divided. And the children of Israel went into the midst of the sea upon the dry ground: and the waters were a wall unto them on their right hand, and on their left. EX 14. 8-14, 21-22

THIRST QUENCHED
Polluted water in the desert purified

So Moses brought Israel from the Red sea, and they went out into the wilderness of Shur; and they went three days in the wilderness, and found no water. When they came to Marah, they could not drink of the waters of Marah, for they were bitter: therefore the name of it was called Marah. And the people murmured against Moses, saying, "What shall we drink?" He cried unto the Lord; and the Lord shewed him a tree, which when he had cast into the waters, the waters were made sweet: there he made for them a statute and an ordinance, and there he proved them, and said, "If thou wilt diligently hearken to the voice of the Lord thy God, and wilt do that which is right in his sight, and wilt give ear to his commandments, and keep all his statutes, I will put none of these diseases upon thee, which I have brought upon the Egyptians: for I am the Lord that healeth thee." EX 15. 22-26

HUNGER SATISFIED
Quails and manna from heaven

The whole congregation of the children of Israel murmured

against Moses and Aaron in the wilderness: and the children of Israel said unto them, "Would to God we had died by the hand of the Lord in the land of Egypt, when we sat by the flesh pots, and when we did eat bread to the full; for ye have brought us forth into this wilderness, to kill this whole assembly with hunger." Then said the Lord unto Moses, "Behold, I will rain bread from heaven for you; and the people shall go out and gather a certain rate every day, that I may prove them whether they will walk in my law, or no. It shall come to pass, that on the sixth day they shall prepare that which they bring in; and it shall be twice as much as they gather daily." And Moses and Aaron said unto all the children of Israel, "At even, then ye shall know that the Lord hath brought you out from the land of Egypt: and in the morning, then ye shall see the glory of the Lord; for that he heareth your murmurings against the Lord: and what are we, that ye murmur against us?" And Moses said, "This shall be, when the Lord shall give you in the evening flesh to eat, and in the morning bread to the full; for that the Lord heareth your murmurings which ye murmur against him: and what are we? your murmurings are not against us, but against the Lord."

Moses spake unto Aaron, "Say unto all the congregation of the children of Israel, 'Come near before the Lord: for he hath heard your murmurings.' " It came to pass, as Aaron spake unto the whole congregation of the children of Israel, that they looked toward the wilderness, and, behold, the glory of the Lord appeared in the cloud. The Lord spake unto Moses, saying, "I have heard the murmurings of the children of Israel: speak unto them, saying, 'At even ye shall eat flesh, and in the morning ye shall be filled with bread; and ye shall know that I am the Lord your God.' "

It came to pass, that at even the quails came up, and covered the camp: and in the morning the dew lay round about the host. When the dew that lay was gone up, behold, upon the face of the wilderness there lay a small round thing, as small as the hoar frost on the ground. When the children of Israel saw it, they said one to another, "It is manna:" for they wist not what it was. And Moses said unto them, "This is the bread which the Lord hath given you to eat. This is the thing which the Lord hath commanded, 'Gather of it every man according to his eating, an omer for every man, according to the number of your persons; take ye every man for them which are in his tents.' " The children of Israel did so, and gathered, some more, some less. When they did mete it with an omer, he that gathered much had nothing over, and he that gathered little had no lack; they gathered every man according to his eating. So the people rested on the seventh day. And the house of Israel called the name thereof manna: and it was like coriander seed, white; and the taste of it was like wafers made with honey. EX 16. 2-18, 30, 31

WITHOUT WATER IN WILDERNESS

Moses obtains water from rock

All the congregation of the children of Israel journeyed from the wilderness of Sin, after their journeys, according to the commandment of the Lord, and pitched in Rephidim: and there was no water for the people to drink. Wherefore the people did chide with Moses, and said, "Give us water that we may drink." And Moses said unto them, "Why chide ye with me? wherefore do ye tempt the Lord?" The people thirsted there for water; and the people murmured against Moses, and said, "Wherefore is this that thou hast brought us up out of Egypt, to kill us and our children and our cattle with thirst?" And Moses cried unto the Lord, saying, "What shall I do unto this people? they be almost ready to stone me." The Lord said unto Moses, "Go on before the people, and take with thee of the elders of Israel; and thy rod, wherewith thou smotest the river, take in thine hand, and go. Behold, I will stand before thee there upon the rock in Horeb; and thou shalt smite the rock, and there shall come water out of it, that the people may drink." And Moses did so in the sight of the elders of Israel. He called the name of the place Massah, and Meribah, because of the chiding of the children of Israel, and because they tempted the Lord, saying, "Is the Lord among us, or not?"

EX 17. 1-7

CARRIED OUT OF SLAVERY IN EGYPT
Escaped as on wings

Moses went up unto God, and the Lord called unto him out of the mountain, saying, "Thus shalt thou say to the house of Jacob, and tell the children of Israel: ye have seen what I did unto the Egyptians, and how I bare you on eagles' wings, and brought you unto myself. Now therefore, if ye will obey my voice indeed, and keep my covenant, then ye shall be a peculiar treasure unto me above all people: for all the earth is mine: and ye shall be unto me a kingdom of priests, and an holy nation. These are the words which thou shalt speak unto the children of Israel." EX 19. 3-6

GOD TAKES SICKNESS AWAY
He sustains during wilderness passage

Behold, I send an angel before thee, to keep thee in the way, and to bring thee into the place which I have prepared. Ye shall serve the Lord your God, and he shall bless thy bread, and thy water; and I will take sickness away from the midst of thee. There shall nothing cast their young, nor be barren, in thy land: the number of thy days I will fulfil. I will send my fear before thee, and will destroy all the people to whom thou shalt come, and I will make all thine enemies turn their backs unto thee. EX 23. 20, 25-27

ALL THE GOODNESS OF THE LORD SHOWN TO MOSES
God's nature is manifested

Moses said unto the Lord, "Thou hast said, 'I know thee

by name, and thou hast also found grace in my sight.' Now therefore, I pray thee, if I have found grace in thy sight, shew me now thy way, that I may know thee, that I may find grace in thy sight: and consider that this nation is thy people." And he said, "My presence shall go with thee, and I will give thee rest." And he said unto him, "If thy presence go not with me, carry us not up hence. For wherein shall it be known here that I and thy people have found grace in thy sight? is it not in that thou goest with us? so shall we be separated, I and thy people, from all the people that are upon the face of the earth." And the Lord said unto Moses, "I will do this thing also that thou hast spoken: for thou hast found grace in my sight, and I know thee by name." And he said, "I beseech thee, shew me thy glory." And he said, "I will make all my goodness pass before thee, and I will proclaim the name of the Lord before thee; and will be gracious to whom I will be gracious, and will shew mercy on whom I will shew mercy."

EX 33. 12-19

THE TEN COMMANDMENTS

Skin of Moses' face shines when he returns with the tablets

The Lord passed by before him, and proclaimed, "The Lord, The Lord God, merciful and gracious, longsuffering, and abundant in goodness and truth, keeping mercy for thousands, forgiving iniquity and transgression and sin, and that will by no means clear the guilty . . . " Moses made haste, and bowed **his head toward the earth, and worshipped. He said, "If now** I have found grace in thy sight, O Lord, let my Lord, I pray thee, go among us; for it is a stiffnecked people; and pardon our iniquity and our sin, and take us for thine inheritance." He said, "Behold, I make a covenant: before all thy people I will do marvels, such as have not been done in all the earth, nor in any nation: and all the people among which thou art **shall see the work of the Lord." . . . He was there with the Lord** forty days and forty nights; he did neither eat bread, nor drink water. And he wrote upon the tables the words of the covenant, the ten commandments. It came to pass, when Moses came down from mount Sinai with the two tables of testimony in Moses' hand, when he came down from the mount, that Moses wist not that the skin of his face shone while he talked with him. When Aaron and all the children of Israel saw Moses, behold, the skin of his face shone; and they were afraid to come nigh him. EX 34. 6-10, 28-30

LEVITICUS

HOLY BECAUSE THE LORD IS HOLY

Man is the reflection of God

I am the Lord your God: ye shall therefore sanctify yourselves, and ye shall be holy; for I am holy: neither shall ye defile yourselves with any manner of creeping thing that creepeth upon the earth. For I am the Lord that bringeth you up out of the land of Egypt, to be your God: ye shall therefore be holy, for I am holy. LEV 11. 44, 45

LIVING SAFELY

If commandments are kept

Wherefore ye shall do my statutes, and keep my judgments, and do them; and ye shall dwell in the land in safety. The land shall yield her fruit, and ye shall eat your fill, and dwell therein in safety. LEV 25. 18, 19

NONE SHALL MAKE YOU AFRAID

God has broken the yoke of slavery

If ye walk in my statutes, and keep my commandments, and do them; then I will give you rain in due season, and the land shall yield her increase, and the trees of the field shall yield their fruit. Your threshing shall reach unto the vintage, and the vintage shall reach unto the sowing time: and ye shall eat your bread to the full, and dwell in your land safely. I will give peace in the land, and ye shall lie down, and none shall make you afraid: and I will rid evil beasts out of the land, neither shall the sword go through your land. I will set my tabernacle among you: and my soul shall not abhor you. I will walk among you, and will be your God, and ye shall be my people. I am the Lord your God, which brought you forth out of the land of Egypt, that ye should not be their bondmen; and I have broken the bands of your yoke, and made you go upright. LEV 26. 3-6, 11-13

NUMBERS

THE LORD BLESS THEE AND KEEP THEE

God's nature transferred to His children

The Lord spake unto Moses, saying, "Speak unto Aaron and unto his sons, saying, on this wise ye shall bless the children of Israel, saying unto them, 'The Lord bless thee, and keep thee: the Lord make his face shine upon thee, and be gracious unto thee: the Lord lift up his countenance upon thee, and give thee peace.' They shall put my name upon the children of Israel; and I will bless them." NUM 6. 22-27

NO EPIDEMIC AMONG THE CHILDREN

When they are near the sanctuary

I have given the Levites as a gift to Aaron and to his sons from among the children of Israel, to do the service of the children of Israel in the tabernacle of the congregation, and to make an atonement for the children of Israel: that there be no plague among the children of Israel, when the children of Israel come nigh unto the sanctuary. NUM 8. 19

MOSES HEALS LEPROSY

His rebellious sister is cured by him

Miriam and Aaron spake against Moses because of the Ethiopian woman whom he had married: for he had married an Ethiopian woman. They said, "Hath the Lord indeed spoken only by Moses? hath he not spoken also by us?" And the Lord heard it. (Now the man Moses was very meek, above all the men which were upon the face of the earth.) The Lord spake suddenly unto Moses, and unto Aaron, and unto Miriam, "Come out ye three unto the tabernacle of the congregation." And they three came out. The Lord came down in the pillar of the cloud, and stood in the door of the tabernacle, and called Aaron and Miriam: and they both came forth. And he said, "Hear now my words: If there be a prophet among you, I the Lord will make myself known unto him in a vision, and will speak unto him in a dream. My servant Moses is not so, who is faithful in all mine house. With him will I speak mouth to mouth, even apparently, and not in dark speeches; and the similitude of the Lord shall he behold: wherefore then were ye not afraid to speak against my servant Moses?" And the anger of the Lord was kindled against them; and he departed. And the cloud departed from off the tabernacle; and, behold, Miriam became leprous, white as snow: and Aaron looked upon Miriam, and, behold, she was leprous. And Aaron said unto Moses, "Alas, my lord, I beseech thee, lay not the sin upon us, wherein we have done foolishly, and wherein we have sinned. Let her not be as one dead, of whom the flesh is half consumed when he cometh out of his mother's womb." And Moses cried unto the Lord, saying, "Heal her now, O God, I beseech thee." And the Lord said unto Moses, "If her father had but spit in her face, should she not be ashamed seven days? let her be shut out from the camp seven days, and after that let her be received in again." And Miriam was shut out from the camp seven days: and the people journeyed not till Miriam was brought in again. NUM 12. 1-15

AN EPIDEMIC IS STOPPED

Aaron makes atonement

On the morrow all the congregation of the children of Israel murmured against Moses and against Aaron, saying, "Ye have killed the people of the Lord." It came to pass, when the congregation was gathered against Moses and against Aaron, that they looked toward the tabernacle of the congregation: and, behold, the cloud covered it, and the glory of the Lord appeared. Moses and Aaron came before the tabernacle of the congregation. Moses said unto Aaron, "Take a censer, and put fire therein from off the altar, and put on incense, and go quickly unto the congregation, and make an atonement for them: for there is wrath gone out from the Lord; the plague is begun." And Aaron took as Moses commanded, and ran into the midst of the congregation; and, behold, the plague was begun among the people: and he put on incense, and made an atonement for the people. He stood between the dead and the living; and the plague was stayed. Now they that died in the plague were fourteen thousand and seven hundred, beside them that died about the matter of Korah. Aaron returned unto Moses unto the door of the tabernacle of the congregation: and the plague was stayed. NUM 16. 41-43, 46-50

SNAKE BITE HEALED

People who follow Moses' instruction recover

They journeyed from mount Hor by the way of the Red sea, to compass the land of Edom: and the soul of the people was much discouraged because of the way. The people spake against God, and against Moses, "Wherefore have ye brought us up out of Egypt to die in the wilderness? for there is no bread, neither is there any water; and our soul loatheth this light bread." And the Lord sent fiery serpents among the people, and they bit the people; and much people of Israel died. Therefore the people came to Moses, and said, "We have sinned, for we have spoken against the Lord, and against thee; pray unto the Lord, that he take away the serpents from us." And Moses prayed for the people. And the Lord said unto Moses, "Make thee a fiery serpent, and set it upon a pole: and it shall come to pass, that every one that is bitten, when he looketh upon it, shall live." Moses made a serpent of brass, and put it upon a pole, and it came to pass, that if a serpent had bitten any man, when he beheld the serpent of brass, he lived.

NUM 21. 4-9

BALAAM'S ASS SAVES HIM

Fatal confrontation with an armed adversary avoided

Balaam rose up in the morning, and saddled his ass, and went with the princes of Moab. God's anger was kindled because he went: and the angel of the Lord stood in the way for an adversary against him. Now he was riding upon his ass, and his two servants were with him. The ass saw the angel of the Lord standing in the way, and his sword drawn in his hand: and the ass turned aside out of the way, and went into the field: and Balaam smote the ass, to turn her into the way. But the angel of the Lord stood in a path of the vineyards, a wall being on this side, and a wall on that side. When the ass saw the angel of the Lord, she thrust herself unto the wall, and crushed Balaam's foot against the wall: and he smote her again. The angel of the Lord went further, and stood in a narrow place, where was no way to turn either to the right hand or to the left. When the ass saw the angel of the Lord, she fell down under Balaam: and Balaam's anger was kindled, and he smote the ass with a staff. The Lord opened the mouth of the ass, and she said unto Balaam, "What have I done unto thee, that thou hast smitten me these three times?" Balaam said unto the ass, "Because thou hast mocked me: I would there were a sword in mine hand, for now would I kill thee." And the ass said unto Balaam, "Am not I thine ass, upon which thou hast ridden ever since I was thine unto this day? was I ever wont to do so unto thee?" And he said, "Nay."

Then the Lord opened the eyes of Balaam, and he saw the angel of the Lord standing in the way, and his sword drawn in his hand: and he bowed down his head, and fell flat on his face. The angel of the Lord said unto him, "Wherefore hast thou smitten thine ass these three times? behold, I went out to withstand thee, because thy way is perverse before me: and the ass saw me, and turned from me these three times: unless she had turned from me, surely now also I had slain thee, and saved her alive." Balaam said unto the angel of the Lord, "I have sinned; for I knew not that thou stoodest in the way against me: now therefore, if it displease thee, I will get me back again." And the angel of the Lord said unto Balaam, "Go with the men: but only the word that I shall speak unto thee, that thou shalt speak." So Balaam went with the princes of Balak.

NUM 22. 21-35

NO HEX AGAINST THE CHILDREN OF GOD
Balaam cannot curse them

The Lord put a word in Balaam's mouth, and said, "Return unto Balak, and thus thou shalt speak." He returned unto him, and, lo, he stood by his burnt sacrifice, he, and all the princes of Moab. He took up his parable, and said, "Balak the king of Moab hath brought me from Aram, out of the mountains of the east, saying, 'Come, curse me Jacob, and come, defy Israel.' How shall I curse, whom God hath not cursed? or how shall I defy, whom the Lord hath not defied?" Balak said unto Balaam, "What hast thou done unto me? I took thee to curse mine enemies, and, behold, thou hast blessed them altogether."

He answered and said, "Must I not take heed to speak that which the Lord hath put in my mouth?"

He took up his parable, and said, "Rise up, Balak, and hear; hearken unto me, thou son of Zippor: God is not a man, that he should lie; neither the son of man, that he should repent: hath he said, and shall he not do it? or hath he spoken, and shall he not make it good? Behold, I have received commandment to bless: and he hath blessed; and I cannot reverse it. He hath not beheld iniquity in Jacob, neither hath he seen perverseness in Israel: the Lord his God is with him, and the shout of a king is among them. God brought them out of Egypt; he hath as it were the strength of an unicorn. Surely there is no enchantment against Jacob, neither is there any divination against Israel: according to this time it shall be said of Jacob and of Israel, What hath God wrought!"

NUM 23. 5-8, 11, 12, 18-23

DEUTERONOMY

Do Not Be Afraid

God shall fight for you

Then I said unto you, "Dread not, neither be afraid of them. The Lord your God which goeth before you, he shall fight for you, according to all that he did for you in Egypt before your eyes; and in the wilderness, where thou hast seen how that the Lord thy God bare thee, as a man doth bear his son, in all the way that ye went, until ye came into this place. Yet in this thing ye did not believe the Lord your God, who went in the way before you, to search you out a place to pitch your tents in, in fire by night, to shew you by what way ye should go, and in a cloud by day." DEUT 1. 29-33

YOU SHALL LACK NOTHING

God has blessed you in all your work

The Lord thy God hath blessed thee in all the works of thy hand: he knoweth thy walking through this great wilderness: these forty years the Lord thy God hath been with thee; thou hast lacked nothing. DEUT 2. 7

GOD BROUGHT YOU OUT OF SLAVERY

With a strong hand

Remember that thou wast a servant in the land of Egypt, and that the Lord thy God brought thee out thence through a mighty hand and by a stretched out arm . . . DEUT 5. 15

THE LORD TAKES AWAY ALL SICKNESS

He will love, bless and multiply you

Wherefore it shall come to pass, if ye hearken to these judgments, and keep, and do them, that the Lord thy God shall keep unto thee the covenant and the mercy which he sware unto thy fathers. He will love thee, and bless thee, and multiply thee: he will also bless the fruit of thy womb, and the fruit of thy land, thy corn, and thy wine, and thine oil, the increase of thy kine, and the flocks of thy sheep, in the land which he sware unto thy fathers to give thee. Thou shalt be blessed above all people: there shall not be male or female barren among you, or among your cattle. The Lord will take away from thee all sickness, and will put none of the evil diseases of Egypt, which thou knowest, upon thee.

DEUT 7. 12-15

GOD HAS DONE GREAT THINGS FOR YOU

So love Him and walk in His ways

Now, Israel, what doth the Lord thy God require of thee, but to fear the Lord thy God, to walk in all his ways, and to love him, and to serve the Lord thy God with all thy heart and with all thy soul, to keep the commandments of the Lord, and his statutes, which I command thee this day for thy good? Behold, the heaven and the heaven of heavens is the Lord's thy God, the earth also, with all that therein is. Only the Lord had a delight in thy fathers to love them, and he chose their seed after them, even you above all people, as it is this day. Circumcise therefore the foreskin of your heart, and be no more stiffnecked. For the Lord your God is God of gods, and Lord of lords, a great God, a mighty, and a terrible, which regardeth not persons, nor taketh reward. He doth execute the judgment of the fatherless and widow, and loveth the stranger, in giving him food and raiment. Love ye therefore the stranger: for ye were strangers in the land of Egypt. Thou shalt fear the Lord thy God; him shalt thou serve, and to him shalt thou cleave, and swear by his name. He is thy praise, and he is thy God, that hath done for thee these great and terrible things, which thine eyes have seen. DEUT 10. 12-21

Being Perfect with God

A prophet shall speak all that God commands

Thou shalt be perfect with the Lord thy God. I will raise them up a prophet from among their brethren, like unto thee, and will put my words in his mouth; and he shall speak unto them all that I shall command him. DEUT 18. 13, 18

Fear Not Nor Tremble

God fights your enemies to save you

It shall be, when ye are come nigh unto the battle, that the priest shall approach and speak unto the people, and shall say unto them, "Hear, O Israel, ye approach this day unto battle against your enemies: let not your hearts faint, fear not, and do not tremble, neither be ye terrified because of them; for the Lord your God is he that goeth with you, to fight for you against your enemies, to save you." DEUT 20. 2-4

SIGNS AND MIRACLES OF DELIVERANCE
Result from the covenant with God

These are the words of the covenant, which the Lord commanded Moses to make with the children of Israel in the land of Moab, beside the covenant which he made with them in Horeb. Moses called unto all Israel, and said unto them, "Ye have seen all that the Lord did before your eyes in the land of Egypt unto Pharaoh, and unto all his servants, and unto all his land; the great temptations which thine eyes have seen, the signs, and those great miracles: yet the Lord hath not given you an heart to perceive, and eyes to see, and ears to hear, unto this day. I have led you forty years in the wilderness: your clothes are not waxen old upon you, and thy shoe is not waxen old upon thy foot. Keep therefore the words of this covenant, and do them, that ye may prosper in all that ye do."

DEUT 29. 1-5, 9

THE CHOICE OF LIFE OR DEATH
Turn to God with all your heart

This commandment which I command thee this day, it is not hidden from thee, neither is it far off. It is not in heaven, that thou shouldest say, "Who shall go up for us to heaven, and bring it unto us that we may hear it, and do it?" Neither is it beyond the sea, that thou shouldest say, "Who shall go over the sea for us, and bring it unto us, that we may hear it, and do it?" But the word is very nigh unto thee, in thy mouth, and in thy heart, that thou mayest do it.

See, I have set before thee this day life and good, and death and evil; in that I command thee this day to love the Lord thy God, to walk in his ways, and to keep his commandments and his statutes and his judgments, that thou mayest live and multiply: and the Lord thy God shall bless thee in the land whither thou goest to possess it. I call heaven and earth to record this day against you, that I have set before you life and death, blessing and cursing: therefore choose life, that both thou and thy seed may live: that thou mayest love the Lord thy God, and that thou mayest obey his voice, and that thou mayest cleave unto him: for he is thy life, and the length of thy days. DEUT 30. 11-16, 19, 20

God Is Your Strength and Refuge

You dwell in safety

Thy shoes shall be iron and brass; and as thy days, so shall thy strength be. There is none like unto the God of Jeshurun, who rideth upon the heaven in thy help, and in his excellency on the sky. The eternal God is thy refuge, and underneath are the everlasting arms: and he shall thrust out the enemy from before thee; and shall say, "Destroy them." Israel then shall dwell in safety alone: the fountain of Jacob shall be upon a land of corn and wine; also his heavens shall drop down dew. Happy art thou, O Israel: who is like unto thee, O people saved by the Lord, the shield of thy help, and who is the sword of thy excellency! and thine enemies shall be found liars unto thee; and thou shalt tread upon their high places.

DEUT 33. 25-29

Faculties Unimpaired in Old Age

Moses at 120 years

Moses was an hundred and twenty years old when he died: his eye was not dim, nor his natural force abated. There arose not a prophet since in Israel like unto Moses, whom the Lord knew face to face, in all the signs and the wonders, which the Lord sent him to do in the land of Egypt to Pharaoh, and to all his servants, and to all his land, and in all that mighty hand, and in all the great terror which Moses shewed in the sight of all Israel. DEUT 34. 7, 10-12

JOSHUA

TAKE COURAGE AND STRENGTH
Read the Book of the Law

Only be thou strong and very courageous, that thou mayest observe to do according to all the law, which Moses my servant commanded thee: turn not from it to the right hand or to the left, that thou mayest prosper whithersoever thou goest. This book of the law shall not depart out of thy mouth; but thou shalt meditate therein day and night, that thou mayest observe to do according to all that is written therein: for then thou shalt make thy way prosperous, and then thou shalt have good success. Have not I commanded thee? Be strong and of a good courage; be not afraid, neither be thou dismayed: for the Lord thy God is with thee whithersoever thou goest.

JOSH 1. 7-9

LIFE AND STRENGTH CONTINUOUS
Caleb is given share of promised land

Then the children of Judah came unto Joshua in Gilgal: and Caleb the son of Jephunneh the Kenezite said unto him, "Thou knowest the thing that the Lord said unto Moses the man of God concerning me and thee in Kadesh-barnea. Forty years old was I when Moses the servant of the Lord sent me from Kadesh-barnea to espy out the land; and I brought him word again as it was in mine heart. Nevertheless my brethren that went up with me made the heart of the people melt: but I wholly followed the Lord my God. And Moses sware on that day, saying, 'Surely the land whereon thy feet have trodden shall be thine inheritance, and thy children's for ever, because thou hast wholly followed the Lord my God.' Now, behold, the Lord hath kept me alive, as he said, these forty and five years, even since the Lord spake this word unto Moses, while the children of Israel wandered in the wilderness: and now, lo, I am this day fourscore and five years old. As yet I am as strong this day as I was in the day that Moses sent me: as my strength was then, even so is my strength now, for war, both to go out, and to come in. Now therefore give me this mountain, whereof the Lord spake in that day; for thou heardest in that day how the Anakims were there, and that the cities were great and fenced: if so be the Lord will be with me, then I shall be able to drive them out, as the Lord said." And Joshua blessed him, and gave unto Caleb the son of Jephunneh Hebron for an inheritance. JOSH 14. 6-13

None of God's Promises Unfulfilled

They all come true

There failed not ought of any good thing which the Lord had spoken unto the house of Israel; all came to pass. And, behold, this day I am going the way of all the earth: and ye know in all your hearts and in all your souls, that not one thing hath failed of all the good things which the Lord your God spake concerning you; all are come to pass unto you, and not one thing hath failed thereof. JOSH 21. 45
23. 14

JUDGES

The Spiritual Conception of Samson

A messenger from the Lord prophesies it

There was a certain man of Zorah, of the family of the Danites, whose name was Manoah; and his wife was barren, and bare not. The angel of the Lord appeared unto the woman, and said unto her, "Behold now, thou art barren, and bearest not: but thou shalt conceive, and bear a son. Now therefore beware, I pray thee, and drink not wine nor strong drink, and eat not any unclean thing: for, lo, thou shalt conceive, and bear a son; and no razor shall come on his head: for the child shall be a Nazarite unto God from the womb: and he shall begin to deliver Israel out of the hand of the Philistines."

Then the woman came and told her husband, saying, "A man of God came unto me, and his countenance was like the countenance of an angel of God, very terrible: but I asked him not whence he was, neither told he me his name. But he said unto me, 'Behold, thou shalt conceive, and bear a son; and now drink no wine nor strong drink, neither eat any unclean thing: for the child shall be a Nazarite to God from the womb to the day of his death.' " Then Manoah intreated the Lord, and said, "O my Lord, let the man of God which thou didst send come again unto us, and teach us what we shall do unto the child that shall be born." And God hearkened to the voice of Manoah; and the angel of God came again unto the woman as she sat in the field: but Manoah her husband was not with her. The woman made haste, and ran, and shewed her husband, and said unto him, "Behold, the man hath appeared unto me, that came unto me the other day." And Manoah arose, and went after his wife, and came to the man, and said unto him, "Art thou the man that spakest unto the woman?" And he said, "I am." And Manoah said, "Now let thy words come to pass. How shall we order the child, and how shall we do unto him?" And the angel of the Lord said unto Manoah, "Of all that I said unto the woman let her beware. She may not eat of any thing that cometh of the vine, neither let her drink wine or strong drink, nor eat any unclean thing: all that I commanded her let her observe." And Manoah said unto the angel of the Lord, "I pray thee, let us detain thee, until we shall have made ready a kid for thee." The angel of the Lord said unto Manoah, "Though thou detain me, I will not eat of thy bread: and if thou wilt offer a burnt offering, thou must offer it unto the Lord." For Manoah knew not that he was an angel of the Lord. Manoah said unto the angel of the Lord, "What is thy name, that when thy sayings come to pass we may do thee honour?" The angel of the Lord said unto him, "Why askest thou thus after my name, seeing it is secret?"

So Manoah took a kid with a meat offering, and offered it upon a rock unto the Lord: and the angel did wonderously; and Manoah and his wife looked on. For it came to pass, when the flame went up toward heaven from off the altar, that the angel of the Lord ascended in the flame of the altar. And Manoah and his wife looked on it, and fell on their faces to the ground. But the angel of the Lord did no more appear to Manoah and to his wife. Then Manoah knew that he was an angel of the Lord. Manoah said unto his wife, "We shall surely die, because we have seen God." But his wife said unto him, "If the Lord were pleased to kill us, he would not have received a burnt offering and a meat offering at our hands, neither would he have shewed us all these things, nor would as at this time have told us such things as these." And the woman bare a son, and called his name Samson: and the child grew, and the Lord blessed him. JUDG 13. 2-24

RUTH

A Full Reward from God

Take refuge under His wings

Boaz answered and said unto her, "It hath fully been showed me, all that thou hast done unto thy mother in law since the death of thine husband: and how thou hast left thy father and thy mother, and the land of thy nativity, and art come unto a people which thou knewest not heretofore. The Lord recompense thy work, and a full reward be given thee of the Lord God of Israel, under whose wings thou art come to trust."

RUTH 2. 11, 12

I SAMUEL

SHEPHERD-BOY SLAYS ARMED GIANT

The battle is the Lord's

David said unto Saul, "Thy servant kept his father's sheep, and there came a lion, and a bear, and took a lamb out of the flock: and I went out after him, and smote him, and delivered it out of his mouth: and when he arose against me, I caught him by his beard, and smote him, and slew him. Thy servant slew both the lion and the bear: and this uncircumcised Philistine shall be as one of them, seeing he hath defied the armies of the living God." David said moreover, "The Lord that delivered me out of the paw of the lion, and out of the paw of the bear, he will deliver me out of the hand of this Philistine." And Saul said unto David, "Go, and the Lord be with thee." Then said David to the Philistine, "Thou comest to me with a sword, and with a spear, and with a shield: but I come to thee in the name of the Lord of hosts, the God of the armies of Israel, whom thou hast defied. This day will the Lord deliver thee into mine hand; and I will smite thee, and take thine head from thee; and I will give the carcases of the host of the Philistines this day unto the fowls of the air, and to the wild beasts of the earth; that all the earth may know that there is a God in Israel. All this assembly shall know that the Lord saveth not with sword and spear: for the battle is the Lord's, and he will give you into our hands."

It came to pass, when the Philistine arose, and came and drew nigh to meet David, that David hasted, and ran toward the army to meet the Philistine. David put his hand in his bag, and took thence a stone, and slang it, and smote the Philistine in his forehead, that the stone sunk into his forehead; and he fell upon his face to the earth. So David prevailed over the Philistine with a sling and with a stone, and smote the Philistine, and slew him; but there was no sword in the hand of David.

I SAM 17. 34-37, 45-50

II SAMUEL

THE TEMPLE PROMISED

Where there will be no more affliction

Moreover I will appoint a place for my people Israel, and will plant them, that they may dwell in a place of their own, and move no more; neither shall the children of wickedness afflict them any more, as beforetime, and as since the time that I commanded judges to be over my people Israel, and have caused thee to rest from all thine enemies. Also the Lord telleth thee that he will make thee an house. Therefore now let it please thee to bless the house of thy servant, that it may continue for ever before thee: for thou, O Lord God, hast spoken it: and with thy blessing let the house of thy servant be blessed for ever. II SAM 7. 10, 11, 29

DRAWN OUT OF DEEP WATERS

Deliverance acknowledged

And David spake unto the Lord the words of this song in the day that the Lord had delivered him out of the hand of all his enemies, and out of the hand of Saul: and he said, "The Lord is my rock, and my fortress, and my deliverer; the God of my rock; in him will I trust: he is my shield, and the horn of my salvation, my high tower, and my refuge, my saviour; thou savest me from violence. I will call on the Lord, who is worthy to be praised: so shall I be saved from mine enemies. When the waves of death compassed me, the floods of ungodly men made me afraid; the sorrows of hell compassed me about; the snares of death prevented me; in my distress I called upon the Lord, and cried to my God: and he did hear my voice out of his temple, and my cry did enter into his ears.

He sent from above, he took me; he drew me out of many waters; he delivered me from my strong enemy, and from them that hated me: for they were too strong for me. They prevented me in the day of my calamity: but the Lord was my stay. He brought me forth also into a large place: he delivered me, because he delighted in me. The Lord rewarded me according to my righteousness: according to the cleanness of my hands hath he recompensed me. Therefore the Lord hath recompensed me according to my righteousness; according to my cleanness in his eye sight. With the merciful thou wilt shew thyself merciful, and with the upright man thou wilt shew thyself upright. With the pure thou wilt shew thyself pure; and with the froward thou wilt shew thyself unsavoury.

The afflicted people thou wilt save: but thine eyes are upon the haughty, that thou mayest bring them down. Thou art my lamp, O Lord: and the Lord will lighten my darkness. For by thee I have run through a troop: by my God have I leaped over a wall.

As for God, his way is perfect; the word of the Lord is tried: he is a buckler to all them that trust in him. For who is God, save the Lord? and who is a rock, save our God? God is my strength and power: and he maketh my way perfect. He maketh my feet like hinds' feet: and setteth me upon my high places. He teacheth my hands to war; so that a bow of steel is broken by mine arms. Thou hast also given me the shield of thy salvation: and thy gentleness hath made me great. Thou hast enlarged my steps under me; so that my feet did not slip. The Lord liveth; and blessed be my rock; and exalted be the God of the rock of my salvation.

II SAM 22. 1-7, 17-21
25-37, 47
PSA 18. 1-49

I KINGS

An Understanding Heart Requested

Right motives rewarded

In Gibeon the Lord appeared to Solomon in a dream by night: and God said, "Ask what I shall give thee." Solomon said, "Thou hast shewed unto thy servant David my father great mercy, according as he walked before thee in truth, and in righteousness, and in uprightness of heart with thee; and thou hast kept for him this great kindness, that thou hast given him a son to sit on his throne, as it is this day. Now, O Lord my God, thou hast made thy servant king instead of David my father: and I am but a little child: I know not how to go out or come in. Thy servant is in the midst of thy people which thou hast chosen, a great people, that cannot be numbered nor counted for multitude. Give therefore thy servant an understanding heart to judge thy people, that I may discern between good and bad: for who is able to judge this thy so great a people?" And the speech pleased the Lord, that Solomon had asked this thing.

God said unto him, "Because thou hast asked this thing, and hast not asked for thyself long life; neither hast asked riches for thyself, nor hast asked the life of thine enemies; but hast asked for thyself understanding to discern judgment; behold, I have done according to thy words. Lo, I have given thee a wise and an understanding heart; so that there was none like thee before thee, neither after thee shall any arise like unto thee. I have also given thee that which thou hast not asked, both riches, and honour: so that there shall not be any among the kings like unto thee all thy days. If thou wilt walk in my ways, to keep my statutes and my commandments, as thy father David did walk, then I will lengthen thy days."

I KINGS 3. 5-14
II CHRON 1. 7-12

The House of God

Church as a place of prayer and healing

He said, "Lord God of Israel, there is no God like thee, in heaven above, or on earth beneath, who keepest covenant and mercy with thy servants that walk before thee with all their heart: who hast kept with thy servant David my father that thou promisedst him: thou spakest also with thy mouth, and hast fulfilled it with thine hand, as it is this day. Yet have thou respect unto the prayer of thy servant, and to his supplication, O Lord my God, to hearken unto the cry and to the prayer, which thy servant prayeth before thee today: that thine eyes may be open toward this house night and day, even toward the place of which thou hast said, 'My name shall be there:' that thou mayest hearken unto the prayer which thy servant shall make toward this place. Hearken thou to the supplication of thy servant, and of thy people Israel, when they shall pray toward this place: and hear thou in heaven thy dwelling place: and when thou hearest, forgive.

"If there be in the land famine, if there be pestilence, blasting, mildew, locust, or if there be caterpiller; if their enemy besiege them in the land of their cities; whatsoever plague, whatsoever sickness there be; what prayer and supplication soever be made by any man, or by all thy people Israel, which shall know every man the plague of his own heart, and spread forth his hands toward this house: then hear thou in heaven thy dwelling place, and forgive, and do, and give to every man according to his ways, whose heart thou knowest; (for thou, even thou only, knowest the hearts of all the children of men). Blessed be the Lord, that hath given rest unto his people Israel, according to all that he promised: there hath not failed one word of all his good promise, which he promised by the hand of Moses his servant. Let your heart therefore be perfect with the Lord our God, to walk in his statutes, and to keep his commandments, as at this day."

I KINGS 8. 23, 24, 28-30, 37-39, 56, 61

The King's Hand Paralyzed

Then restored by the man of God

Behold, there came a man of God out of Judah by the word of the Lord unto Bethel: and Jeroboam stood by the altar to burn incense. He cried against the altar in the word of the Lord, and said, "O altar, altar, thus saith the Lord; behold, a child shall be born unto the house of David, Josiah by name; and upon thee shall he offer the priests of the high places that burn incense upon thee, and men's bones shall be burnt upon thee." He gave a sign the same day, saying, "This is the sign which the Lord hath spoken; behold, the altar shall be rent, and the ashes that are upon it shall be poured out."

It came to pass, when king Jeroboam heard the saying of the man of God, which had cried against the altar in Bethel, that he put forth his hand from the altar, saying, "Lay hold on him." And his hand, which he put forth against him, dried up, so that he could not pull it in again to him. The altar also was rent, and the ashes poured out from the altar, according to the sign which the man of God had given by the word of the Lord. The king answered and said unto the man of God, "Intreat now the face of the Lord thy God, and pray for me, that my hand may be restored me again." And the man of God besought the Lord, and the king's hand was restored him again, and became as it was before. I KINGS 13. 1-6

Nourished in the Wilderness

Elijah fed by the ravens

Elijah the Tishbite, who was of the inhabitants of Gilead, said unto Ahab, "As the Lord God of Israel liveth, before whom I stand, there shall not be dew nor rain these years, but according to my word." The word of the Lord came unto him, saying, "Get thee hence, and turn thee eastward, and hide thyself by the brook Cherith, that is before Jordan. It shall be, that thou shalt drink of the brook; and I have commanded the ravens to feed thee there." So he went and did according unto the word of the Lord: for he went and dwelt by the brook Cherith, that is before Jordan. The ravens brought him bread and flesh in the morning, and bread and flesh in the evening; and he drank of the brook. It came to pass after a while, that the brook dried up, because there had been no rain in the land.

I KINGS 17. 1-7

SUPPLY EXTENDED
Indigent widow feeds Elijah

The word of the Lord came unto him, saying, "Arise, get thee to Zarephath, which belongeth to Zidon, and dwell there: behold, I have commanded a widow woman there to sustain thee." So he arose and went to Zarephath. And when he came to the gate of the city, behold, the widow woman was there gathering of sticks: and he called to her, and said, "Fetch me, I pray thee, a little water in a vessel, that I may drink." As she was going to fetch it, he called to her, and said, "Bring me, I pray thee, a morsel of bread in thine hand." She said, "As the Lord thy God liveth, I have not a cake, but an handful of meal in a barrel, and a little oil in a cruse: and, behold, I am gathering two sticks, that I may go in and dress it for me and my son, that we may eat it, and die." And Elijah said unto her, "Fear not; go and do as thou hast said: but make me thereof a little cake first, and bring it unto me, and after make for thee and for thy son. For thus saith the Lord God of Israel, The barrel of meal shall not waste, neither shall the cruse of oil fail, until the day that the Lord sendeth rain upon the earth." She went and did according to the saying of Elijah: and she, and he, and her house, did eat many days. The barrel of meal wasted not, neither did the cruse of oil fail, according to the word of the Lord, which he spake by Elijah.

I KINGS 17. 8-16

DEAD RAISED

Prophet restores life of a child

It came to pass after these things, that the son of the woman, the mistress of the house, fell sick; and his sickness was so sore, that there was no breath left in him. She said unto Elijah, "What have I to do with thee, O thou man of God? art thou come unto me to call my sin to remembrance, and to slay my son?" He said unto her, "Give me thy son." And he took him out of her bosom, and carried him up into a loft, where he abode, and laid him upon his own bed. He cried unto the Lord, and said, "O Lord my God, hast thou also brought evil upon the widow with whom I sojourn, by slaying her son?" He stretched himself upon the child three times, and cried unto the Lord, and said, "O Lord my God, I pray thee, let this child's soul come into him again." The Lord heard the voice of Elijah; and the soul of the child came into him again, and he revived. Elijah took the child, and brought him down out of the chamber into the house, and delivered him unto his mother: and Elijah said, "See, thy son liveth." The woman said to Elijah, "Now by this I know that thou art a man of God, and that the word of the Lord in thy mouth is truth." I KINGS 17. 17-24

PRAYER FOR RAIN

Elijah ends three-year drought

It came to pass after many days, that the word of the Lord came to Elijah in the third year, saying, "Go, shew thyself unto Ahab; and I will send rain upon the earth." And Elijah said unto Ahab, "Get thee up, eat and drink; for there is a sound of abundance of rain." So Ahab went up to eat and to drink. And Elijah went up to the top of Carmel; and he cast himself down upon the earth, and put his face between his knees, and said to his servant, "Go up now, look toward the sea." And he went up, and looked, and said, "There is nothing." And he said, "Go again seven times." And it came to pass at the seventh time, that he said, "Behold, there ariseth a little cloud out of the sea, like a man's hand." And he said, "Go up, say unto Ahab, Prepare thy chariot, and get thee down, that the rain stop thee not." It came to pass in the meanwhile, that the heaven was black with clouds and wind, and there was a great rain. And Ahab rode, and went to Jezreel. The hand of the Lord was on Elijah; and he girded up his loins, and ran before Ahab to the entrance of Jezreel.

I KINGS 18. 1, 41-46

ELIJAH DISCOURAGED BUT SUICIDE AVERTED
God preserves him during flight from enemies

Ahab told Jezebel all that Elijah had done, and withal how he had slain all the prophets with the sword. Then Jezebel sent a messenger unto Elijah, saying, "So let the gods do to me, and more also, if I make not thy life as the life of one of them by tomorrow about this time." When he saw that, he arose, and went for his life, and came to Beer-sheba, which belongeth to Judah, and left his servant there. But he himself went a day's journey into the wilderness, and came and sat down under a juniper tree: and he requested for himself that he might die; and said, "It is enough; now, O Lord, take away my life; for I am not better than my fathers." And as he lay and slept under a juniper tree, behold, then an angel touched him, and said unto him, "Arise and eat." He looked, and, behold, there was a cake baken on the coals, and a cruse of water at his head. And he did eat and drink, and laid him down again. The angel of the Lord came again the second time, and touched him, and said, "Arise and eat; because the journey is too great for thee." He arose, and did eat and drink, and went in the strength of that meat forty days and forty nights unto Horeb the mount of God.

I KINGS 19. 1-8

II KINGS

Ascension of Elijah Witnessed by Elisha

They cross over Jordan on dry ground

It came to pass, when the Lord would take up Elijah into heaven by a whirlwind, that Elijah went with Elisha from Gilgal. And Elijah said unto Elisha, "Tarry here, I pray thee; for the Lord hath sent me to Beth-el." And Elisha said unto him, "As the Lord liveth, and as thy soul liveth, I will not leave thee." So they went down to Beth-el. And the sons of the prophets that were at Beth-el came forth to Elisha, and said unto him, "Knowest thou that the Lord will take away thy master from thy head today?" And he said, "Yea, I know it; hold ye your peace." And Elijah said unto him, "Elisha, tarry here, I pray thee; for the Lord hath sent me to Jericho." And he said, "As the Lord liveth, and as thy soul liveth, I will not leave thee." So they came to Jericho. And the sons of the prophets that were at Jericho came to Elisha, and said unto him, "Knowest thou that the Lord will take away thy master from thy head today?" And he answered, "Yea, I know it; hold ye your peace." Elijah said unto him, "Tarry, I pray thee, here; for the Lord hath sent me to Jordan." And he said, "As the Lord liveth, and as thy soul liveth, I will not leave thee." And they two went on.

Fifty men of the sons of the prophets went, and stood to view afar off: and they two stood by Jordan. Elijah took his mantle, and wrapped it together, and smote the waters, and they were divided hither and thither, so that they two went over on dry ground. And it came to pass, when they were gone over, that Elijah said unto Elisha, "Ask what I shall do for thee, before I be taken away from thee." And Elisha said, "I pray thee, let a double portion of thy spirit be upon me." And he said, "Thou hast asked a hard thing: nevertheless, if thou see me when I am taken from thee, it shall be so unto thee; but if not, it shall not be so." And it came to pass, as they still went on, and talked, that, behold, there appeared a chariot of fire, and horses of fire, and parted them both asunder; and Elijah went up by a whirlwind into heaven. II KINGS 2. 1-11

SPIRIT OF ELIJAH TRANSFERRED TO ELISHA

Elisha divides the waters of Jordan too

Elisha saw it, and he cried, "My father, my father, the chariot of Israel, and the horsemen thereof." And he saw him no more: and he took hold of his own clothes, and rent them in two pieces. He took up also the mantle of Elijah that fell from him, and went back, and stood by the bank of Jordan; he took the mantle of Elijah that fell from him, and smote the waters, and said, "Where is the Lord God of Elijah?" and when he also had smitten the waters, they parted hither and thither: and Elisha went over. And when the sons of the prophets which were to view at Jericho saw him, they said, "The spirit of Elijah doth rest on Elisha." And they came to meet him, and bowed themselves to the ground before him.

II KINGS 2. 12-15

POISONED SPRING PURIFIED

Elisha heals waters

The men of the city said unto Elisha, "Behold, I pray thee, the situation of this city is pleasant, as my lord seeth: but the water is naught, and the ground barren." And he said, "Bring me a new cruse, and put salt therein." And they brought it to him. And he went forth unto the spring of the waters, and cast the salt in there, and said, "Thus saith the Lord, I have healed these waters; there shall not be from thence any more death or barren land." So the waters were healed unto this day, according to the saying of Elisha which he spake.

II KINGS 2. 19-22

IRRIGATION DITCHES FILLED

Elisha causes water to flow without rain

But Jehoshaphat said, "Is there not here a prophet of the

Lord, that we may enquire of the Lord by him?" And one of the king of Israel's servants answered and said, "Here is Elisha the son of Shaphat, which poured water on the hands of Elijah." He said, "Thus saith the Lord, 'Make this valley full of ditches.' For thus saith the Lord, 'Ye shall not see wind, neither shall ye see rain; yet that valley shall be filled with water, that ye may drink, both ye, and your cattle, and your beasts.' This is but a light thing in the sight of the Lord: he will deliver the Moabites also into your hand. Ye shall smite every fenced city, and every choice city, and shall fell every good tree, and stop all wells of water, and mar every good piece of land with stones." And it came to pass in the morning, when the meat offering was offered, that, behold, there came water by the way of Edom, and the country was filled with water.

II KINGS 3. 11, 16-20

Debts Paid

Elisha causes flow of oil for widow to sell

Now there cried a certain woman of the wives of the sons of the prophets unto Elisha, saying, "Thy servant my husband is dead; and thou knowest that thy servant did fear the Lord: and the creditor is come to take unto him my two sons to be bondmen." And Elisha said unto her, "What shall I do for thee? tell me, what hast thou in the house?" And she said, "Thine handmaid hath not anything in the house, save a pot of oil." Then he said, "Go, borrow thee vessels abroad of all thy neighbours, even empty vessels; borrow not a few. When thou art come in, thou shalt shut the door upon thee and upon thy sons, and shalt pour out into all those vessels, and thou shalt set aside that which is full." So she went from him, and shut the door upon her and upon her sons, who brought the vessels to her; and she poured out. It came to pass, when the vessels were full, that she said unto her son, "Bring me yet a vessel." And he said unto her, "There is not a vessel more." And the oil stayed. Then she came and told the man of God. And he said, "Go, sell the oil, and pay thy debt, and live thou and thy children of the rest."

II KINGS 4. 1-7

LIFE RESTORED

Elisha raises benefactor's child from death

It fell on a day, that Elisha passed to Shunem, where was a great woman; and she constrained him to eat bread. And so it was, that as oft as he passed by, he turned in thither to eat bread. She said unto her husband, "Behold now, I perceive that this is an holy man of God, which passeth by us continually. Let us make a little chamber, I pray thee, on the wall; and let us set for him there a bed, and a table, and a stool, and a candlestick: and it shall be, when he cometh to us, that he shall turn in thither." It fell on a day, that he came thither, and he turned into the chamber, and lay there. He said to Gehazi his servant, "Call this Shunammite." And when he had called her, she stood before him. And he said unto him, "Say now unto her, 'Behold, thou hast been careful for us with all this care; what is to be done for thee? wouldest thou be spoken for to the king? or to the captain of the host?' " And she answered, "I dwell among mine own people." He said, "What then is to be done for her?" And Gehazi answered, "Verily she hath no child, and her husband is old." He said, "Call her." And when he had called her, she stood in the door. He said, "About this season, according to the time of life, thou shalt embrace a son." And she said, "Nay, my lord, thou man of God, do not lie unto thine handmaid." And the woman conceived, and bare a son at that season that Elisha had said unto her, according to the time of life.

And when the child was grown, it fell on a day, that he went out to his father to the reapers. And he said unto his father, "My head, my head." And he said to a lad, "Carry him to his mother." And when he had taken him, and brought him to his mother, he sat on her knees till noon, and then died. She went up, and laid him on the bed of the man of God, and shut the door upon him, and went out. She called unto her husband, and said, "Send me, I pray thee, one of the young men, and one of the asses, that I may run to the man of God, and come again. And he said, "Wherefore wilt thou go to him today? it is neither new moon, nor sabbath." And she said, "It shall be well." Then she saddled an ass, and said to her servant, "Drive, and go forward; slack not thy riding for me, except I bid thee." So she went and came unto the man of God to mount Carmel. And it came to pass, when the man of God saw her afar off, that he said to Gehazi his servant, "Behold, yonder is that Shunammite. Run now, I pray thee, to meet her, and say unto her, 'Is it well with thee? is it well with thy husband? is it well with the child?'" And she answered, "It is well." When she came to the man of God to the hill, she caught him by the feet: but Gehazi came near to thrust her away. And the man of God said, "Let her alone; for her soul is vexed within her: and the Lord hath hid it from me, and hath not told me." Then she said, "Did I desire a son of my lord? did I not say, 'Do not deceive me'?" Then he said to Gehazi, "Gird up thy loins, and take my staff in thine hand, and go thy way: if thou meet any man, salute him not; and if any salute thee, answer him not again: and lay my staff upon the face of the child." The mother of the child said, "As the Lord liveth, and as thy soul liveth, I will not leave thee." And he arose, and followed her.

Gehazi passed on before them, and laid the staff upon the face of the child; but there was neither voice, nor hearing. Wherefore he went again to meet him, and told him, saying, "The child is not awaked." When Elisha was come into the house, behold, the child was dead, and laid upon his bed. He went in therefore, and shut the door upon them twain, and prayed unto the Lord. He went up, and lay upon the child, and put his mouth upon his mouth, and his eyes upon his eyes, and his hands upon his hands: and he stretched himself upon the child; and the flesh of the child waxed warm. Then he returned, and walked in the house to and fro; and went up, and stretched himself upon him: and the child sneezed seven times, and the child opened his eyes. He called Gehazi, and said, "Call this Shunammite." So he called her. And when she was come in unto him, he said, "Take up thy son." Then she went in, and fell at his feet, and bowed herself to the ground, and took up her son, and went out. II KINGS 4. 8-37

POISONED FOOD RENDERED HARMLESS
Elisha saves his disciples from death

Elisha came again to Gilgal: and there was a dearth in the land; and the sons of the prophets were sitting before him: and he said unto his servant, "Set on the great pot, and seethe pottage for the sons of the prophets." One went out into the field to gather herbs, and found a wild vine, and gathered thereof wild gourds his lap full, and came and shred them into the pot of pottage: for they knew them not. So they poured out for the men to eat. And it came to pass, as they were eating of the pottage, that they cried out, and said, "O thou man of God, there is death in the pot." And they could not eat thereof. But he said, "Then bring meal." And he cast it into the pot; and he said, "Pour out for the people, that they may eat." And there was no harm in the pot. II KINGS 4. 38-41

FOOD SUPPLY EXPANDED
Elisha feeds 100 men with 20 rolls

There came a man from Baal-shalisha, and brought the man of God bread of the firstfruits, twenty loves of barley, and full ears of corn in the husk thereof. And he said, "Give unto the people, that they may eat." And his servitor said, "What, should I set this before an hundred men?" He said again, "Give the people, that they may eat: for thus saith the Lord, 'They shall eat, and shall leave thereof.' " So he set it before them, and they did eat, and left thereof, according to the word of the Lord. II KINGS 4. 42-44

Skin Disease Healed
Elisha cures Naaman, captain of Syrian army

Now Naaman, captain of the host of the king of Syria, was a great man with his master, and honourable, because by him the Lord had given deliverance unto Syria: he was also a mighty man in valour, but he was a leper. The Syrians had gone out by companies, and had brought away captive out of the land of Israel a little maid; and she waited on Naaman's wife. And she said unto her mistress, "Would God my lord were with the prophet that is in Samaria! for he would recover him of his leprosy." And one went in, and told his lord, saying, Thus and thus said the maid that is of the land of Israel. And the king of Syria said, "Go to, go, and I will send a letter unto the king of Israel." And he departed, and took with him ten talents of silver, and six thousand pieces of gold, and ten changes of raiment. He brought the letter to the king of Israel, saying, "Now when this letter is come unto thee, behold, I have therewith sent Naaman my servant to thee, that thou mayest recover him of his leprosy." It came to pass, when the king of Israel had read the letter, that he rent his clothes, and said, "Am I God, to kill and to make alive, that this man doth send unto me to recover a man of his leprosy? wherefore consider, I pray you, and see how he seeketh a quarrel against me."

It was so, when Elisha the man of God had heard that the king of Israel had rent his clothes, that he sent to the king, saying, "Wherefore hast thou rent thy clothes? let him come now to me, and he shall know that there is a prophet in Israel." So Naaman came with his horses and with his chariot, and stood at the door of the house of Elisha. Elisha sent a messenger unto him, saying, "Go and wash in Jordan seven times, and thy flesh shall come again to thee, and thou shalt be clean." But Naaman was wroth, and went away, and said, "Behold, I thought, He will surely come out to me, and stand, and call on the name of the Lord his God, and strike his hand over the place, and recover the leper. Are not Abana and Pharpar, rivers of Damascus, better than all the waters of Israel? may I not wash in them, and be clean?" So he turned and went away in a rage. His servants came near, and spake unto him, and said, "My father, if the prophet had bid thee do some great thing, wouldest thou not have done it? how much rather then, when he saith to thee, 'Wash, and be clean'?" Then went he down, and dipped himself seven times in Jordan, according to the saying of the man of God: and his flesh came again like unto the flesh of a little child, and he was clean. He returned to the man of God, he and all his company, and came, and stood before him: and he said, "Behold, now I know that there is no God in all the earth, but in Israel: now therefore, I pray thee, take a blessing of thy servant." II KINGS 5. 1-15

AXE HEAD FLOATS

Elisha recovers a borrowed tool lost in river

The sons of the prophets said unto Elisha, "Behold now, the place where we dwell with thee is too strait for us. Let us go, we pray thee, unto Jordan, and take thence every man a beam, and let us make us a place there, where we may dwell." And he answered, "Go ye." And one said, "Be content, I pray thee, and go with thy servants." And he answered, "I will go." So he went with them. And when they came to Jordan, they cut down wood. But as one was felling a beam, the axe head fell into the water: and he cried, and said, "Alas, master! for it was borrowed." And the man of God said, "Where fell it?" And he shewed him the place. And he cut down a stick, and cast it in thither; and the iron did swim. Therefore said he, "Take it up to thee." And he put out his hand, and took it.

II KINGS 6. 1-7

ISRAEL PRESERVED FROM ENEMY INVASION

Elisha traps Syrian army sent to capture him

Then the king of Syria warred against Israel, and took

counsel with his servants, saying, In such and such a place shall be my camp. And the man of God sent unto the king of Israel, saying, Beware that thou pass not such a place; for thither the Syrians are come down. The king of Israel sent to the place which the man of God told him and warned him of, and saved himself there, not once nor twice. Therefore the heart of the king of Syria was sore troubled for this thing; and he called his servants, and said unto them, "Will ye not shew me which of us is for the king of Israel?" And one of his servants said, "None, my lord, O king: but Elisha, the prophet that is in Israel, telleth the king of Israel the words that thou speakest in thy bedchamber." And he said, "Go and spy where he is, that I may send and fetch him." And it was told him, saying, "Behold, he is in Dothan." Therefore sent he thither horses, and chariots, and a great host: and they came by night, and compassed the city about.

When the servant of the man of God was risen early, and gone forth, behold, an host compassed the city both with horses and chariots. And his servant said unto him, "Alas, my master! how shall we do?" And he answered, "Fear not: for they that be with us are more than they that be with them." Elisha prayed, and said, "Lord, I pray thee, open his eyes, that he may see." And the Lord opened the eyes of the young man; and he saw: and, behold, the mountain was full of horses and chariots of fire round about Elisha. When they came down to him, Elisha prayed unto the Lord, and said, "Smite this people, I pray thee with blindness." And he smote them with blindness according to the word of Elisha. Elisha said unto them, "This is not the way, neither is this the city: follow me, and I will bring you to the man whom ye seek." But he led them to Samaria. It came to pass, when they were come into Samaria, that Elisha said, "Lord, open the eyes of these men, that they may see." And the Lord opened their eyes, and they saw; and, behold, they were in the midst of Samaria. The king of Israel said unto Elisha, when he saw them, "My father, shall I smite them? shall I smite them?" And he answered, "Thou shalt not smite them: wouldest thou smite those whom thou hast taken captive with thy sword and with thy bow? set bread and water before them, that they may eat and drink, and go to their master." He prepared great provision for them: and when they had eaten and drunk, he sent them away, and they went to their master. So the bands of Syria came no more into the land of Israel. II KINGS 6. 8-23

PROOF THAT ELISHA RAISED THE DEAD

His servant and the mother of the child testify

Then spake Elisha unto the woman, whose son he had restored to life, saying, "Arise, and go thou and thine household, and sojourn wheresoever thou canst sojourn: for the Lord hath called for a famine; and it shall also come upon the land seven years." The woman arose, and did after the saying of the man of God: and she went with her household, and sojourned in the land of the Philistines seven years. It came to pass at the seven years' end, that the woman returned out of the land of the Philistines: and she went forth to cry unto the king for her house and for her land. The king talked with Gehazi the servant of the man of God, saying, "Tell me, I pray thee, all the great things that Elisha hath done." It came to pass, as he was telling the king how he had restored a dead body to life, that, behold, the woman, whose son he had restored to life, cried to the king for her house and for her land. And Gehazi said, "My lord, O king, this is the woman, and this is her son, whom Elisha restored to life." And when the king asked the woman, she told him. So the king appointed unto her a certain officer, saying, "Restore all that was hers, and all the fruits of the field since the day that she left the land, even until now." II KINGS 8. 1-6

Assyrian Army Retreats
Isaiah prays for deliverance

Then Isaiah the son of Amoz sent to Hezekiah, saying, "Thus saith the Lord God of Israel, that which thou hast prayed to me against Sennacherib king of Assyria I have heard. The remnant that is escaped of the house of Judah shall yet again take root downward, and bear fruit upward. For out of Jerusalem shall go forth a remnant, and they that escape out of mount Zion: the zeal of the Lord of hosts shall do this. Therefore thus saith the Lord concerning the king of Assyria, He shall not come into this city, nor shoot an arrow there, nor come before it with shield, nor cast a bank against it. By the way that he came, by the same shall he return, and shall not come into this city, saith the Lord. For I will defend this city, to save it, for mine own sake, and for my servant David's sake." It came to pass that night, that the angel of the Lord went out, and smote in the camp of the Assyrians an hundred fourscore and five thousand: and when they arose early in the morning, behold, they were all dead corpses. So Sennacherib king of Assyria departed, and went and returned and dwelt at Nineveh.

II KINGS 19. 20, 30-36

II CHRONICLES

Prayer Heals Sores, Sickness and Misery
God hears and His saints rejoice

If there be dearth in the land, if there be pestilence, if there be blasting, or mildew, locusts, or caterpillers; if their enemies besiege them in the cities of their land; whatsoever sore or whatsoever sickness there be: then what prayer or what supplication soever shall be made of any man, or of all thy people Israel, when everyone shall know his own sore and his own grief, and shall spread forth his hands in this house: then hear thou from heaven thy dwelling place, and forgive, and render unto every man according unto all his ways, whose heart thou knowest; (for thou only knowest the hearts of the children of men:) that they may fear thee, to walk in thy ways, so long as they live in the land which thou gavest unto our fathers. Now therefore arise, O Lord God, into thy resting place, thou, and the ark of thy strength: let thy priests, O Lord God, be clothed with salvation, and let thy saints rejoice in goodness.

II CHRON 6. 28-31, 41

The Country Healed and People Forgiven

By humble prayer to God

If my people, which are called by my name, shall humble themselves, and pray, and seek my face, and turn from their wicked ways; then will I hear from heaven, and will forgive their sin, and will heal their land. II CHRON 7. 14

Asa Dies of Foot Disease

He did not turn to the Lord

And, behold, the acts of Asa, first and last, lo, they are written in the book of the kings of Judah and Israel. Asa in the thirty and ninth year of his reign was diseased in his feet, until his disease was exceeding great: yet in his disease he sought not to the Lord, but to the physicians. Asa slept with his fathers, and died in the one and fortieth year of his reign.

II CHRON 16. 11-13

Protection in War

The battle is not yours but God's

Then upon Jahaziel the son of Zechariah, . . . came the Spirit of the Lord in the midst of the congregation; and he said, "Hearken ye, all Judah, and ye inhabitants of Jerusalem, and thou king Jehoshaphat, thus saith the Lord unto you, 'Be not afraid nor dismayed by reason of this great multitude; for the battle is not yours, but God's. Tomorrow go ye down against them: behold, they come up by the cliff of Ziz; and ye shall find them at the end of the brook, before the wilderness of Jeruel. Ye shall not need to fight in this battle: set yourselves, stand ye still, and see the salvation of the Lord with you, O Judah and Jerusalem: fear not, nor be dismayed; tomorrow go out against them: for the Lord will be with you.' " Jehoshaphat bowed his head with his face to the ground: and all Judah and the inhabitants of Jerusalem fell before the Lord, worshipping the Lord.

II CHRON 20. 14-18

The Lord Healed the People

When Hezekiah prayed for pardon

Hezekiah prayed for them, saying, "The good Lord pardon every one that prepareth his heart to seek God, the Lord God of his fathers, though he be not cleansed according to the purification of the sanctuary." The Lord hearkened to Hezekiah, and healed the people.

II CHRON 30. 18-20

God Fights our Battles

Don't panic; be strong and courageous

When Hezekiah saw that Sennacherib was come, and that he was purposed to fight against Jerusalem, he set captains of war over the people, and gathered them together to him in the street of the gate of the city, and spake comfortably to them, saying, "Be strong and courageous, be not afraid nor dismayed for the king of Assyria, nor for all the multitude that is with him: for there be more with us than with him: with him is an arm of flesh; but with us is the Lord our God to help us, and to fight our battles." And the people rested themselves upon the words of Hezekiah king of Judah.

II CHRON 32. 2, 6-8

GOD SAVES FROM TYRANNY

Isaiah's prayer answered by an angel

Thus saith Sennacherib king of Assyria, "Whereon do ye trust, that ye abide in the siege in Jerusalem? Doth not Hezekiah persuade you to give over yourselves to die by famine and by thirst, saying, 'The Lord our God shall deliver us out of the hand of the king of Assyria?' Know ye not what I and my fathers have done unto all the people of other lands? were the gods of the nations of those lands any ways able to deliver their lands out of mine hand? Who was there among all the gods of those nations that my fathers utterly destroyed, that could deliver his people out of mine hand, that your God should be able to deliver you out of mine hand? Now therefore let not Hezekiah deceive you, nor persuade you on this manner, neither yet believe him: for no god of any nation or kingdom was able to deliver his people out of mine hand, and out of the hand of my fathers: how much less shall your God deliver you out of mine hand?" For this cause Hezekiah the king, and the prophet Isaiah the son of Amoz, prayed and cried to heaven. The Lord sent an angel, which cut off all the mighty men of valour, and the leaders and captains in the camp of the king of Assyria. So he returned with shame of face to his own land. And when he was come into the house of his god, they that came forth of his own bowels slew him there with the sword. Thus the Lord saved Hezekiah and the inhabitants of Jerusalem from the hand of Sennacherib the king of Assyria, and from the hand of all other, and guided them on every side.

II CHRON 32. 10, 11, 13-15, 20-22

NEHEMIAH

STRENGTH TO REBUILD

Derived from God

Then said I unto them, "Ye see the distress that we are in, how Jerusalem lieth waste, and the gates thereof are burned with fire: come, and let us build up the wall of Jerusalem, that we be no more a reproach." Then I told them of the hand of my God which was good upon me; as also the king's words that he had spoken unto me. And they said, "Let us rise up and build." So they strengthened their hands for this good work. But when Sanballat the Horonite, and Tobiah the servant, the Ammonite, and Geshem the Arabian, heard it, they laughed us to scorn, and despised us, and said, "What is this thing that ye do? will ye rebel against the king?" Then answered I them, and said unto them, "The God of heaven, he will prosper us; therefore we his servants will arise and build." NEH 2. 17-20

OUR WORK IS FINISHED

When accomplished by God

. . . Now therefore, O God, strengthen my hands. So the wall was finished in the twenty and fifth day of the month Elul, in fifty and two days. It came to pass, that when all our enemies heard thereof, and all the heathen that were about us saw these things, they were much cast down in their own eyes: for they perceived that this work was wrought of our God. NEH 6. 9, 15, 16

JOY IN THE LORD IS YOUR STRENGTH

It comes from understanding God's law

Ezra the priest brought the law before the congregation both of men and women, and all that could hear with understanding, upon the first day of the seventh month. He read therein before the street that was before the water gate from the morning until midday, before the men and the women, and those that could understand; and the ears of all the people were attentive unto the book of the law. Ezra the scribe stood upon a pulpit of wood, . . . and Ezra opened the book in the sight of all the people; (for he was above all the people;) and when he opened it, all the people stood up. Ezra blessed the Lord, the great God. And all the people answered, "Amen, Amen," with lifting up their hands: and they bowed their heads, and worshipped the Lord with their faces to the ground. So they read in the book in the law of God distinctly, and gave the sense, and caused them to understand the reading. Nehemiah, which is the Tirshatha, and Ezra the priest the scribe, and the Levites that taught the people, said unto all the people, "This day is holy unto the Lord your God; mourn not, nor weep." For all the people wept, when they heard the words of the law. Then he said unto them, "Go your way, eat the fat, and drink the sweet, and send portions unto them for whom nothing is prepared: for this day is holy unto our Lord: neither be ye sorry; for the joy of the Lord is your strength."

NEH 8. 2-6, 8-10

ESTHER

JUSTICE TRIUMPHS

Enemies of those who are good are punished

So the king and Haman came to banquet with Esther the queen. The king said again unto Esther on the second day at the banquet of wine, "What is thy petition, queen Esther? and it shall be granted thee: and what is thy request? and it shall be performed, even to the half of the kingdom." Then Esther the queen answered and said, "If I have found favour in thy sight, O king, and if it please the king, let my life be given me at my petition, and my people at my request: for we are sold, I and my people, to be destroyed, to be slain, and to perish. But if we had been sold for bondmen and bond-women, I had held my tongue, although the enemy could not countervail the king's damage."

Then the king Ahasuerus answered and said unto Esther the queen, "Who is he, and where is he, that durst presume in his heart to do so?" Esther said, "The adversary and enemy is this wicked Haman." Then Haman was afraid before the king and the queen. The king arising from the banquet of wine in his wrath went into the palace garden: and Haman stood up to make request for his life to Esther the queen; for he saw that there was evil determined against him by the king. Then the king returned out of the palace garden into the place of the banquet of wine; and Haman was fallen upon the bed whereon Esther was. Then said the king, "Will he force the queen also before me in the house?" As the word went out of the king's mouth, they covered Haman's face. And Harbonah, one of the chamberlains, said before the king, "Behold also, the gallows fifty cubits high, which Haman had made for Mordecai, who had spoken good for the king, standeth in the house of Haman." Then the king said, "Hang him thereon." So they hanged Haman on the gallows that he had prepared for Mordecai. Then was the king's wrath pacified.

ESTHER 7. 1-10

JOB

JOB AFFLICTED WITH SORE BOILS
Resigns himself temporarily

So went Satan forth from the presence of the Lord, and smote Job with sore boils from the sole of his foot unto his crown. And he took him a potsherd to scrape himself withal; and he sat down among the ashes. JOB 2. 7, 8

THE THING I FEARED IS COME
Job insecure and restless

Why is light given to a man whose way is hid, and whom God hath hedged in? For my sighing cometh before I eat, and my roarings are poured out like the waters. For the thing which I greatly feared is come upon me, and that which I was afraid of is come unto me. I was not in safety, neither had I rest, neither was I quiet; yet trouble came. JOB 3. 23-26

JOB'S GOOD DEEDS RECALLED
To strengthen him

Then Eliphaz the Temanite answered and said, "If we assay to commune with thee, wilt thou be grieved? but who can withhold himself from speaking? Behold, thou hast instructed many, and thou hast strengthened the weak hands. Thy words have upholden him that was falling, and thou hast strengthened the feeble knees. But now it is come upon thee, and thou faintest; it toucheth thee, and thou art troubled. Is not this thy fear, thy confidence, thy hope, and the uprightness of thy ways? Remember, I pray thee, who ever perished, being innocent? or where were the righteous cut off?" JOB 4. 1-7

GOD DELIVERS MAN FROM MANY TROUBLES

You need not fear violence

I would seek unto God, and unto God would I commit my cause: which doeth great things and unsearchable; marvellous things without number: who giveth rain upon the earth, and sendeth waters upon the fields: to set up on high those that be low; that those which mourn may be exalted to safety. But he saveth the poor from the sword, from their mouth, and from the hand of the mighty. So the poor hath hope, and iniquity stoppeth her mouth. Behold, happy is the man whom God correcteth: therefore despise not thou the chastening of the Almighty: for he maketh sore, and bindeth up: he woundeth, and his hands make whole. He shall deliver thee in six troubles: yea, in seven there shall no evil touch thee. In famine he shall redeem thee from death: and in war from the power of the sword. Thou shalt be hid from the scourge of the tongue: neither shalt thou be afraid of destruction when it cometh. At destruction and famine thou shalt laugh: neither shalt thou be afraid of the beasts of the earth. JOB 5. 8-11, 15-22

GOD VISITS MAN EVERY MORNING

He tests him every hour

What is man, that thou shouldest magnify him? and that thou shouldest set thine heart upon him? and that thou shouldest visit him every morning, and try him every moment?

JOB 7. 17, 18

GOD MOVES MOUNTAINS

From Him comes strength and justice

Then Job answered and said, "I know it is so of a truth: but how should man be just with God? If he will contend with him, he cannot answer him one of a thousand. He is wise in heart, and mighty in strength: who hath hardened himself against him, and hath prospered? Which removeth the mountains, and they know not: which overturneth them in his anger. If I speak of strength, lo, he is strong: and if of judgment, who shall set me a time to plead?" JOB 9. 1-5, 19

LIFE GIVEN BY GOD
He preserves body and spirit

Thou hast clothed me with skin and flesh, and hast fenced me with bones and sinews. Thou hast granted me life and favour, and thy visitation hath preserved my spirit.

JOB 10. 11, 12

LIE DOWN TO REST WITHOUT FEAR
Then lift your face without spot

If thou prepare thine heart, and stretch out thine hands toward him; if iniquity be in thine hand, put it far away, and let not wickedness dwell in thy tabernacles. For then shalt thou lift up thy face without spot; yea, thou shalt be stedfast, and shalt not fear: because thou shalt forget thy misery, and remember it as waters that pass away. Thine age shall be clearer than the noonday; thou shalt shine forth, thou shalt be as the morning. Thou shalt be secure, because there is hope; yea, thou shalt dig about thee, and thou shalt take thy rest in safety. Also thou shalt lie down, and none shall make thee afraid.

JOB 11. 13-19

LIGHT SHINED ON THE SHADOW OF DEATH
Longevity from understanding

And Job answered and said, "No doubt but ye are the people, and wisdom shall die with you. But I have understanding as well as you; I am not inferior to you: yea, who knoweth not such things as these? Who knoweth not in all these that the hand of the Lord hath wrought this? In whose hand is the soul of every living thing, and the breath of all mankind. Doth not the ear try words? and the mouth taste his meat? With the ancient is wisdom; and in length of days understanding.

With him is wisdom and strength, he hath counsel and understanding. With him is strength and wisdom: the deceived and the deceiver are his. He discovereth deep things out of darkness, and bringeth out to light the shadow of death."

JOB 12. 1-3, 9-13, 16, 22

The Pure Become Stronger

The righteous maintains his course

The righteous also shall hold on his way, and he that hath clean hands shall be stronger and stronger. JOB 17. 9

My Redeemer Lives

In his flesh Job sees God expressed in health

My bone cleaveth to my skin and to my flesh, and I am escaped with the skin of my teeth. Oh that my words were now written! oh that they were printed in a book! That they were graven with an iron pen and lead in the rock forever! For I know that my redeemer liveth, and that he shall stand at the latter day upon the earth: and though after my skin worms destroy this body, yet in my flesh shall I see God.

JOB 19. 20, 23-26

God Is the One Mind

He performs my assignments

Then Job answered and said, "Even today is my complaint bitter: my stroke is heavier than my groaning. Oh that I knew where I might find him! that I might come even to his seat! I would order my cause before him, and fill my mouth with arguments. I would know the words which he would answer me, and understand what he would say unto me. Will he plead against me with his great power? No; but he would put strength in me. But he knoweth the way that I take: when he hath tried me, I shall come forth as gold. My foot hath held his steps, his way have I kept, and not declined. Neither have I gone back from the commandment of his lips; I have esteemed the words of his mouth more than my necessary food. But he is in one mind, and who can turn him? and what his soul desireth, even that he doeth. For he performeth the thing that is appointed for me: and many such things are with him."

JOB 23. 1-6, 10-14

SPIRIT CREATES AND GIVES LIFE

Flesh shall be refreshed

Wherefore, Job, I pray thee, hear my speeches, and hearken to all my words. Behold, now I have opened my mouth, my tongue hath spoken in my mouth. My words shall be of the uprightness of my heart: and my lips shall utter knowledge clearly. The Spirit of God hath made me, and the breath of the Almighty hath given me life. For God speaketh once, yea twice, yet man perceiveth it not. In a dream, in a vision of the night, when deep sleep falleth upon men, in slumberings upon the bed; then he openeth the ears of men, and sealeth their instruction, that he may withdraw man from his purpose, and hide pride from man. He keepeth back his soul from the pit, and his life from perishing by the sword. Yea, his soul draweth near unto the grave, and his life to the destroyers If there be a messenger with him, an interpreter, one among a thousand, to shew unto man his uprightness: then he is gracious unto him, and saith, "Deliver him from going down to the pit: I have found a ransom." His flesh shall be fresher than a child's: he shall return to the days of his youth: he shall pray unto God, and he will be favourable unto him: and he shall see his face with joy: for he will render unto man his righteousness. He will deliver his soul from going into the pit, and his life shall see the light. Lo, all these things worketh God oftentimes with man, to bring back his soul from the pit, to be enlightened with the light of the living.

JOB 33. 1-4, 14-18, 22-26, 28-30

GOD DOES NOT AFFLICT
He is all-powerful and just

Touching the Almighty, we cannot find him out: he is excellent in power, and in judgment, and in plenty of justice: he will not afflict. JOB 37. 23

GOD RESTORES JOB'S FORTUNES
He blessed his end more than his beginning

The Lord turned the captivity of Job, when he prayed for his friends: also the Lord gave Job twice as much as he had before. Then came there unto him all his brethren, and all his sisters, and all they that had been of his acquaintance before, and did eat bread with him in his house: and they bemoaned him, and comforted him over all the evil that the Lord had brought upon him: every man also gave him a piece of money, and every one an earring of gold. So the Lord blessed the latter end of Job more than his beginning. JOB 42. 10-12

PSALMS

GOD SHALL PROSPER A GOOD MAN
Like a tree that withers not

Blessed is the man
        that walketh not in the counsel of the ungodly,
        nor standeth in the way of sinners,
        nor sitteth in the seat of the scornful.
But his delight is in the law of the Lord;
    and in his law doth he meditate day and night.
He shall be like a tree
        planted by the rivers of water,
        that bringeth forth his fruit in his season;
    his leaf also shall not wither;
    and whatsoever he doeth shall prosper.

LIVING IN SECURITY
He helps us sleep in peace

There be many that say, "Who will shew us any good?"
Lord, lift thou up the light of thy countenance upon us.
Thou hast put gladness in my heart,
More than in the time that their corn and their wine increased.
I will both lay me down in peace, and sleep:
for thou, Lord, only makest me dwell in safety. PSA 4. 6-8

APPEAL TO GOD TO HEAL WEAKNESS
Bones also can be healed

Have mercy upon me, O Lord; for I am weak:
O Lord, heal me; for my bones are vexed. PSA 6. 2

THE SLEEP OF DEATH AVOIDED
By trust in God's mercy

Consider and hear me, O Lord my God:
lighten mine eyes, lest I sleep the sleep of death;
but I have trusted in thy mercy;
my heart shall rejoice in thy salvation.
I will sing unto the Lord,
because he hath dealt bountifully with me. PSA 13. 3, 5, 6

SHOWN THE PATH OF LIFE
Fullness of joy in God's presence

The Lord is the portion of mine inheritance and of my cup:
thou maintainest my lot.
The lines are fallen unto me in pleasant places;
yea, I have a goodly heritage.
I will bless the Lord, who hath given me counsel:
my reins also instruct me in the night seasons.
I have set the Lord always before me:
because he is at my right hand, I shall not be moved.
Therefore my heart is glad, and my glory rejoiceth:

my flesh also shall rest in hope.
For thou wilt not leave my soul in hell;
neither wilt thou suffer thine Holy One to see corruption.
Thou wilt shew me the path of life:
in thy presence is fulness of joy;
at thy right hand there are pleasures for evermore. PSA 16. 5-11

Put Trust in God
Then awake in His likeness

Shew thy marvellous lovingkindness,
O thou that savest by thy right hand them which put their trust in thee.
As for me, I will behold thy face in righteousness:
I shall be satisfied, when I awake, with thy likeness. PSA 17. 7, 15

We Can Rise and Stand Upright
With the saving strength of His right hand

We will rejoice in thy salvation,
and in the name of our God we will set up our banners:
the Lord fulfil all thy petitions.
Now know I that the Lord saveth his anointed;
he will hear him from his holy heaven
with the saving strength of his right hand.
Some trust in chariots, and some in horses:
but we will remember the name of the Lord our God.
They are brought down and fallen:
but we are risen, and stand upright. PSA 20. 5-8

Your Heart Shall Live Forever
Because of trust in God

Our fathers trusted in thee:
they trusted, and thou didst deliver them.
They cried unto thee, and were delivered:
they trusted in thee, and were not confounded.

The meek shall eat and be satisfied:
they shall praise the Lord that seek him:
your heart shall live forever. PSA 22. 4, 5, 26

IN THE VALLEY OF THE SHADOW OF DEATH

Thou art with me

The Lord is my shepherd; I shall not want.
He maketh me to lie down in green pastures:
he leadeth me beside the still waters.
He restoreth my soul:
He leadeth me in the paths of righteousness for his name's sake.
Yea, though I walk through the valley of the shadow of death,
I will fear no evil:
for thou art with me;
thy rod and thy staff they comfort me. PSA 23. 1-4

GOD OUR SALVATION FROM AFFLICTION AND PAIN

He brings us out of distress

Shew me thy ways, O Lord; teach me thy paths.
Lead me in thy truth, and teach me:
for thou art the God of my salvation;
on thee do I wait all the day.
Remember, O Lord, thy tender mercies and thy lovingkindnesses;
for they have been ever of old.
The meek will he guide in judgment:
and the meek will he teach his way.
All the paths of the Lord are mercy and truth
unto such as keep his covenant and his testimonies.
For thy name's sake, O Lord, pardon mine iniquity;
for it is great.

What man is he that feareth the Lord?
him shall he teach in the way that he shall choose.
His soul shall dwell at ease;
and his seed shall inherit the earth.
The secret of the Lord is with them that fear him;

and he will shew them his covenant.
Mine eyes are ever toward the Lord;
for he shall pluck my feet out of the net.
Turn thee unto me, and have mercy upon me;
for I am desolate and afflicted.
The troubles of my heart are enlarged:
O bring thou me out of my distresses.
Look upon mine affliction and my pain;
and forgive all my sins.

PSA 25. 4-6, 9-18

He Shall Strengthen Your Heart

What then shall you dread?

The Lord is my light and my salvation;
whom shall I fear?
the Lord is the strength of my life;
of whom shall I be afraid?
When the wicked, even mine enemies and my foes,
came upon me to eat up my flesh,
they stumbled and fell.
Though an host should encamp against me,
my heart shall not fear:
though war should rise against me,
in this will I be confident.
One thing have I desired of the Lord,
that will I seek after;
that I may dwell in the house of the Lord
all the days of my life,
to behold the beauty of the Lord,
and to enquire in his temple.
For in the time of trouble he shall hide me in his pavilion:
in the secret of his tabernacle shall he hide me;
he shall set me up upon a rock.
I had fainted, unless I had believed
to see the goodness of the Lord in the land of the living.
Wait on the Lord:
be of good courage, and he shall strengthen thine heart:
wait, I say, on the Lord.

PSA 27. 1-5, 13, 14

GOD IS THE SAVING STRENGTH OF HIS ANOINTED

Therefore my heart trusts in Him

The Lord is my strength and my shield;
my heart trusted in him, and I am helped:
therefore my heart greatly rejoiceth;
and with my song will I praise him.
The Lord is their strength,
and he is the saving strength of his anointed. PSA 28. 7, 8

GOD HAS HEALED ME

For in His favor is life

I will extol thee, O Lord;
for thou hast lifted me up,
and hast not made my foes to rejoice over me.
O Lord my God, I cried unto thee,
and thou hast healed me.
O Lord, thou hast brought up my soul from the grave:
thou hast kept me alive,
that I should not go down to the pit.
Sing unto the Lord, O ye saints of his,
and give thanks at the remembrance of his holiness.
For his anger endureth but a moment;
in his favour is life:
weeping may endure for a night,
but joy cometh in the morning.
Hear, O Lord, and have mercy upon me:
Lord, be thou my helper.
Thou hast turned for me my mourning into dancing:
thou hast put off my sackcloth,
and girded me with gladness;
to the end that my glory may sing praise to thee,
and not be silent.
O Lord my God, I will give thanks unto thee forever.

PSA 30. 1-5, 10-12

OUR HEART SHALL REJOICE
We trust in His nature

Behold, the eye of the Lord
is upon them that fear him,
upon them that hope in his mercy;
to deliver their soul from death,
and to keep them alive in famine.
Our soul waiteth for the Lord:
he is our help and our shield.
For our heart shall rejoice in him,
because we have trusted in his holy name.

PSA 33. 18-21

NO BONES BROKEN
Delivered from all afflictions

O magnify the Lord with me,
and let us exalt his name together.
I sought the Lord, and he heard me,
and delivered me from all my fears.
They looked unto him, and were lightened:
and their faces were not ashamed.
This poor man cried, and the Lord heard him,
and saved him out of all his troubles.
O fear the Lord, ye his saints:
for there is no want to them that fear him.
The young lions do lack, and suffer hunger:
but they that seek the Lord shall not want any good thing.
The righteous cry, and the Lord heareth,
and delivereth them out of all their troubles.
The Lord is nigh unto them that are of a broken heart;
and saveth such as be of a contrite spirit.
Many are the afflictions of the righteous:
but the Lord delivereth him out of them all.
He keepeth all his bones: not one of them is broken.
Evil shall slay the wicked:
and they that hate the righteous shall be desolate.
The Lord redeemeth the soul of his servants:
and none of them that trust in him shall be desolate.

PSA 34. 3-6, 9, 10, 17-22

My Bones Delivered by the Lord

Who is like Him?

All my bones shall say,
"Lord, who is like unto thee,
which deliverest the poor
from him that is too strong for him,
yea, the poor and the needy from him that spoileth him?"

PSA 35. 10

The Fountain of Life

In Thy light shall we see light

Thy mercy, O Lord, is in the heavens;
and thy faithfulness reacheth unto the clouds.
Thy righteousness is like the great mountains;
thy judgments are a great deep:
O Lord, thou preservest man and beast.
How excellent is thy lovingkindness, O God!
therefore the children of men put their trust
under the shadow of thy wings.
They shall be abundantly satisfied with the fatness of thy house;
and thou shalt make them drink of the river of thy pleasures.
For with thee is the fountain of life:
in thy light shall we see light.
O continue thy lovingkindness unto them that know thee;
and thy righteousness to the upright in heart. PSA 36. 5-10

Your Heart's Desire Granted

Trust in the Lord

Trust in the Lord, and do good;
so shalt thou dwell in the land,
and verily thou shalt be fed.
Delight thyself also in the Lord;
and he shall give thee the desires of thine heart.
Commit thy way unto the Lord;
trust also in him; and he shall bring it to pass.
He shall bring forth thy righteousness as the light,

and thy judgment as the noonday.
Rest in the Lord, and wait patiently for him:
fret not thyself because of him who prospereth in his way,
because of the man who bringeth wicked devices to pass.
Cease from anger, and forsake wrath:
fret not thyself in any wise to do evil.
For evildoers shall be cut off:
but those that wait upon the Lord,
they shall inherit the earth.
For yet a little while, and the wicked shall not be:
Yea, thou shalt diligently consider his place, and it shall not be.
But the meek shall inherit the earth;
and shall delight themselves in the abundance of peace.

PSA 37. 3-11

MARK THE PERFECT MAN
Upheld by God's hand

They shall not be ashamed in the evil time:
and in the days of famine they shall be satisfied.
But the wicked shall perish,
and the enemies of the Lord shall be as the fat of lambs:
they shall consume; into smoke shall they consume away.
The wicked borroweth, and payeth not again:
but the righteous sheweth mercy, and giveth.
For such as be blessed of him shall inherit the earth;
and they that be cursed of him shall be cut off.
The steps of a good man are ordered by the Lord:
and he delighteth in his way.
Though he fall, he shall not be utterly cast down:
for the Lord upholdeth him with his hand.
I have been young, and now am old;
yet have I not seen the righteous forsaken,
nor his seed begging bread.
He is ever merciful, and lendeth;
and his seed is blessed.

Depart from evil, and do good:
and dwell forevermore.

For the Lord loveth judgment,
and forsaketh not his saints;
they are preserved forever:
but the seed of the wicked shall be cut off.
The righteous shall inherit the land,
and dwell therein forever.
The law of his God is in his heart;
none of his steps shall slide.
Mark the perfect man, and behold the upright:
for the end of that man is peace.
But the transgressors shall be destroyed together:
the end of the wicked shall be cut off.
But the salvation of the righteous is of the Lord:
he is their strength in the time of trouble.
The Lord shall help them, and deliver them:
he shall deliver them from the wicked, and save them,
because they trust in him. PSA 37. 19-29, 31, 37-40

HE BROUGHT ME UP OUT OF THE PIT

And set my feet upon a rock

I waited patiently for the Lord;
and he inclined unto me, and heard my cry.
He brought me up also out of an horrible pit,
out of the miry clay,
and set my feet upon a rock,
and established my goings.
He hath put a new song in my mouth,
even praise unto our God:
many shall see it, and fear,
and shall trust in the Lord.
Blessed is that man that maketh the Lord his trust,
and respecteth not the proud,
nor such as turn aside to lies.
Many, O Lord my God,
are thy wonderful works which thou hast done,
and thy thoughts which are to us-ward.
They cannot be reckoned up in order unto thee:

if I would declare and speak of them,
they are more than can be numbered.
Sacrifice and offering thou didst not desire;
mine ears hast thou opened.
Withhold not thou thy tender mercies from me, O Lord:
Let thy lovingkindness and thy truth continually preserve me.

PSA 40. 1-6, 11

STRENGTHENED ON THE SICK-BED

Kept alive by the Lord

The Lord will preserve him,
and keep him alive;
and he shall be blessed upon the earth:
and thou wilt not deliver him unto the will of his enemies.
The Lord will strengthen him upon the bed of languishing:
thou wilt make all his bed in his sickness.
I said, "Lord, be merciful unto me: heal my soul." PSA 41. 2-4

THE HEALTH OF MY COUNTENANCE

Thy light and thy truth lead me

O send out thy light and thy truth:
let them lead me;
let them bring me unto thy holy hill, and to thy tabernacles.
Why art thou cast down, O my soul?
Why art thou disquieted within me?
Hope in God: for I shall yet praise him,
Who is the health of my countenance, and my God. PSA 43. 3, 5

A VERY PRESENT HELP IN TROUBLE

God in the midst of her

God is our refuge and strength,
a very present help in trouble.
Therefore will not we fear,
though the earth be removed,
and though the mountains
be carried into the midst of the sea;

though the waters thereof roar and be troubled,
though the mountains shake with the swelling thereof.
There is a river,
the streams whereof shall make glad the city of God,
the holy place of the tabernacles of the most High.
God is in the midst of her;
she shall not be moved:
God shall help her, and that right early.
The heathen raged, the kingdoms were moved:
he uttered his voice, the earth melted.

The Lord of hosts is with us;
the God of Jacob is our refuge.
Come, behold the works of the Lord,
what desolations he hath made in the earth.
He maketh wars to cease unto the end of the earth;
he breaketh the bow, and cutteth the spear in sunder;
he burneth the chariot in the fire.
Be still, and know that I am God:
I will be exalted among the heathen,
I will be exalted in the earth.
The Lord of hosts is with us;
the God of Jacob is our refuge. PSA 46. 1-11

REDEEMED FROM THE GRAVE
God ransoms our lives

God will redeem my soul
from the power of the grave:
for he shall receive me. PSA 49. 15

TRUTH IN THE IWARD PARTS
Renew my spirit within me

Behold, thou desirest truth in the inward parts:
and in the hidden part thou shalt make me to know wisdom.
Purge me with hyssop, and I shall be clean:
wash me, and I shall be whiter than snow.

Create in me a clean heart, O God;
  and renew a right spirit within me. PSA 51. 6, 7, 10

THEY WERE IN GREAT FEAR
Though there was no need for fear

There were they in great fear,
  where no fear was. PSA 53. 5

MY HEART IS SORE PAINED
But the Lord shall save me

My heart is sore pained within me:
  and the terrors of death are fallen upon me.
Fearfulness and trembling are come upon me,
    and horror hath overwhelmed me.
I said, "Oh that I had wings like a dove!
    for then would I fly away, and be at rest."
As for me, I will call upon God;
  and the Lord shall save me.
Evening, and morning, and at noon, will I pray, and cry aloud:
  and he shall hear my voice.
He hath delivered my soul in peace
    from the battle that was against me:
  for there were many with me. PSA 55. 4-6, 16-18

NO FEAR OF WHAT FLESH CAN DO
My feet delivered from falling

What time I am afraid, I will trust in thee.
In God I will praise his word,
    in God I have put my trust;
  I will not fear what flesh can do unto me.
When I cry unto thee, then shall mine enemies turn back:
  this I know; for God is for me.
In God will I praise his word:
  in the Lord will I praise his word.
In God have I put my trust:

I will not be afraid what man can do unto me.
Thy vows are upon me, O God:
I will render praises unto thee.
For thou hast delivered my soul from death:
wilt not thou deliver my feet from falling,
that I may walk before God in the light of the living?

PSA 56. 3, 4, 9-13

MY HEART IS FIXED
God performs all things for me

Be merciful unto me, O God,
be merciful unto me: for my soul trusteth in thee:
yea, in the shadow of thy wings will I make my refuge
until these calamities be overpast.
I will cry unto God most high;
unto God that performeth all things for me.
He shall send from heaven, and save me
from the reproach of him that would swallow me up.
God shall send forth his mercy and his truth.
My heart is fixed, O God, my heart is fixed:
I will sing and give praise.
Awake up, my glory;
awake, psaltery and harp:
I myself will awake early.
I will praise thee, O Lord, among the people:
I will sing unto thee among the nations.
For thy mercy is great unto the heavens,
and thy truth unto the clouds.
Be thou exalted, O God, above the heavens:
let thy glory be above all the earth.

PSA 57. 1-3, 7-11

THE ROCK OF MY STRENGTH
I shall not be shaken

Truly my soul waiteth upon God:
from him cometh my salvation.

He only is my rock and my salvation;
he is my defence;
I shall not be greatly moved.
My soul, wait thou only upon God;
for my expectation is from him.
He only is my rock and my salvation:
he is my defence; I shall not be moved.
In God is my salvation and my glory:
the rock of my strength, and my refuge, is in God.
Trust in him at all times;
ye people, pour out your heart before him:
God is a refuge for us.
God hath spoken once; twice have I heard this;
that power belongeth unto God.
Also unto thee, O Lord, belongeth mercy:
for thou renderest to every man according to his work.

PSA 62. 1, 2, 5-8, 11, 12

MY FLESH LONGS FOR THEE
Thy right hand upholds me

O God, thou art my God; early will I seek thee:
my soul thirsteth for thee.
My flesh longeth for thee
in a dry and thirsty land, where no water is;
to see thy power and thy glory,
so as I have seen thee in the sanctuary.
Because thy lovingkindness is better than life,
my lips shall praise thee.
Thus will I bless thee while I live:
I will lift up my hands in thy name.
My soul shall be satisfied as with marrow and fatness;
and my mouth shall praise thee with joyful lips.
When I remember thee upon my bed,
and meditate on thee in the night watches.
Because thou hast been my help,
therefore in the shadow of thy wings will I rejoice.
My soul followeth hard after thee:
thy right hand upholdeth me.

PSA 63. 1-8

HE KEEPS OUR FEET FROM STUMBLING
He holds our soul in life

Make a joyful noise unto God, all ye lands:
sing forth the honour of his name:
make his praise glorious.
Say unto God, "How terrible art thou in thy works!
through the greatness of thy power
shall thine enemies submit themselves unto thee.
All the earth shall worship thee, and shall sing unto thee;
they shall sing to thy name."
Come and see the works of God:
he is terrible in his doing toward the children of men.
He turned the sea into dry land:
they went through the flood on foot:
there did we rejoice in him.
He ruleth by his power forever;
his eyes behold the nations:
let not the rebellious exalt themselves.
O bless our God, ye people,
and make the voice of his praise to be heard:
which holdeth our soul in life,
and suffereth not our feet to be moved.
For thou, O God, hast proved us:
thou hast tried us, as silver is tried.

PSA 66. 1-10

THY SAVING HEALTH KNOWN TO ALL NATIONS
His face shines on us

God be merciful unto us, and bless us;
and cause his face to shine upon us;
that thy way may be known upon earth,
thy saving health among all nations.
Let the people praise thee, O God;
let all the people praise thee.
O let the nations be glad and sing for joy:
for thou shalt judge the people righteously,
and govern the nations upon earth.

Let the people praise thee, O God;
  let all the people praise thee.
Then shall the earth yield her increase;
  and God, even our own God, shall bless us.
God shall bless us; and all the ends of the earth shall fear him.

PSA 67. 1-7

THE ISSUES FROM DEATH

He brings out those bound with chains

God setteth the solitary in families:
  he bringeth out those which are bound with chains.
He that is our God is the God of salvation;
  and unto God the Lord belong the issues from death.
The God of Israel is he that giveth strength and power
    unto his people.
Blessed be God.

PSA 68. 6, 20, 35

WHEN MY FLESH AND HEART FAIL

God is the strength of my heart

Nevertheless I am continually with thee:
  thou hast holden me by my right hand.
Thou shalt guide me with thy counsel,
    and afterward receive me to glory.
Whom have I in heaven but thee?
    and there is none upon earth that I desire beside thee.
My flesh and my heart faileth:
  but God is the strength of my heart, and my portion forever.
It is good for me to draw near to God:
  I have put my trust in the Lord God,
    that I may declare all thy works.

PSA 73. 23-26, 28

FOOD AND WATER FURNISHED

God spreads a table even in the wilderness

Yea, they spake against God;
  they said, "Can God furnish a table in the wilderness?"

Behold, he smote the rock, that the waters gushed out,
and the streams overflowed.
"Can he give bread also? can he provide flesh for his people?"
He led them on safely,
so that they feared not.
So he fed them according to the integrity of his heart;
and guided them by the skilfulness of his hands.

PSA 78. 19, 20, 53, 72

HEART AND FLESH CRY FOR THE LIVING GOD
No good thing will He withhold

How amiable are thy tabernacles, O Lord of hosts!
My soul longeth, yea, even fainteth for the courts of the Lord:
my heart and my flesh crieth out for the living God.
Yea, the sparrow hath found an house,
and the swallow a nest for herself,
where she may lay her young,
even thine altars, O Lord of hosts, my King, and my God.
Blessed are they that dwell in thy house:
they will be still praising thee.
Blessed is the man whose strength is in thee;
in whose heart are the ways of them.
Who passing through the valley of Baca make it a well;
the rain also filleth the pools.
They go from strength to strength,
every one of them in Zion appeareth before God.

O Lord God of hosts, hear my prayer:
give ear, O God of Jacob.
Behold, O God our shield,
and look upon the face of thine anointed.
For a day in thy courts is better than a thousand.
I had rather be a doorkeeper in the house of my God,
than to dwell in the tents of wickedness.
For the Lord God is a sun and shield:
the Lord will give grace and glory:
no good thing will he withhold from them that walk uprightly.
O Lord of hosts, blessed is the man that trusteth in thee. PSA 84. 1-12

THEY SHALL WALK IN THE LIGHT OF THY PRESENCE
Might and strength are from God

Thou hast a mighty arm:
strong is thy hand, and high is thy right hand.
Justice and judgment are the habitation of thy throne:
mercy and truth shall go before thy face.
Blessed is the people that know the joyful sound:
they shall walk, O Lord, in the light of thy countenance.

PSA 89. 13-15

DELIVERY FROM CONTAGION
By dwelling in the shelter of the Most High

He that dwelleth in the secret place of the most High
shall abide under the shadow of the Almighty.
I will say of the Lord, He is my refuge and my fortress: my God;
in him will I trust.
Surely he shall deliver thee from the snare of the fowler,
and from the noisome pestilence.
He shall cover thee with his feathers,
and under his wings shalt thou trust:
his truth shall be thy shield and buckler.
Thou shalt not be afraid for the terror by night;
nor for the arrow that flieth by day;
nor for the pestilence that walketh in darkness;
nor for the destruction that wasteth at noonday.

A thousand shall fall at thy side,
and ten thousand at thy right hand;
but it shall not come nigh thee.
Only with thine eyes
shalt thou behold and see the reward of the wicked.
Because thou hast made the Lord,
which is my refuge, even the most High, thy habitation;
there shall no evil befall thee,
neither shall any plague come nigh thy dwelling.
For he shall give his angels charge over thee,
to keep thee in all thy ways.

They shall bear thee up in their hands,
lest thou dash thy foot against a stone.
Thou shalt tread upon the lion and adder:
the young lion and the dragon shalt thou trample under feet.

Because he hath set his love upon me,
therefore will I deliver him:
I will set him on high, because he hath known my name.
He shall call upon me, and I will answer him:
I will be with him in trouble;
I will deliver him, and honour him.
With long life will I satisfy him,
and shew him my salvation. PSA 91. 1-16

FRUITAGE IN OLD AGE

Because planted in the house of the Lord

It is a good thing to give thanks unto the Lord,
and to sing praises unto thy name, O most High:
to shew forth thy lovingkindness in the morning,
and thy faithfulness every night,
upon an instrument of ten strings, and upon the psaltery;
upon the harp with a solemn sound.
For thou, Lord, hast made me glad through thy work:
I will triumph in the works of thy hands.

O Lord, how great are thy works!
and thy thoughts are very deep.
The righteous shall flourish like the palm tree:
he shall grow like a cedar in Lebanon.
Those that be planted in the house of the Lord
shall flourish in the courts of our God.
They shall still bring forth fruit in old age;
they shall be fat and flourishing. PSA 92. 1-5, 12-14

GOD THAT FORMED THE EAR AND EYE

He hears and He sees

He that planted the ear,
shall he not hear?
he that formed the eye,
shall he not see?
Unless the Lord had been my help,
my soul had almost dwelt in silence.
When I said, "My foot slippeth,"
thy mercy, O Lord, held me up.
In the multitude of my thoughts within me
thy comforts delight my soul.
But the Lord is my defence;
and my God is the rock of my refuge. PSA 94. 9, 17-19, 22

IT IS GOD THAT MADE US

Give thanks to Him

Make a joyful noise unto the Lord, all ye lands.
Serve the Lord with gladness:
come before his presence with singing.
Know ye that the Lord he is God:
it is he that hath made us, and not we ourselves;
we are his people, and the sheep of his pasture.
Enter into his gates with thanksgiving,
and into his courts with praise:
be thankful unto him, and bless his name.
For the Lord is good; his mercy is everlasting;
and his truth endureth to all generations. PSA 100. 1-5

I WILL WALK WITH A PERFECT HEART

Behave myself in a perfect way

I will sing of mercy and judgment:
unto thee, O Lord, will I sing.
I will behave myself wisely in a perfect way.
O when wilt thou come unto me?

I will walk within my house with a perfect heart.
I will set no wicked thing before mine eyes:
I hate the work of them that turn aside;
it shall not cleave to me.
A froward heart shall depart from me:
I will not know a wicked person. PSA 101. 1-4

He Heals All Your Diseases

His mercy extends to children's children

Bless the Lord, O my soul:
and all that is within me, bless his holy name.
Bless the Lord, O my soul, and forget not all his benefits:
who forgiveth all thine iniquities;
who healeth all thy diseases;
who redeemeth thy life from destruction;
who crowneth thee with lovingkindness and tender mercies;
who satisfieth thy mouth with good things;
so that thy youth is renewed like the eagle's. PSA 103. 1-5

Recovery and Renewal

When God sends forth His spirit

O Lord, how manifold are thy works!
in wisdom hast thou made them all:
the earth is full of thy riches.
That thou givest them they gather:
thou openest thine hand, they are filled with good.
Thou sendest forth thy spirit, they are created:
and thou renewest the face of the earth. PSA 104. 24, 28, 30

Not One Feeble Person

All led out with joy

There was not one feeble person among their tribes.
The people asked, and he brought quails,
and satisfied them with the bread of heaven.

He opened the rock, and the waters gushed out;
they ran in the dry places like a river.
For he remembered his holy promise, and Abraham his servant.
And he brought forth his people with joy,
and his chosen with gladness. PSA 105. 37, 40-43

HE SENT HIS WORD TO HEAL THEM
Delivered from their distress

O give thanks unto the Lord, for he is good;
for his mercy endureth forever.
Let the redeemed of the Lord say so,
whom he hath redeemed from the hand of the enemy;
and gathered them out of the lands,
from the east, and from the west,
from the north, and from the south.
They wandered in the wilderness in a solitary way;
they found no city to dwell in.
Hungry and thirsty, their soul fainted in them.
Then they cried unto the Lord in their trouble,
and he delivered them out of their distresses.
And he led them forth by the right way,
that they might go to a city of habitation.
Oh that men would praise the Lord for his goodness,
and for his wonderful works to the children of men!
For he satisfieth the longing soul,
and filleth the hungry soul with goodness.

Such as sit in darkness and in the shadow of death,
being bound in affliction and iron;
because they rebelled against the words of God,
and contemned the counsel of the most High,
therefore he brought down their heart with labour;
they fell down, and there was none to help.
Then they cried unto the Lord in their trouble,
and he saved them out of their distresses.
He brought them out of darkness and the shadow of death,
and brake their bands in sunder.

Oh that men would praise the Lord for his goodness,
and for his wonderful works to the children of men!
For he hath broken the gates of brass,
and cut the bars of iron in sunder.

Fools because of their transgression,
and because of their iniquities, are afflicted.
Their soul abhorreth all manner of meat;
and they draw near unto the gates of death.
Then they cry unto the Lord in their trouble,
and he saveth them out of their distresses.
He sent his word,
and healed them,
and delivered them from their destructions.
Oh that men would praise the Lord for his goodness,
and for his wonderful works to the children of men!
And let them sacrifice the sacrifices of thanksgiving,
and declare his works with rejoicing.
They that go down to the sea in ships,
that do business in great waters;
these see the works of the Lord,
and his wonders in the deep. PSA 107. 1-24

PRESERVED FROM PAIN AND DEATH

To take the cup of salvation

The sorrows of death compassed me,
and the pains of hell gat hold upon me:
I found trouble and sorrow.
Then called I upon the name of the Lord;
O Lord, I beseech thee, deliver my soul.
Gracious is the Lord, and righteous;
yea, our God is merciful.
The Lord preserveth the simple:
I was brought low, and he helped me.
Return unto thy rest, O my soul,
for the Lord hath dealt bountifully with thee.

For thou hast delivered my soul from death,
mine eyes from tears, and my feet from falling.
I will walk before the Lord in the land of the living.
I believed, therefore have I spoken:
I was greatly afflicted:
What shall I render unto the Lord for all his benefits toward me?
I will take the cup of salvation,
and call upon the name of the Lord. PSA 116. 3-10, 12, 13

SET FREE FROM MY DISTRESS

I shall not die but live

O give thanks unto the Lord;
for he is good:
because his mercy endureth forever.
I called upon the Lord in distress:
the Lord answered me, and set me in a large place.
The Lord is on my side;
I will not fear: what can man do unto me?
The Lord is my strength and song,
and is become my salvation.
The voice of rejoicing and salvation
is in the tabernacles of the righteous:
the right hand of the Lord doeth valiantly.
The right hand of the Lord is exalted:
the right hand of the Lord doeth valiantly.
I shall not die, but live,
and declare the works of the Lord. PSA 118. 1, 5, 6, 14-17

AFFLICTION HELPS ME LEARN YOUR LAWS

Your precepts give me life

Before I was afflicted I went astray:
but now have I kept thy word.
Thou art good, and doest good;
teach me thy statutes.
It is good for me that I have been afflicted;
that I might learn thy statutes.

Unless thy law had been my delights,
I should then have perished in mine affliction.
I will never forget thy precepts:
for with them thou hast quickened me.
Thy word is a lamp unto my feet,
and a light unto my path.
The entrance of thy words giveth light;
it giveth understanding unto the simple.
Great peace have they which love thy law:
and nothing shall offend them.

PSA 119. 67, 68, 71, 92, 93, 105, 130, 165

Preserved from All Evil

The Lord is your guardian

I will lift up mine eyes unto the hills.
From whence cometh my help?
My help cometh from the Lord, which made heaven and earth.
He will not suffer thy foot to be moved:
he that keepeth thee will not slumber.
Behold, he that keepeth Israel shall neither slumber nor sleep.
The Lord is thy keeper:
the Lord is thy shade upon thy right hand.
The sun shall not smite thee by day, nor the moon by night.
The Lord shall preserve thee from all evil:
he shall preserve thy soul.
The Lord shall preserve thy going out and thy coming in
from this time forth, and even forevermore.

PSA 121. 1-8

He Gives His Beloved Sleep

God keeps watch over the city

Except the Lord build the house,
they labour in vain that build it.
Except the Lord keep the city,
the watchman waketh but in vain.
It is vain for you to rise up early,
to sit up late, to eat the bread of sorrows:
for so he giveth his beloved sleep.

PSA 127. 1, 2

GOD STRENGTHENED ME
He perfects all that concerns me

In the day when I cried thou answeredst me,
and strengthenedst me with strength in my soul.
The Lord will perfect that which concerneth me:
thy mercy, O Lord, endureth forever. PSA 138. 3, 8

EVER-PRESENCE OF SPIRIT
It includes my substance

Whither shall I go from thy spirit?
or whither shall I flee from thy presence?
If I ascend up into heaven, thou art there:
if I make my bed in hell, behold, thou art there.
If I take the wings of the morning,
and dwell in the uttermost parts of the sea;
even there shall thy hand lead me,
and thy right hand shall hold me.
I will praise thee; for I am fearfully and wonderfully made:
marvellous are thy works;
and that my soul knoweth right well.
My substance was not hid from thee, when I was made in secret,
and curiously wrought in the lowest parts of the earth.
Thine eyes did see my substance, yet being unperfect;
and in thy book all my members were written,
which in continuance were fashioned,
when as yet there was none of them.
How precious also are thy thoughts unto me, O God!
how great is the sum of them!
If I should count them, they are more in number than the sand:
when I awake, I am still with thee. PSA 139. 7-10, 14-18

HE HOLDS UP THOSE WHO STUMBLE
The Lord watches over all who love Him

The Lord upholdeth all that fall,
and raiseth up all those that be bowed down.

The eyes of all wait upon thee;
and thou givest them their meat in due season.
Thou openest thine hand,
and satisfiest the desire of every living thing.
The Lord is righteous in all his ways,
and holy in all his works.
The Lord is nigh unto all them that call upon him,
to all that call upon him in truth.
He will fulfil the desire of them that fear him:
he also will hear their cry, and will save them.
PSA 145. 14-19

GOD RESTORES SIGHT

He straightens backs which are bent

Happy is he that hath the God of Jacob for his help,
whose hope is in the Lord his God:
Which made heaven, and earth, the sea, and all that therein is:
which keepeth truth forever:
which executeth judgment for the oppressed:
which giveth food to the hungry.
The Lord looseth the prisoners.
The Lord openeth the eyes of the blind.
The Lord raiseth them that are bowed down.
The Lord loveth the righteous.
The Lord preserveth the strangers;
he relieveth the fatherless and widow.
PSA 146. 5-9

GOD HEALS BROKEN HEARTS

He binds up wounds

He healeth the broken in heart,
and bindeth up their wounds.
He telleth the number of the stars;
he calleth them all by their names.
Great is our Lord, and of great power:
his understanding is infinite.
PSA 147. 3-5

PROVERBS

HEALTH TO BONES AND NAVEL
Understanding is a tree of life

My son, forget not my law; but let thine heart keep my commandments: for length of days, and long life, and peace, shall they add to thee. Let not mercy and truth forsake thee: bind them about thy neck; write them upon the table of thine heart: so shalt thou find favour and good understanding in the sight of God and man.

Trust in the Lord with all thine heart; and lean not unto thine own understanding. In all thy ways acknowledge him, and he shall direct thy paths. Be not wise in thine own eyes: fear the Lord, and depart from evil. It shall be health to thy navel, and marrow to thy bones.

Happy is the man that findeth wisdom, and the man that getteth understanding. My son, let not them depart from thine eyes: keep sound wisdom and discretion: so shall they be life unto thy soul, and grace to thy neck. Then shalt thou walk in thy way safely, and thy foot shall not stumble. When thou liest down, thou shalt not be afraid: yea, thou shalt lie down, and thy sleep shall be sweet. Be not afraid of sudden fear.

PROV 3. 1-8, 13, 21-25

THE FATHER'S WORDS ARE HEALTH TO THE WHOLE BODY
And they give life to those who know them

When thou goest, thy steps shall not be straitened; and when thou runnest, thou shalt not stumble. Take fast hold of instruction; let her not go: keep her; for she is thy life. But the path of the just is as the shining light, that shineth more and more unto the perfect day.

My son, attend to my words; incline thine ear unto my sayings. Let them not depart from thine eyes; keep them in the midst of thine heart. For they are life unto those that find them, and health to all their flesh. PROV 4. 12, 13, 18, 20-22

The Years of Life Increased

By understanding God

The fear of the Lord is the beginning of wisdom: and the knowledge of the holy is understanding. For by me thy days shall be multiplied, and the years of thy life shall be increased.

PROV 9. 10, 11

The Tongue of the Wise Heals

A kind word makes the heart glad

There is that speaketh like the piercings of a sword: but the tongue of the wise is health. The lip of truth shall be established forever: but a lying tongue is but for a moment. Heaviness in the heart of man maketh it stoop: but a good word maketh it glad. In the way of righteousness is life; and in the pathway thereof there is no death. PROV 12. 18, 19, 25, 28

Hope Deferred Makes the Heart Sick

A faithful ambassador imparts health

Hope deferred maketh the heart sick: but when the desire cometh, it is a tree of life. A wicked messenger falleth into mischief: but a faithful ambassador is health. PROV 13. 12, 17

Bones Decayed by Envy

A sound heart puts flesh on a man

The fear of the Lord is a fountain of life, to depart from the snares of death. In the multitude of people is the king's honour: but in the want of people is the destruction of the prince. He that is slow to wrath is of great understanding: but he that is hasty of spirit exalteth folly. A sound heart is the life of the flesh: but envy the rottenness of the bones.

PROV 14. 27-30

WHOLESOME CONVERSATION IS A STAFF OF LIFE

Good news warms the marrow

A wholesome tongue is a tree of life: but perverseness therein is a breach in the spirit. The light of the eyes rejoiceth the heart: and a good report maketh the bones fat. PROV 15. 4, 30

UNDERSTANDING IS A WELLSPRING OF LIFE

Kind words are health to the bones

Understanding is a wellspring of life unto him that hath it: but the instruction of fools is folly. The heart of the wise teacheth his mouth, and addeth learning to his lips. Pleasant words are as an honeycomb, sweet to the soul, and health to the bones. PROV 16. 22-24

CHEERFULNESS HAS A GOOD EFFECT

Like a medicine

A merry heart doeth good like a medicine: but a broken spirit drieth the bones. PROV 17. 22

THE SEEING EYE AND THE HEARING EAR

God made them both

Wine is a mocker, strong drink is raging: and whosoever is deceived thereby is not wise. The hearing ear, and the seeing eye, the Lord hath made even both of them. Say not thou, I will recompense evil; but wait on the Lord, and he shall save thee. The spirit of man is the candle of the Lord, searching all the inward parts of the belly. PROV 20. 1, 12, 22, 27

ECCLESIASTES

GOD REQUIRES PAST
What He does is forever

There is no remembrance of former things; neither shall there be any remembrance of things that are to come with those that shall come after. I know that, whatsoever God doeth, it shall be forever: nothing can be put to it, nor any thing taken from it: and God doeth it, that men should fear before him. That which hath been is now and that which is to be hath already been; and God requireth that which is past.

ECCLES 1. 11
3. 14, 15

THE RIGHTEOUS ARE IN THE HAND OF GOD
Also their works are under His control

All this I considered in my heart even to declare all this, that the righteous, and the wise, and their works, are in the hand of God.

ECCLES 9. 1

ISAIAH

RELIEF FROM PAIN, FEAR AND SLAVERY
The Lord's purpose cannot be annulled

It shall come to pass that the Lord shall give thee rest from thy sorrow, and from thy fear, and from the hard bondage wherein thou wast made to serve. The Lord of hosts hath sworn, saying, "Surely as I have thought, so shall it come to pass; and as I have purposed, so shall it stand: that I will break the Assyrian in my land, and upon my mountains tread him under foot: then shall his yoke depart from off them, and his burden depart from off their shoulders." This is the purpose that is purposed upon the whole earth: and this is the hand that is stretched out upon all the nations. For the Lord of hosts hath purposed, and who shall disannul it? and his hand is stretched out, and who shall turn it back? ISA 14. 3, 24-27

A Saviour to Deliver Them

He shall heal those that ask

In that day shall there be an altar to the Lord in the midst of the land of Egypt, and a pillar at the border thereof to the Lord. It shall be for a sign and for a witness unto the Lord of hosts in the land of Egypt: for they shall cry unto the Lord because of the oppressors, and he shall send them a saviour, and a great one, and he shall deliver them. The Lord shall be known to Egypt, and the Egyptians shall know the Lord in that day, and shall do sacrifice and oblation; yea, they shall vow a vow unto the Lord, and perform it. The Lord shall smite Egypt: he shall smite and heal it: and they shall return even to the Lord, and he shall be intreated of them, and shall heal them. ISA 19. 19-22

Deaf Shall Hear and Blind See

Even the erring gain understanding

Wherefore the Lord said, "Forasmuch as this people draw near me with their mouth, and with their lips do honour me, but have removed their heart far from me, and their fear toward me is taught by the precept of men: woe unto them that seek deep to hide their counsel from the Lord, and their works are in the dark, and they say, 'Who seeth us?' and 'Who knoweth us?' Surely your turning of things upside down shall be esteemed as the potter's clay: for shall the work say of him that made it, 'He made me not'? or shall the thing framed say of him that framed it, 'He had no understanding'? Is it not yet a very little while, and Lebanon shall be turned into a fruitful field, and the fruitful field shall be esteemed as a forest? In that day shall the deaf hear the words of the book, and the eyes of the blind shall see out of obscurity, and out of darkness. The meek also shall increase their joy in the Lord, and the poor among men shall rejoice in the Holy One of Israel. They also that erred in spirit shall come to understanding, and they that murmured shall learn doctrine." ISA 29. 13, 15-19, 24

STROKE HEALED

Confidence in God shall be your strength

Thus saith the Lord God, the Holy One of Israel, "In returning and rest shall ye be saved; in quietness and in confidence shall be your strength. Moreover the light of the moon shall be as the light of the sun, and the light of the sun shall be sevenfold, as the light of seven days, in the day that the Lord bindeth up the breach of his people, and healeth the stroke of their wound." ISA 30. 15, 26

EYES SEE, EARS HEAR

Those who stammer speak plainly

The eyes of them that see shall not be dim, and the ears of them that hear shall hearken. The heart also of the rash shall understand knowledge, and the tongue of the stammerers shall be ready to speak plainly. ISA 32. 3, 4

THE LORD WILL SAVE US

No one shall say, "I am sick."

The Lord is exalted; for he dwelleth on high: he hath filled Zion with judgment and righteousness. Wisdom and knowledge shall be the stability of thy times, and strength of salvation: the fear of the Lord is his treasure. Look upon Zion, the city of our solemnities: thine eyes shall see Jerusalem a quiet habitation, a tabernacle that shall not be taken down; not one of the stakes thereof shall ever be removed, neither shall any of the cords thereof be broken. But there the glorious Lord will be unto us a place of broad rivers and streams; wherein shall go no galley with oars, neither shall gallant ship pass thereby. For the Lord is our judge, the Lord is our lawgiver, the Lord is our king; he will save us. The inhabitant shall not say, "I am sick." The people that dwell therein shall be forgiven their iniquity.

ISA 33. 5, 6
20-22, 24

STRENGTHEN WEAK HANDS AND FEEBLE KNEES

Be strong, fear not

The wilderness and the solitary place shall be glad for them; and the desert shall rejoice, and blossom as the rose. It shall blossom abundantly, and rejoice even with joy and singing: the glory of Lebanon shall be given unto it, the excellency of Carmel and Sharon, they shall see the glory of the Lord, and the excellency of our God.

Strengthen ye the weak hands, and confirm the feeble knees. Say to them that are of a fearful heart, be strong, fear not: behold, your God will come with vengeance, even God with a recompence; he will come and save you. Then the eyes of the blind shall be opened, and the ears of the deaf shall be unstopped. Then shall the lame man leap as an hart, and the tongue of the dumb sing: for in the wilderness shall waters break out, and streams in the desert. The parched ground shall become a pool, and the thirsty land springs of water: in the habitation of dragons, where each lay, shall be grass with reeds and rushes. An highway shall be there, and a way, and it shall be called the way of holiness; the unclean shall not pass over it; but it shall be for those, the wayfaring men; though fools shall not err therein. No lion shall be there, nor any ravenous beast shall go up thereon, it shall not be found there; but the redeemed shall walk there: and the ransomed of the Lord shall return, and come to Zion with songs and everlasting joy upon their heads. They shall obtain joy and gladness, and sorrow and sighing shall flee away.

ISA 35. 1-10

GOD WILL RECOVER ME AND MAKE ME LIVE

The living shall praise thee

In those days was Hezekiah sick unto death. And Isaiah the prophet the son of Amoz came unto him, and said unto him, "Thus saith the Lord, Set thine house in order: for thou shalt die, and not live." Then Hezekiah turned his face toward the wall, and prayed unto the Lord, and said, "Remember now, O Lord, I beseech thee, how I have walked before thee in truth and with a perfect heart, and have done that which is good in thy sight." And Hezekiah wept sore. Then came the word of the Lord to Isaiah, saying, "Go, and say to Hezekiah, Thus saith the Lord, the God of David thy father: I have heard thy prayer, I have seen thy tears: behold, I will add unto thy days fifteen years." Isaiah had said, "Let them take a lump of figs, and lay it for a plaister upon the boil, and he shall recover." Hezekiah also had said, What is the sign that I shall go up to the house of the Lord? "This shall be a sign unto thee from the Lord, that the Lord will do this thing that he hath spoken. Behold, I will bring again the shadow of the degrees, which is gone down in the sun dial of Ahaz, ten degrees backward." So the sun returned ten degrees, by which degrees it was gone down.

The writing of Hezekiah king of Judah, when he had been sick, and was recovered of his sickness: I said in the cutting off of my days, I shall go to the gates of the grave: I am deprived of the residue of my years. I said, I shall not see the Lord, even the Lord, in the land of the living: I shall behold man no more with the inhabitants of the world. Mine age is departed, and is removed from me as a shepherd's tent: I have cut off like a weaver my life: he will cut me off with pining sickness: from day even to night wilt thou make an end of me. I reckoned till morning, that, as a lion, so will he break all my bones. From day even to night wilt thou make an end of me. Like a crane or a swallow, so did I chatter: I did mourn as a dove: mine eyes fail with looking upward: O Lord, I am oppressed;

undertake for me. What shall I say? he hath both spoken unto me, and himself hath done it: I shall go softly all my years in the bitterness of my soul. O Lord, by these things men live, and in all these things is the life of my spirit: so wilt thou recover me, and make me to live. Behold, for peace I had great bitterness: but thou hast in love to my soul delivered it from the pit of corruption: for thou hast cast all my sins behind thy back. For the grave cannot praise thee, death cannot celebrate thee: they that go down into the pit cannot hope for thy truth. The living, the living, he shall praise thee, as I do this day: the father to the children shall make known thy truth. The Lord was ready to save me: therefore we will sing my songs to the stringed instruments all the days of our life in the house of the Lord. ISA 38. 1-5, 21, 22, 7-20
II KINGS 20. 1-11

THE SICK KING RECOVERED
His friend rejoices

At that time Merodach-baladan, the son of Baladan, king of Babylon, sent letters and a present to Hezekiah: for he had heard that he had been sick, and was recovered. ISA 39. 1

RUN AND NOT TIRE, WALK AND NOT FAINT
When waiting on the Lord

Hast thou not known? hast thou not heard, that the everlasting God, the Lord, the creator of the ends of the earth, fainteth not, neither is weary? there is no searching of his understanding. He giveth power to the faint; and to them that have no might he increaseth strength. Even the youths shall faint and be weary, and the young men shall utterly fall: but they that wait upon the Lord shall renew their strength; they shall mount up with wings as eagles; they shall run, and not be weary; and they shall walk, and not faint. ISA 40. 28-31

HELP FROM THE LORD
Fear nothing for I am with you

Fear thou not; for I am with thee: be not dismayed; for I am thy God: I will strengthen thee; yea, I will help thee; yea, I will uphold thee with the right hand of my righteousness. Behold, all they that were incensed against thee shall be ashamed and confounded: they shall be as nothing; and they that strive with thee shall perish. Thou shalt seek them, and shalt not find them, even them that contended with thee: they that war against thee shall be as nothing, and as a thing of nought. For I the Lord thy God will hold thy right hand, saying unto thee, Fear not; I will help thee, saith the Lord, and thy redeemer, the Holy One of Israel.

Behold, I will make thee a new sharp threshing instrument having teeth: thou shalt thresh the mountains, and beat them small, and shalt make the hills as chaff. Thou shalt fan them, and the wind shall carry them away, and the whirlwind shall scatter them: and thou shalt rejoice in the Lord, and shalt glory in the Holy One of Israel. When the poor and needy seek water, and there is none, and their tongue faileth for thirst, I the Lord will hear them, I the God of Israel will not forsake them. I will open rivers in high places, and fountains in the midst of the valleys: I will make the wilderness a pool of water, and the dry land springs of water. I will plant in the wilderness the cedar, the shittah tree, and the myrtle, and the oil tree; I will set in the desert the fir tree, and the pine, and the box tree together: that they may see, and know, and consider, and understand together, that the hand of the Lord hath done this, and the Holy One of Israel hath created it. ISA 41. 10-20

HEAR, YE DEAF, AND LOOK, YE BLIND
Bring out the prisoners

Thus saith God the Lord, he that created the heavens, and stretched them out; he that spread forth the earth, and that which cometh out of it; he that giveth breath unto the people upon it, and spirit to them that walk therein: I the Lord have called thee in righteousness, and will hold thine hand, and will keep thee, and give thee for a covenant of the people, for a light of the Gentiles; to open the blind eyes, to bring out the prisoners from the prison, and them that sit in darkness out of the prison house. I am the Lord: that is my name: and my glory will I not give to another, neither my praise to graven images. Behold, the former things are come to pass, and new things do I declare: before they spring forth I tell you of them. I will bring the blind by a way that they knew not; I will lead them in paths that they have not known: I will make darkness light before them, and crooked things straight. These things will I do unto them, and not forsake them. They shall be turned back, they shall be greatly ashamed, that trust in graven images, that say to the molten images, Ye are our gods. Hear, ye deaf; and look, ye blind, that ye may see.

ISA 42. 5-9, 16-18

Rivers Shall Not Overflow nor Fire Burn

You are my witnesses

But now thus saith the Lord that created thee, O Jacob, and he that formed thee, O Israel, Fear not: for I have redeemed thee, I have called thee by thy name; thou art mine. When thou passest through the waters, I will be with thee; and through the rivers, they shall not overflow thee: when thou walkest through the fire, thou shalt not be burned; neither shall the flame kindle upon thee. For I am the Lord thy God the Holy One of Israel, thy Saviour: I gave Egypt for thy ransom, Ethiopia and Seba for thee. Since thou wast precious in my sight, thou hast been honourable, and I have loved thee: therefore will I give men for thee, and people for thy life. Fear not: for I am with thee. Ye are my witnesses, saith the Lord, and my servant whom I have chosen: that ye may know and believe me, and understand that I am he. Before me there was no God formed, neither shall there be after me. I, even I, am the Lord; and beside me there is no saviour. I have declared, and have saved, and I have shewed, when there was no strange god among you: therefore ye are my witnesses, saith the Lord, that I am God. Yea, before the day was I am he; and there is none that can deliver out of my hand: I will work, and who shall let it?

I am the Lord, your Holy One, the creator of Israel, your king. Thus saith the Lord, which maketh a way in the sea, and a path in the mighty waters; which bringeth forth the chariot and horse, the army and the power; they shall lie down together, they shall not rise: they are extinct, they are quenched as tow. Remember ye not the former things, neither consider the things of old. Behold, I will do a new thing; now it shall spring forth; shall ye not know it? I will even make a way in the wilderness, and rivers in the desert. The beast of the field shall honour me, the dragons and the owls: because I give waters in the wilderness, and rivers in the desert, to give drink to my people, my chosen. This people have I formed for myself; they shall shew forth my praise.

ISA 43. 1-5, 10-13, 15-21

LOOK TO ME AND BE SAVED, ALL THE EARTH

For I am God and there is none else

Look unto me, and be ye saved, all the ends of the earth: for I am God, and there is none else. I have sworn by myself, the word is gone out of my mouth in righteousness, and shall not return, that unto me every knee shall bow, every tongue shall swear. Surely, shall one say, in the Lord have I righteousness and strength: even to him shall men come; and all that are incensed against him shall be ashamed. In the Lord shall all the seed of Israel be justified, and shall glory.

ISA 45. 22-25

WHEN WHITE HAIRS COME, I WILL STILL CARRY YOU

My purpose shall stand firm

Hearken unto me, O house of Jacob, and all the remnant of the house of Israel, which are borne by me from the belly, which are carried from the womb: and even to your old age I am he; and even to hoar hairs will I carry you: I have made, and I will bear; even I will carry, and will deliver you. To whom will ye liken me, and make me equal, and compare me, that we may be like? Remember this, and shew yourselves men: bring it again to mind, O ye transgressors. Remember the former things of old: for I am God, and there is none else; I am God, and there is none like me, declaring the end from the beginning, and from ancient times the things that are not yet done, saying, "My counsel shall stand, and I will do all my pleasure." ISA 46. 3-5, 8-10

GOD WILL HELP AND PRESERVE YOU

He will not forget you

Thus saith the Lord, "In an acceptable time have I heard thee, and in a day of salvation have I helped thee: and I will preserve thee, and give thee for a covenant of the people, to establish the earth, to cause to inherit the desolate heritages; that thou mayest say to the prisoners, 'Go forth'; to them that are in darkness, 'Shew yourselves.' They shall feed in the ways, and their pastures shall be in all high places. They shall not hunger nor thirst; neither shall the heat nor sun smite them: for he that hath mercy on them shall lead them, even by the springs of water shall he guide them. I will make all my mountains a way, and my highways shall be exalted." ISA 49. 8-11

GOD HAS OPENED MY EAR

He has power to deliver

Is my hand shortened at all, that it cannot redeem? Or have I no power to deliver? The Lord God hath given me the tongue of the learned, that I should know how to speak a word in season to him that is weary: he wakeneth morning by morning, he wakeneth mine ear to hear as the learned. The Lord God hath opened mine ear, and I was not rebellious, neither turned away back. ISA 50. 2, 4, 5

AN EVERLASTING SIGN OF GOD'S GOODNESS

My word shall accomplish my purpose

As the heavens are higher than the earth, so are my ways higher than your ways, and my thoughts than your thoughts. For as the rain cometh down, and the snow from heaven, and returneth not thither, but watereth the earth, and maketh it bring forth and bud, that it may give seed to the sower, and bread to the eater: so shall my word be that goeth forth out of my mouth: it shall not return unto me void, but it shall accomplish that which I please, and it shall prosper in the thing whereto I sent it. For ye shall go out with joy, and be led forth with peace: the mountains and the hills shall break forth before you into singing, and all the trees of the field shall clap their hands. Instead of the thorn shall come up the fir tree, and instead of the brier shall come up the myrtle tree: and it shall be to the Lord for a name, for an everlasting sign that shall not be cut off. ISA 55. 9-13

COMFORT RESTORED

I will heal him, saith the Lord

Thus saith the high and lofty one that inhabiteth eternity, whose name is holy; I dwell in the high and holy place, with him also that is of a contrite and humble spirit, to revive the spirit of the humble, and to revive the heart of the contrite ones. I have seen his ways, and will heal him: I will lead him also, and restore comforts unto him and to his mourners. I create the fruit of the lips; peace, peace to him that is far off, and to him that is near, saith the Lord; and I will heal him. ISA 57. 15, 18, 19

HEALTH SHALL SPRING FORTH SPEEDILY

Built up by the repairer of the breach

Is not this the fast that I have chosen? to loose the bands of wickedness, to undo the heavy burdens, and to let the oppressed go free, and that ye break every yoke? Is it not to deal thy bread to the hungry, and that thou bring the poor that are cast out to thy house? when thou seest the naked, that thou cover him; and that thou hide not thyself from thine own flesh? Then shall thy light break forth as the morning, and thine health shall spring forth speedily: and thy righteousness shall go before thee; the glory of the Lord shall be thy rereward. Then shalt thou call, and the Lord shall answer; thou shalt cry, and he shall say, "Here I am." If thou take away from the midst of thee the yoke, the putting forth of the finger, and speaking vanity; and if thou draw out thy soul to the hungry, and satisfy the afflicted soul; then shall thy light rise in obscurity, and thy darkness be as the noonday. The Lord shall guide thee continually, and satisfy thy soul in drought, and make fat thy bones: and thou shalt be like a watered garden, and like a spring of water, whose waters fail not. They that shall be of thee shall build the old waste places: thou shalt raise up the foundations of many generations; and thou shalt be called the repairer of the breach, the restorer of paths to dwell in.

ISA 58. 6-12

FLOOD OVERCOME

Spirit lifts a standard against it

When the enemy shall come in like a flood, the Spirit of the Lord shall lift up a standard against him. And the Redeemer shall come to Zion, and unto them that turn from transgression in Jacob, saith the Lord. As for me, this is my covenant with them, saith the Lord: my spirit that is upon thee, and my words which I have put in thy mouth, shall not depart out of thy mouth, nor out of the mouth of thy seed, nor out of the mouth of thy seed's seed, saith the Lord, from henceforth and forever.

ISA 59. 19-21

NORMAL CHILDBIRTH

Delivery cared for by God's motherhood

"Shall I bring to the birth, and not cause to bring forth?" saith the Lord. "Shall I cause to bring forth, and shut the womb?" saith thy God. Rejoice ye with Jerusalem, and be glad with her, all ye that love her: rejoice for joy with her, all ye that mourn for her: that ye may suck, and be satisfied with the breasts of her consolations; that ye may milk out, and be delighted with the abundance of her glory. For thus saith the Lord, "Behold, I will extend peace to her like a river, and the glory of the Gentiles like a flowing stream: then shall ye suck, ye shall be borne upon her sides, and be dandled upon her knees. As one whom his mother comforteth, so will I comfort you; and ye shall be comforted in Jerusalem." When ye see this, your heart shall rejoice, and your bones shall flourish like an herb: and the hand of the Lord shall be known toward his servants, and his indignation toward his enemies. For, behold, the Lord will come with fire, and with his chariots like a whirlwind.

ISA 66. 9-15

JEREMIAH

FORMED BY GOD BEFORE BIRTH

Fear not. I am with you to keep you safe

Then the word of the Lord came unto me, saying, "Before I formed thee in the belly I knew thee; and before thou camest forth out of the womb I sanctified thee, and I ordained thee a prophet unto the nations." Then said I, "Ah, Lord God! behold, I cannot speak: for I am a child." But the Lord said unto me, "Say not, I am a child: for thou shalt go to all that I shall send thee, and whatsoever I command thee thou shalt speak. Be not afraid of their faces: for I am with thee to deliver thee," saith the Lord. Then the Lord put forth his hand, and touched my mouth. And the Lord said unto me, "Behold, I have put my words in thy mouth. They shall fight against thee; but they shall not prevail against thee; for I am with thee," saith the Lord, "to deliver thee." JER 1. 4-9, 19

WARNING AGAINST FALSE HEALERS

They only partially alleviate

Thus saith the Lord of hosts, "To whom shall I speak, and give warning, that they may hear? behold, their ear is uncircumcised, and they cannot hearken: behold, the word of the Lord is unto them a reproach; they have no delight in it. . . . From the prophet even unto the priest every one dealeth falsely. They have healed also the hurt of the daughter of my people slightly, saying, 'Peace, peace'; when there is no peace."

JER 6. 9, 10, 13, 14

WHY IS HEALTH NOT RECOVERED?

There is no true balm in an idolatrous land

They have healed the hurt of the daughter of my people slightly, saying, "Peace, peace"; when there is no peace. When I would comfort myself against sorrow, my heart is faint in me. Behold the voice of the cry of the daughter of my people because of them that dwell in a far country: is not the Lord in Zion? is not her king in her? Why have they provoked me to anger with their graven images, and with strange vanities? The harvest is past, the summer is ended, and we are not saved. For the hurt of the daughter of my people am I hurt; I am black; astonishment hath taken hold on me. Is there no balm in Gilead? Is there no physician there? Why then is not the health of the daughter of my people recovered? JER 8. 11, 18-22

My Refuge in Time of Trouble

God is my strength and fortress

O Lord, my strength, and my fortress, and my refuge in the day of affliction, the Gentiles shall come unto thee from the ends of the earth. JER 16. 19

Truly Healed if God Does It

Happy the man who trusts Him

Blessed is the man that trusteth in the Lord, and whose hope the Lord is. Heal me, O Lord, and I shall be healed; save me, and I shall be saved: for thou art my praise. JER 17. 7, 14

Your Wounds Healed

I am with you to save you

Therefore fear thou not, O my servant Jacob, saith the Lord; neither be dismayed, O Israel: for, lo, I will save thee from afar, and thy seed from the land of their captivity. Jacob shall return, and shall be in rest, and be quiet, and none shall make him afraid. For I am with thee, saith the Lord, to save thee. For I will restore health unto thee, and I will heal thee of thy wounds, saith the Lord. JER 30. 10, 11, 17

Is Anything Impossible to God?

Nothing is too hard for Him

Ah Lord God! behold, thou hast made the heaven and the earth by thy great power and stretched out arm, and there is nothing too hard for thee. Thou shewest lovingkindness unto thousands, and recompensest the iniquity of the fathers into the bosom of their children after them: the Great, the Mighty God, the Lord of hosts, is his name, great in counsel, and mighty in work. Thine eyes are open upon all the ways of the sons of men: to give every one according to his ways, and according to the fruit of his doings: which hast set signs and wonders in the land of Egypt, even unto this day, and in Israel, and among other men; and hast made thee a name, as at this day; and hast brought forth thy people Israel out of the land of Egypt with signs, and with wonders, and with a strong hand, and with a stretched out arm, and with great terror; and hast given them this land, which thou didst swear to their fathers to give them, a land flowing with milk and honey. Then came the word of the Lord unto Jeremiah, saying, "Behold, I am the Lord, the God of all flesh: is there anything too hard for me?" JER 32. 17-22, 26, 27

GOD WILL HEAL, CURE AND CLEANSE

He procures goodness and prosperity

Moreover the word of the Lord came unto Jeremiah the second time, while he was yet shut up in the court of the prison, saying, "Thus saith the Lord the maker thereof, the Lord that formed it, to establish it; the Lord is his name: call unto me, and I will answer thee, and shew thee great and mighty things, which thou knowest not." For thus saith the Lord, the God of Israel, concerning the houses of this city, "Behold, I will bring it health and cure, and I will cure them, and will reveal unto them the abundance of peace and truth." JER 33. 1-4, 6

MANY MEDICINES USED IN VAIN

You will not be cured by these

Go up into Gilead, and take balm, O virgin, the daughter of Egypt: in vain shalt thou use many medicines; for thou shalt not be cured. JER 46. 11

LAMENTATIONS

FEAR NOT. YOUR LIFE REDEEMED
His compassion doesn't fail

It is of the Lord's mercies that we are not consumed, because his compassions fail not. They are new every morning: great is thy faithfulness. The Lord is my portion, saith my soul; therefore will I hope in him. The Lord is good unto them that wait for him, to the soul that seeketh him. It is good that a man should both hope and quietly wait for the salvation of the Lord. Wherefore doth a living man complain, a man for the punishment of his sins? Let us search and try our ways, and turn again to the Lord. Let us lift up our heart with our hands unto God in the heavens. Thou drewest near in the day that I called upon thee: thou saidst, "Fear not." O Lord, thou hast pleaded the causes of my soul; thou hast redeemed my life.

LAM 3. 22-26, 39-41, 57, 58

EZEKIEL

POWER OF SPEECH RESTORED
When God opens your mouth

But thou, O son of man, behold, they shall put bands upon thee, and shall bind thee with them, and thou shalt not go out among them. I will make thy tongue cleave to the roof of thy mouth, that thou shalt be dumb, and shalt not be to them a reprover: for they are a rebellious house. But when I speak with thee, I will open thy mouth, and thou shalt say unto them, Thus saith the Lord God, "He that heareth, let him hear; and he that forbeareth, let him forbear: for they are a rebellious house."

EZEK 3. 25-27

NO HEREDITARY ILLS

When the son is lawful and right

The word of the Lord came unto me again, saying, what mean ye, that ye use this proverb concerning the land of Israel, saying, The fathers have eaten sour grapes, and the children's teeth are set on edge? As I live, saith the Lord God, ye shall not have occasion any more to use this proverb in Israel. Behold, all souls are mine; as the soul of the father, so also the soul of the son is mine: the soul that sinneth, it shall die. But if a man be just, and do that which is lawful and right, . . . and hath walked in my statutes and hath kept my judgments, to deal truly; he is just, he shall surely live, saith the Lord God. Now, lo, if he beget a son, that seeth all his father's sins which he hath done, and considereth, and doeth not such like, . . . he shall not die for the iniquity of his father, he shall surely live.

As for his father, because he cruelly oppressed, spoiled his brother by violence, and did that which is not good among his people, lo, even he shall die in his iniquity. Yet say ye, "Why? doth not the son bear the iniquity of the father?" When the son hath done that which is lawful and right, and hath kept all my statutes, and hath done them, he shall surely live. The soul that sinneth, it shall die. The son shall not bear the iniquity of the father, neither shall the father bear the iniquity of the son: the righteousness of the righteous shall be upon him, and the wickedness of the wicked shall be upon him. But if the wicked will turn from all his sins that he hath committed, and keep all my statutes, and do that which is lawful and right, he shall surely live, he shall not die. All his transgressions that he hath committed, they shall not be mentioned unto him: in his righteousness that he hath done he shall live. Have I any pleasure at all that the wicked should die? saith the Lord God: and not that he should return from his ways and live.

EZEK 18. 1-5, 9, 14, 17-23

THE DUMB CAN SPEAK AGAIN

By knowing the Lord

Thus Ezekiel is unto you a sign: according to all that he hath done shall ye do: and when this cometh, ye shall know that I am the Lord God. Also, thou son of man, shall it not be in the day when I take from them their strength, the joy of their glory, the desire of their eyes, and that whereupon they set their minds, their sons and their daughters, that he that escapeth in that day shall come unto thee, to cause thee to hear it with thine ears? In that day shall thy mouth be opened to him which is escaped, and thou shalt speak, and be no more dumb: and thou shalt be a sign unto them; and they shall know that I am the Lord. EZEK 24. 24-27

WALK BY THE RULES THAT ENSURE LIFE

The wrongdoers die

Say unto them, As I live, saith the Lord God, I have no pleasure in the death of the wicked; but that the wicked turn from his way and live: turn ye, turn ye from your evil ways; for why will ye die, O house of Israel? Therefore, thou son of man, say unto the children of thy people, The righteousness of the righteous shall not deliver him in the day of his transgression: as for the wickedness of the wicked, he shall not fall thereby in the day that he turneth from his wickedness; neither shall the righteous be able to live for his righteousness in the day that he sinneth. When I shall say to the righteous, that he shall surely live; if he trust to his own righteousness, and commit iniquity, all his righteousnesses shall not be remembered; but for his iniquity that he hath committed, he shall die for it. Again, when I say unto the wicked, thou shalt surely die; if he turn from his sin, and do that which is lawful and right; if the wicked restore the pledge, give again that he had robbed, walk in the statutes of life, without committing iniquity; he shall surely live, he shall not die. None of his sins that he hath committed shall be mentioned unto him: he hath done that which is lawful and right; he shall surely live.

Yet the children of thy people say, The way of the Lord is not equal: but as for them, their way is not equal. When the righteous turneth from his righteousness, and committeth iniquity, he shall even die thereby. But if the wicked turn from his wickedness, and do that which is lawful and right, he shall live thereby.

EZEK 33. 11-19

SPEECH RESTORED

God judges us according to our deeds

Yet ye say, The way of the Lord is not equal. O ye house of Israel, I will judge you every one after his ways. And it came to pass in the twelfth year of our captivity, in the tenth month, in the fifth day of the month, that one that had escaped out of Jerusalem came unto me, saying, "The city is smitten." Now the hand of the Lord was upon me in the evening, afore he that was escaped came; and had opened my mouth, until he came to me in the morning; and my mouth was opened, and I was no more dumb.

EZEK 33. 20-22

GOD, LIKE A SHEPHERD, CARES FOR HIS SHEEP

They shall dwell safely

The word of the Lord came unto me, saying, son of man, prophesy against the shepherds of Israel, prophesy, and say unto them, thus saith the Lord God unto the shepherds: Woe be to the shepherds of Israel that do feed themselves! Should not the shepherds feed the flocks? Ye eat the fat, and ye clothe you with the wool, ye kill them that are fed: but ye feed not the flock. The diseased have ye not strengthened, neither have ye healed that which was sick, neither have ye bound up that which was broken, neither have be brought again that which was driven away, neither have ye sought that which was lost; but with force and with cruelty have ye ruled them.

As I live, saith the Lord God, surely because my flock became a prey, and my flock became meat to every beast of the field, because there was no shepherd, neither did my shepherds search for my flock, but the shepherds fed themselves, and fed not my flock; . . . behold, I, even I, will both search my sheep, and seek them out. As a shepherd seeketh out his flock in the day that he is among his sheep that are scattered; so will I seek out my sheep, and will deliver them out of all places where they have been scattered in the cloudy and dark day. I will bring them out from the people, and gather them from the countries, and will bring them to their own land, and feed them upon the mountains of Israel by the rivers, and in all the inhabited places of the country. I will feed them in a good pasture, and upon the high mountains of Israel shall their fold be: there shall they lie in a good fold, and in a fat pasture shall they feed upon the mountains of Israel. I will feed my flock, and I will cause them to lie down, saith the Lord God. I will seek that which was lost, and bring again that which was driven away, and will bind up that which was broken, and will strengthen that which was sick. I will make with them a covenant of peace, and will cause the evil beasts to cease out of the land: and they shall dwell safely in the wilderness, and sleep in the woods.

I will make them and the places round about my hill a blessing; and I will cause the shower to come down in his season; there shall be showers of blessing. The tree of the field shall yield her fruit, and the earth shall yield her increase, and they shall be safe in their land, and shall know that I am the Lord, when I have broken the bands of their yoke, and delivered them out of the hand of those that served themselves of them. They shall no more be a prey to the heathen, neither shall the beast of the land devour them; but they shall dwell safely, and none shall make them afraid. Thus shall they know that I the Lord their God am with them, and that they, even the house of Israel, are my people, saith the Lord God.

Ye my flock, the flock of my pasture, are men, and I am your God, saith the Lord God. EZEK 34. 1-4, 8, 11-16, 25-28, 30, 31

I WILL GIVE YOU A NEW HEART

I will put my spirit within you

Then will I sprinkle clean water upon you, and ye shall be clean from all your filthiness, and from all your idols will I cleanse you. A new heart also will I give you, and a new spirit will I put within you: and I will take away the stony heart out of your flesh, and I will give you an heart of flesh. I will put my spirit within you, and cause you to walk in my statutes, and ye shall keep my judgments, and do them. Ye shall dwell in the land that I gave to your fathers; and ye shall be my people, and I will be your God. I will also save you from all your uncleannesses: and I will call for the corn, and will increase it, and lay no famine upon you. I will multiply the fruit of the tree, and the increase of the field, that ye shall receive no more reproach of famine among the heathen.

EZEK 36. 25-30

GOD COVERS DRY BONES WITH FLESH

God, the source of breath

The hand of the Lord was upon me, and carried me out in the spirit of the Lord, and set me down in the midst of the valley which was full of bones, and caused me to pass by them round about: and, behold, there were very many in the open valley; and, lo, they were very dry. He said unto me, "Son of man, can these bones live?" And I answered, "O Lord God, thou knowest." Again he said unto me, "Prophesy upon these bones, and say unto them, O ye dry bones, hear the word of the Lord. Thus saith the Lord God unto these bones; behold, I will cause breath to enter into you, and ye shall live: and I will lay sinews upon you, and will bring up flesh upon you, and cover you with skin, and put breath in you, and ye shall live; and ye shall know that I am the Lord." So I prophesied as I was commanded: and as I prophesied, there was a noise, and behold a shaking, and the bones came together, bone to his bone. When I beheld, lo, the sinews and the flesh came up upon them, and the skin covered them above: but there was no breath in them.

Then said he unto me, "Prophesy unto the wind, prophesy, son of man, and say to the wind, Thus saith the Lord God; come from the four winds, O breath, and breathe upon these slain, that they may live." So I prophesied as he commanded me, and the breath came into them, and they lived, and stood up upon their feet, an exceeding great army. Then he said unto me, "Son of man, these bones are the whole house of Israel: behold, they say 'Our bones are dried, and our hope is lost: we are cut off for our parts.' Therefore prophesy and say unto them, Thus saith the Lord God: "Behold, O my people, I will open your graves, and cause you to come up out of your graves, and bring you into the land of Israel. And ye shall know that I am the Lord, when I have opened your graves, O my people, and brought you up out of your graves, and shall put my spirit in you, and ye shall live, and I shall place you in your own land: then shall ye know that I the Lord have spoken it, and performed it," saith the Lord. EZEK 37. 1-14

THE HEALING RIVER WATERS

Medicine from the waters of the sanctuary

Afterward he brought me again unto the door of the house; and, behold, waters issued out from under the threshold of the house eastward: for the forefront of the house stood toward the east, and the waters came down from under from the right side of the house, at the south side of the altar. Then brought he me out of the way of the gate northward, and led me about the way without unto the utter gate by the way that looketh eastward; and, behold, there ran out waters on the right side. When the man that had the line in his hand went forth eastward, he measured a thousand cubits, and he brought me through the waters; the waters were to the ankles. Again he measured a thousand, and brought me through the waters; the waters were to the knees. Again he measured a thousand, and brought me through; the waters were to the loins. Afterward he measured a thousand; and it was a river that I could not pass over: for the waters were risen, waters to swim in, a river that could not be passed over.

He said unto me, "Son of man, hast thou seen this?" Then he brought me, and caused me to return to the brink of the river. Now when I had returned, behold, at the bank of the river were very many trees on the one side and on the other. Then said he unto me, "These waters issue out toward the east country, and go down into the desert, and go into the sea: which being brought forth into the sea, the waters shall be healed. It shall come to pass, that everything that liveth, which moveth, whithersoever the rivers shall come, shall live: and there shall be a very great multitude of fish, because these waters shall come thither: for they shall be healed; and everything shall live whither the river cometh. It shall come to pass, that the fishers shall stand upon it from En-gedi even unto En-eglaim; they shall be a place to spread forth nets; their fish shall be according to their kinds, as the fish of the great sea, exceeding many. But the miry places thereof and the marishes thereof shall not be healed; they shall be given to salt. By the river upon the bank thereof, on this side and on that side, shall grow all trees for meat, whose leaf shall not fade, neither shall the fruit thereof be consumed. It shall bring forth new fruit according to his months, because their waters they issued out of the sanctuary. The fruit thereof shall be for meat, and the leaf thereof for medicine." EZEK 47. 1-12

DANIEL

SPECIAL DIET NOT NECESSARY

Well-being improved without eating prescribed foods

In the third year of the reign of Jehoiakim, king of Judah, came Nebuchadnezzar, king of Babylon, unto Jerusalem, and besieged it. The Lord gave Jehoiakim, king of Judah, into his hand, with part of the vessels of the house of God: which he carried into the land of Shinar to the house of his god; and he brought the vessels into the treasure house of his god. The king spake unto Ashpenaz the master of his eunuchs, that he should bring certain of the children of Israel, and of the king's seed, and of the princes; children in whom was no blemish, but well-favoured, and skillful in all wisdom, and cunning in knowledge, and understanding science, and such as had ability in them to stand in the king's palace, and whom they might teach the learning and the tongue of the Chaldeans. The king appointed them a daily provision of the king's meat, and of the wine which he drank: so nourishing them three years, that at the end thereof they might stand before the king. Now among these were of the children of Judah, Daniel, Hananiah, Mishael, and Azariah: unto whom the prince of the eunuchs gave names: for he gave unto Daniel the name of Belteshazzar; and to Hananiah, of Shadrach; and to Mishael, of Meshach; and to Azariah, of Abed-nego.

But Daniel purposed in his heart that he would not defile himself with the portion of the king's meat, nor with the wine which he drank: therefore he requested of the prince of the eunuchs that he might not defile himself. Now God had brought Daniel into favour and tender love with the prince of the eunuchs. The prince of the eunuchs said unto Daniel, "I fear my lord the king, who hath appointed your meat and your drink: for why should he see your faces worse liking than the children which are of your sort? then shall ye make me endanger my head to the king." Then said Daniel to Melzar, whom the prince of the eunuchs had set over Daniel, Hananiah, Mishael, and Azariah, "Prove thy servants, I beseech thee, ten days; and let them give us pulse to eat, and water to drink. Then let our countenances be looked upon before thee, and the countenance of the children that eat of the portion of the king's meat: and as thou seest, deal with thy servants." So he consented to them in this matter, and proved them ten days. At the end of ten days their countenances appeared fairer and fatter in flesh than all the children which did eat the portion of the king's meat. Thus Melzar took away the portion of their meat, and the wine that they should drink; and gave them pulse.

As for these four children, God gave them knowledge and skill in all learning and wisdom: and Daniel had understanding in all visions and dreams. Now at the end of the days that the king had said he should bring them in, then the prince of the eunuchs brought them in before Nebuchadnezzar. The king communed with them; and among them all was found none like Daniel, Hananiah, Mishael, and Azariah: therefore stood they before the king. In all matters of wisdom and understanding, that the king enquired of them, he found them ten times better than all the magicians and astrologers that were in all his realm. Daniel continued even unto the first year of king Cyrus.

DAN 1. 1-21

UNHARMED BY FIRE

Through absolute reliance on one God

Nebuchadnezzar the king made an image of gold, whose height was threescore cubits, and the breadth thereof six cubits. He set it up in the plain of Dura, in the province of Babylon. Then Nebuchadnezzar the king sent to gather together the princes, the governors, and the captains, the judges, the treasurers, the counsellors, the sheriffs, and all the rulers of the provinces, to come to the dedication of the image which Nebuchadnezzar the king had set up. Then the princes, the governors, and captains, the judges, the treasurers, the counsellors, the sheriffs, and all the rulers of the provinces, were gathered together unto the dedication of the image that Nebuchadnezzar the king had set up; and they stood before the image that Nebuchadnezzar had set up. Then an herald cried aloud, "To you it is commanded, O people, nations, and languages, that at what time ye hear the sound of the cornet, flute, harp, sackbut, psaltery, dulcimer, and all kinds of musick, ye fall down and worship the golden image that Nebuchadnezzar the king hath set up. Whoso falleth not down and worshippeth shall the same hour be cast into the midst of a burning fiery furnace." Therefore at that time, when all the people heard the sound of the cornet, flute, harp, sackbut, psaltery, and all kinds of musick, all the people, the nations, and the languages, fell down and worshipped the golden image that Nebuchadnezzar the king had set up.

Wherefore at that time certain Chaldeans came near, and accused the Jews. They spake and said to the king Nebuchadnezzar, "O king, live forever. Thou, O king, hast made a decree, that every man that shall hear the sound of the cornet, flute, harp, sackbut, psaltery, and dulcimer, and all kinds of musick, shall fall down and worship the golden image: and whoso falleth not down and worshippeth, that he should be cast into the midst of a burning fiery furnace. There are certain Jews whom thou hast set over the affairs of the province of Babylon, Shadrach, Meshach, and Abed-nego; these men, O king, have not regarded thee. They serve not thy gods, nor worship the golden image which thou hast set up." Then Nebuchadnezzar in his rage and fury commanded to bring Shadrach, Meshach, and Abed-nego. Then they brought these men before the king. Nebuchadnezzar spake and said unto them, "Is it true, O Shadrach, Meshach, and Abed-nego, do not ye serve my gods, nor worship the golden image which I have set up? Now if ye be ready that at what time ye hear the sound of the cornet, flute, harp, sackbut, psaltery, and dulcimer, and all kinds of musick, ye fall down and worship the image which I have made; well. But if ye worship not, ye shall be cast the same hour into the midst of a burning fiery furnace; and who is that God that shall deliver you out of my hands?" Shadrach, Meshach, and Abed-nego answered and said to the king, "O Nebuchadnezzar, we are not careful to answer thee in this matter. If it be so, our God whom we serve is able to deliver us from the burning fiery furnace, and he will deliver us out of thine hand, O king. But if not, be it known unto thee, O king, that we will not serve thy gods, nor worship the golden image which thou hast set up.

Then was Nebuchadnezzar full of fury, and the form of his visage was changed against Shadrach, Meshach, and Abed-nego: therefore he spake, and commanded that they should heat the furnace one seven times more than it was wont to be heated. He commanded the most mighty men that were in his army to bind Shadrach, Meshach, and Abed-nego, and to cast them into the burning fiery furnace. Then these men were bound in their coats, their hosen, and their hats, and their other garments, and were cast into the midst of the burning fiery furnace. Therefore because the king's commandment was urgent, and the furnace exceeding hot, the flame of the fire slew those men that took up Shadrach, Meshach, and Abed-nego. These three men, Shadrach, Meshach, and Abed-nego, fell down bound into the midst of the burning fiery furnace. Then Nebuchadnezzar the king was astonied, and rose up in haste, and spake, and said unto his counsellors, "Did not we cast three men bound into the midst of the fire?" They answered and said unto the king, "True, O king." He answered and said, "Lo, I see four men loose, walking in the midst of the fire, and they have no hurt; and the form of the fourth is like the Son of God."

Then Nebuchadnezzar came near to the mouth of the burning fiery furnace, and spake, and said, "Shadrach, Meshach, and Abednego, ye servants of the most high God, come forth, and come hither." And Shadrach, Meshach, and Abednego came forth of the midst of the fire. The princes, governors, and captains, and the king's counsellors, being gathered together, saw these men, upon whose bodies the fire had no power, nor was an hair of their head singed, neither were their coats changed, nor the smell of fire had passed on them. Then Nebuchadnezzar spake, and said, "Blessed be the God of Shadrach, Meshach, and Abednego, who hath sent his angel, and delivered his servants that trusted in him, and have changed the king's word, and yielded their bodies, that they might not serve nor worship any god, except their own God. Therefore I make a decree, that every people, nation, and language, which speak anything amiss against the God of Shadrach, Meshach, and Abednego, shall be cut in pieces and their houses shall be made a dunghill: because there is no other God that can deliver after this sort." Then the king promoted Shadrach, Meshach, and Abednego, in the province of Babylon. DAN 3. 1-30

INSANITY HEALED

By turning to the Most High

All this came upon the king Nebuchadnezzar. At the end of twelve months he walked in the palace of the kingdom of Babylon. The king spake, and said, "Is not this great Babylon, that I have built for the house of the kingdom by the might of my power and for the honour of my majesty?" While the word was in the king's mouth, there fell a voice from heaven, saying, "O king Nebuchadnezzar, to thee it is spoken; the kingdom is departed from thee. They shall drive thee from men, and thy dwelling shall be with the beasts of the field. They shall make thee to eat grass as oxen, and seven times shall pass over thee, until thou know that the most High ruleth in the kingdom of men, and giveth it to whomsoever he will." The same hour was the thing fulfilled upon Nebuchadnezzar: and he was driven from men, and did eat grass as oxen, and his body was wet with the dew of heaven, till his hairs were grown like eagles' feathers, and his nails like birds' claws. At the end of the days I, Nebuchadnezzar, lifted up mine eyes unto heaven, and mine understanding returned unto me, and I blessed the most High, and I praised and honoured him that liveth forever, whose dominion is an everlasting dominion, and his kingdom is from generation to generation. All the inhabitants of the earth are reputed as nothing: and he doeth according to his will in the army of heaven, and among the inhabitants of the earth: and none can stay his hand, or say unto him, "What doest thou?" At the same time my reason returned unto me; and for the glory of my kingdom, mine honour and brightness returned unto me; and my counsellors and my lords sought unto me; and I was established in my kingdom, and excellent majesty was added unto me. Now I Nebuchadnezzar praise and extol and honour the king of heaven, all whose works are truth, and his ways judgment: and those that walk in pride he is able to abase. DAN 4. 28-37

PRESERVED IN LIONS' DEN

Because of God's protecting power

It pleased Darius to set over the kingdom an hundred and twenty princes, which should be over the whole kingdom; and over these three presidents; of whom Daniel was first: that the princes might give accounts unto them, and the king should have no damage. Then this Daniel was preferred above the presidents and princes, because an excellent spirit was in him; and the king thought to set him over the whole realm. Then the presidents and princes sought to find occasion against Daniel concerning the kingdom; but they could find none occasion nor fault; forasmuch as he was faithful, neither was there any error or fault found in him. Then said these men, "We shall not find any occasion against this Daniel, except we find it against him concerning the law of his God." Then these presidents and princes assembled together to the king, and said thus unto him, "King Darius, live forever. All the presidents of the kingdom, the governors, and the princes, the counsellors, and the captains, have consulted together to establish a royal statute, and to make a firm decree, that whosoever shall ask a petition of any God or man for thirty days, save of thee, O king, he shall be cast into the den of lions. Now, O king, establish the decree, and sign the writing, that it be not changed, according to the law of the Medes and Persians, which altereth not." Wherefore king Darius signed the writing and the decree.

Now when Daniel knew that the writing was signed, he went into his house; and his windows being open in his chamber toward Jerusalem, he kneeled upon his knees three times a day, and prayed, and gave thanks before his God, as he did aforetime. Then these men assembled, and found Daniel praying and making supplication before his God. Then they came near, and spake before the king concerning the king's decree, "Hast thou not signed a decree, that every man that shall ask a petition of any God or man within thirty days, save of thee, O king, shall be cast into the den of lions?" The king answered and said, "The thing is true, according to the law of the Medes and Persians, which altereth not." Then answered they and said before the king, "That Daniel, which is of the children of the captivity of Judah, regardeth not thee, O king, nor the decree that thou hast signed, but maketh his petition three times a day." Then the king, when he heard these words, was sore displeased with himself, and set his heart on Daniel to deliver him: and he laboured till the going down of the sun to deliver him. Then these men assembled unto the king, and said unto the king, "Know, O king, that the law of the Medes and Persians is, that no decree nor statute which the king establisheth may be changed." Then the king commanded, and they brought Daniel, and cast him into the den of lions. Now the king spake and said unto Daniel, "Thy God whom thou servest continually, he will deliver thee." A stone was brought, and laid upon the mouth of the den; and the king sealed it with his own signet, and with the signet of his lords; that the purpose might not be changed concerning Daniel.

Then the king went to his palace, and passed the night fasting: neither were instruments of musick brought before him: and his sleep went from him. Then the king arose very early in the morning, and went in haste unto the den of lions. When he came to the den, he cried with a lamentable voice unto Daniel: and the king spake and said to Daniel, "O Daniel, servant of the living God, is thy God, whom thou servest continually, able to deliver thee from the lions?" Then said Daniel unto the king, "O king, live forever. My God hath sent his angel, and hath shut the lions' mouths, that they have not hurt me: forasmuch as before him innocency was found in me; and also before thee, O king, have I done no hurt." Then was the king exceeding glad for him, and commanded that they should take Daniel up out of the den. So Daniel was taken up out of the den, and no manner of hurt was found upon him, because he believed in his God. The king commanded, and they brought those men which had accused Daniel, and they cast them into the den of lions, them, their children, and their wives; and the lions had the mastery of them, and brake all their bones in pieces or ever they came at the bottom of the den. Then king Darius wrote unto all people, nations, and languages, that dwell in all the earth; "Peace be multiplied unto you. I make a decree that in every dominion of my kingdom men tremble and fear before the God of Daniel: for he is the living God, and steadfast forever, and his kingdom that which shall not be destroyed, and his dominion shall be even unto the end. He delivereth and rescueth, and he worketh signs and wonders in heaven and in earth, who hath delivered Daniel from the power of the lions." So this Daniel prospered in the reign of Darius, and in the reign of Cyrus the Persian.

DAN 6. 1-28

I WAS STRENGTHENED

By the truth in the Scriptures

Then there came again and touched me one like the appearance of a man, and he strengthened me, and said, "O man greatly beloved, fear not: peace be unto thee, be strong, yea, be strong." When he had spoken unto me, I was strengthened, and said, "Let my lord speak; for thou hast strengthened me." Then said he, "I will shew thee that which is noted in the scripture of truth." DAN 10. 18-21

HOSEA

WE SHALL LIVE IN HIS PRESENCE

He will heal us

Come, and let us return unto the Lord: for he hath torn, and he will heal us; he hath smitten, and he will bind us up. After two days will he revive us: in the third day he will raise us up, and we shall live in his sight. HOSEA 6. 1, 2

LED WITH BONDS OF LOVE

They did not know it was God who healed them

When Israel was a child, then I loved him, and called my son out of Egypt. As they called them, so they went from them: they sacrificed unto Baalim, and burned incense to graven images. I taught Ephraim also to go, taking them by their arms; but they knew not that I healed them. I drew them with cords of a man, with bands of love: and I was to them as they that take off the yoke on their jaws, and I laid meat unto them.

HOSEA 11. 1-4

REDEEMED FROM DEATH
There is no saviour other than God

Yet I am the Lord thy God from the land of Egypt, and thou shalt know no god but me: for there is no saviour beside me. I will be thy king: where is any other that may save thee in all thy cities? I will ransom them from the power of the grave; I will redeem them from death. O death, I will be thy plagues; O grave, I will be thy destruction: repentance shall be hid from mine eyes. HOSEA 13. 4, 10, 14

JOEL

SPIRIT POURED UPON FLESH
Not wounded by falls

When they fall upon the sword, they shall not be wounded. I will restore to you the years that the locust hath eaten, and ye shall eat in plenty, and be satisfied, and praise the name of the Lord your God, that hath dealt wondrously with you: and my people shall never be ashamed. Ye shall know that I am in the midst of Israel, and that I am the Lord your God, and none else: and my people shall never be ashamed. It shall come to pass afterward, that I will pour out my spirit upon all flesh; and your sons and your daughters shall prophesy, your old men shall dream dreams, your young men shall see visions. Also upon the servants and upon the handmaids in those days will I pour out my spirit. I will shew wonders in the heavens and in the earth. JOEL 2. 8, 25-30

AMOS

TO LIVE SEEK GOOD
God shall be with you

Seek good, and not evil, that ye may live: and so the Lord, the God of hosts, shall be with you, as ye have spoken. Hate the evil, and love the good, and establish judgment in the gate: it may be that the Lord God of hosts will be gracious unto the remnant of Joseph. AMOS 5. 14, 15

JONAH

MY LIFE BROUGHT UP FROM CORRUPTION
Salvation is of the Lord

Then Jonah prayed unto the Lord his God out of the fish's belly, and said, I cried by reason of mine affliction unto the Lord, and he heard me; out of the belly of hell cried I, and thou heardest my voice. For thou hadst cast me into the deep, in the midst of the seas; and the floods compassed me about: all thy billows and thy waves passed over me. Then I said, I am cast out of thy sight; yet I will look again toward thy holy temple. The waters compassed me about, even to the soul: the depth closed me round about, the weeds were wrapped about my head. I went down to the bottoms of the mountains; the earth with her bars was about me forever: yet hast thou brought up my life from corruption, O Lord my God. When my soul fainted within me I remembered the Lord: and my prayer came in unto thee, into thine holy temple. They that observe lying vanities forsake their own mercy. But I will sacrifice unto thee with the voice of thanksgiving; I will pay that that I have vowed. Salvation is of the Lord. The Lord spake unto the fish, and it vomited out Jonah upon the dry land.

JONAH 2. 1-10

MICAH

GOD GATHERS ALL AFFLICTED

The Lord shall be established

But in the last days it shall come to pass that the mountain of the house of the Lord shall be established in the top of the mountains, and it shall be exalted above the hills; and people shall flow unto it. Many nations shall come, and say, "Come, and let us go up to the mountain of the Lord, and to the house of the God of Jacob; and he will teach us of his ways, and we will walk in his paths." For the law shall go forth of Zion, and the word of the Lord from Jerusalem. He shall judge among many people, and rebuke strong nations afar off; and they shall beat their swords into plowshares, and their spears into pruninghooks. Nation shall not lift up a sword against nation, neither shall they learn war any more. But they shall sit every man under his vine and under his fig tree; and none shall make them afraid: for the mouth of the Lord of hosts hath spoken it. For all people will walk every one in the name of his god, and we will walk in the name of the Lord our God forever and ever. In that day, saith the Lord, will I assemble her that halteth, and I will gather her that is driven out, and her that I have afflicted; and I will make her that halted a remnant, and her that was cast far off a strong nation: and the Lord shall reign over them in mount Zion from henceforth, even forever. Thou, O tower of the flock, the stronghold of the daughter of Zion, unto thee shall it come, even the first dominion; the kingdom shall come to the daughter of Jerusalem.

MICAH 4. 1-8

WHEN I FALL I SHALL ARISE
In darkness the Lord is my light

Therefore I will look unto the Lord; I will wait for the God of my salvation: my God will hear me. Rejoice not against me, O mine enemy: when I fall, I shall arise; when I sit in darkness, the Lord shall be a light unto me. MICAH 7. 7, 8

NAHUM

AFFLICTION SHALL NOT OCCUR A SECOND TIME
Once its yoke is broken

The Lord is good, a stronghold in the day of trouble; and he knoweth them that trust in him. What do ye imagine against the Lord? he will make an utter end: affliction shall not rise up the second time. For now will I break his yoke from off thee, and will burst thy bonds in sunder. Behold upon the mountains the feet of him that bringeth good tidings, that publisheth peace! NAHUM 1. 7, 9, 13, 15

HABAKKUK

WE SHALL NOT DIE
God too pure to behold evil

Art thou not from everlasting, O Lord my God, mine Holy One? we shall not die. O Lord, thou hast ordained them for judgment; and, O mighty God, thou hast established them for correction. Thou art of purer eyes than to behold evil, and canst not look on iniquity. HAB 1. 12, 13

The Just Shall Live by Being Faithful

The vision will surely appear

I will stand upon my watch, and set me upon the tower, and will watch to see what he will say unto me, and what I shall answer when I am reproved. The Lord answered me, and said, "Write the vision, and make it plain upon tables, that he may run that readeth it. For the vision is yet for an appointed time, but at the end it shall speak, and not lie: though it tarry, wait for it; because it will surely come, it will not tarry. The just shall live by his faith." HAB 2. 1-4

God Is My Strength

He will enable me to scale the heights

Yet I will rejoice in the Lord, I will joy in the God of my salvation. The Lord God is my strength, and he will make my feet like hinds' feet, and he will make me to walk upon mine high places. HAB 3. 18, 19

ZEPHANIAH

God Sweeps Away Your Enemy

God is in your midst

Sing, O daughter of Zion; shout, O Israel; be glad and rejoice with all the heart, O daughter of Jerusalem. The Lord hath taken away thy judgments, he hath cast out thine enemy: the king of Israel, even the Lord, is in the midst of thee: thou shalt not see evil any more. In that day it shall be said to Jerusalem, fear thou not: and to Zion, let not thine hands be slack. The Lord thy God in the midst of thee is mighty; he will save, he will rejoice over thee with joy; he will rest in his love, he will joy over thee with singing. I will gather them that are sorrowful for the solemn assembly, who are of thee, to whom the reproach of it was a burden. Behold, at that time I will undo all that afflict thee: and I will save her that halteth, and gather her that was driven out; and I will get them praise and fame in every land where they have been put to shame. At that time will I bring you again, even in the time that I gather you: for I will make you a name and a praise among all people of the earth, when I turn back your captivity before your eyes, saith the Lord. ZEPH 3. 14-20

ZECHARIAH

THEY SHALL WALK UNFETTERED

Strengthened by the Lord

I will strengthen them in the Lord; and they shall walk up and down in his name, saith the Lord. ZECH 10. 12

MALACHI

GOD'S SONS ARE NOT CONSUMED

He is unchanging

Behold, I will send my messenger, and he shall prepare the way before me: and the Lord, whom ye seek, shall suddenly come to his temple, even the messenger of the covenant, whom ye delight in: behold, he shall come, saith the Lord of hosts. But who may abide the day of his coming? And who shall stand when he appeareth? For he is like a refiner's fire, and like fullers' soap: and he shall sit as a refiner and purifier of silver: and he shall purify the sons of Levi, and purge them as gold and silver, that they may offer unto the Lord an offering in righteousness. Then shall the offering of Judah and Jerusalem be pleasant unto the Lord, as in the days of old, and as in former years. I will come near to you to judgment; and I will be a swift witness against the sorcerers, and against the adulterers, and against false swearers, and against those that oppress the hireling in his wages, the widow, and the fatherless, and that turn aside the stranger from his right, and fear not me, saith the Lord of hosts. For I am the Lord, I change not; therefore ye sons of Jacob are not consumed. Even from the days of your fathers ye are gone away from mine ordinances, and have not kept them. Return unto me, and I will return unto you, saith the Lord of hosts. MAL 3. 1-7

HEALING COMES

From the rising sun of justice

Unto you that fear my name shall the sun of righteousness arise with healing in his wings. . . . MAL 4. 2

INDEX

A

Aaron 111, 117, 118
Abdomen (try belly)
Abide 56, 179
Ability 80
Abimelech 102
Abraham 101, 102, 183
Abundance 20, 30, 112, 114, 137, 162, 168, 169, 195, 204, 207, 213
Accident 71
Acts 60
Adam 78
Adversary 119
Aeneas 66
Affliction 14, 15, 31, 44, 49, 87, 91, 131, 132, 156, 161, 167, 185, 186, 206, 226, 228, 230
Afraid 7, 40, 47, 56, 116, 121, 126, 151, 157, 174, 179, 204, 227
Age 26, 101, 102, 125, 126, 158, 180, 201
Ahab 135, 137
Ahasuerus 155
Alive 167, 171
All in all 95
All manner of sicknesses 1, 3, 4, 7, 19, 20, 31, 34, 63, 122
All-powerful 161
Allergy (see flesh)
Alleviate 205
Almighty 179
Altar 129, 135, 178, 193
Amos 226
Amputation 37
Ananias 64
Andrew 46
Angels 12, 26, 39, 67, 103, 113, 138, 149, 152, 179, 223
Ankle 61, 215 (also see limb)
Annulled 192
Anointed 28, 29, 89, 91, 166
Antagonism 105
Anxiety (see fear)
Arise 66, 228, 231
Arm, arms 31, 105, 122, 125, 151, 179, 206, 207, 224
Armor 85
Arrest 56
Arthritis (see joints, bones, pain, deformity)
Asa 150
Ascension 25, 26, 41, 58, 60, 139, 187
Assassination 28, 65
Assemble 227
Asthma (see breath)
Astonished 18, 29, 30, 39, 64
Atonement 24, 25, 117, 118
Authority 13, 31, 34, 45
Awake 52, 85, 163
Axe head 146

B

Back injury 36
Balaam 119, 120
Bald 5
Balm 205, 207
Bands 116, 183, 203, 208, 212
Baptism 28
Barnabas 68
Barrenness 26, 101, 113, 122, 127, 140
Bars of iron 184, 226
Bartimaeus 23
Battle 123, 130, 150, 151, 173
Beasts 73, 116, 157
Beelzebub 6, 16
Believing 4, 11, 18, 23, 24, 42, 43, 49, 51-54, 57, 59, 63, 66, 70, 71, 80, 88, 92, 106, 165, 199
Belly 191, 201, 204, 226
Bethesda 44
Bind 188, 208, 224
Birth 26, 49, 90, 142, 204
Bitter 110
Blemish 158
Bless 116, 161, 176, 212
Blind 3, 4, 6, 10, 21, 23, 49-51, 64, 147, 194, 195
Blood 18, 74
Body 3, 4, 19, 75-81, 84-86, 148, 158, 189
Boils 156, 196
Bondage 75, 83, 89, 90, 102, 141, 155, 192, 224, 228
Bones 61, 90, 189, 190, 191, 204, 213, 214
Born blind 49
Bosom 106, 107
Bowed 36, 188
Boy 22, 43, 130
Brain (see mind, nerves)
Brain tumor 142
Breach 203
Bread 8, 20, 21, 40, 46, 47, 111, 113, 136
Breakfast 59, 60
Breastplate 85
Breasts 204
Breath 58, 137, 158, 160, 199, 213, 214
Broken 167, 184, 188, 191, 228
Brothers (see family)
Brow (see head)
Bruised 29
Build 153, 186
Burdened 5, 80, 81, 192, 203, 230
Burial 11, 24, 57
Burn 106, 199, 217-219
Bursitis (see joints, pain)
Bush 106
Business 104, 105

C

Calamities 76, 132, 174
Caleb 126
Calf (see limb)
Cancer (see flesh, blood, bones)
Captivity 29, 146, 161, 206, 230
Carmel 137, 143, 195
Carnally minded 75
Cataract (see eyes, sight, blind)
Caterpillar 134, 149
Centurion 31, 73
Chains 16, 177
Change 79, 231
Chastening 157
Cheerful 191
Chest (see body)
Children 8, 17, 18, 22, 23, 43, 137, 143, 204

Children of God 2, 75, 120
Children's diseases (see contagion)
Chronic 19, 36, 44
II Chronicles 149
Church 85, 95, 134
Circulation (see blood, heart, etc.)
City 172, 183, 186
Clean 4, 5, 14, 33, 37, 132, 146, 172, 207, 213
Cleopas 39
Clothes 124
Cloud 109, 118, 121, 138
Colds (see contagion)
Colossians 87
Comfort 2, 23, 55, 79, 81, 82, 87, 88, 161, 164, 202, 204
Comforter 55, 56
Commandments 55, 60, 110, 115, 123, 134, 189
Commands 13, 69, 123, 124, 128
Communion 48, 60
Companionship 9
Compassed 147, 226
Compassion 10, 32, 208
Confidence 81, 94, 165, 194
Consolation 79, 204
Contagion 14, 117, 118
Contrite 167, 191, 202
Control 192
Conversation 86, 191
Convinced 58
Convulsion 22
Cords 195, 224
Corinthians 77
Correction 228
Corruption 61, 75, 78, 79, 163, 197, 226
Countenance 104, 114, 115, 116, 125, 150, 158, 160, 162, 167, 171, 178, 179, 204, 217
Courage 126, 151, 165
Covenant 90, 114, 122, 124, 134, 164, 199, 201, 212, 230
Cover 179
Cripple 61, 68
Crooked 28, 199
Cross 11
Crown 95, 156, 182
Crucifixion 11, 24, 25, 38, 57, 62, 83
Cures 21, 22, 34, 117
Curse 120
Cut 184

D

Damascus 64
Daniel 216, 221, 223
Darius 221, 222, 223
Darkness 28, 41, 47, 87, 132, 183, 203, 228
Daughter 8, 18, 205
David 27, 130, 131, 133, 134, 149, 196
Deaf 5, 20, 23, 33, 107, 193, 195, 198
Death 17, 28, 31-33, 35, 43, 45, 49, 52-54, 60, 66, 68, 71-76, 78-80, 86-90, 95, 108, 124, 143, 144, 150, 164, 177, 183, 190, 196, 197, 209, 210, 225, 228
Debts 141
Decay 190
Defile 216
Deformity 31, 36, 135
Deliverance 74, 79, 81, 89, 109, 124, 145, 157, 167, 180, 183, 184, 200, 201, 205, 220, 223
Demoniac 17, 71
Depression 1, 22
Desire 160, 165-168, 188
Desolate 165, 167, 172
Despair 80
Destruction 155, 157, 179, 182, 184, 225
Deuteronomy 121
Devils 3, 4, 8, 16, 17, 25, 33, 34, 85, 90, 93
Diet 3, 216nDisability 44
Disciples 16, 30, 31, 34, 35, 39, 41, 46, 49, 51, 52, 54, 55, 57, 58
Disciples heal 66, 92
Discouragement 22, 138
Dislocation 103
Dismayed 126, 151, 198, 206
Disquieted 171
Dissolved 81
Distress 76, 82, 87, 131, 153, 165, 183, 184, 185
Divided 6, 16, 139
Doctors 18
Dominion 93, 221, 227
Dorcas 66
Dothan 147
Doubt 5, 7, 13, 23, 24, 33, 52, 59, 72
Driven out 227, 230
Dropsy 36
Drought 137, 138, 203
Dumb 4, 6, 23, 26, 27, 107, 208, 210, 211

E

Ears 5, 20, 21, 33, 37, 95, 171, 191, 194, 195, 202
Earthquake 12, 69, 70
Eat 3, 95, 108, 111, 112, 136, 144, 209
Ecclesiastes 192
Edema 36
Egypt 104, 111, 193, 207, 225
Elbow (see arm, joint)
Elders 91
Elisha (Eliseus) 29, 139, 140, 141, 142, 145, 146
Elijah (Elias) 21, 29, 34, 92, 135, 136, 137, 138, 139, 140
Elisabeth 26
Eloquence 107
Emmaus 39
Enchantment 121
Enemies 113, 165
Energy 138, 197 (also see strength)
Ephesians 84
Epidemics 107, 116, 118
Epilepsy 22
Esaias 6, 28, 29
Esau 104
Escape 28, 65, 67, 73, 113
Esther 154
Eutychus 71
Ever-presence 37, 106, 126, 163, 164, 187, 188, 224
Evil 31, 83, 85, 88, 89, 116, 124, 164, 167, 169, 179, 186, 189, 226, 228, 229
Exalted 132, 167, 172, 185, 227
Exodus 106
Exorcists 71
Eyes 3, 4, 6, 10, 21, 23, 24, 49-51, 64, 65, 80, 125, 147, 191
Ezekiel 208
Ezra 153

F

Face 104, 114, 115, 116, 125, 150, 158, 160, 162, 167, 171, 178, 179, 204, 216, 217
Faculties 10, 107, 125, 158, 171, 191
Fail 22, 127, 134, 136, 177, 208
Faint 80, 165, 178, 183, 197

Faith 4, 7, 8, 17, 19, 22-25, 32, 33, 37, 59, 62, 83-85, 87, 90-93
Falling 5, 29, 56, 71, 73, 165, 173, 174, 179, 185, 187, 225, 228
Family 104, 105
Famine 76, 134, 157, 167, 169, 213
Fasting 23, 203, 216
Fat 191, 203
Father 43, 209, 231
Fatigue (see strength)
Fault 221
Fear 5, 18, 26, 40, 75, 82, 86, 88-90, 94, 103, 106, 136, 147, 156, 158, 164, 165, 167, 171, 173, 185, 189, 198, 199, 206, 208, 224, 229, 231
Feeding 46, 96, 135, 136, 144, 148, 168, 178, 212
Feet 28, 40, 61, 68, 85, 106, 132, 165, 174, 176, 180, 185, 189, 228, 229
Fetters 16, 70
Fever 3, 43, 74
Fig tree 11
Finger (see hand)
Fire 90, 92, 118, 121, 140, 172, 199, 217, 230
First-born 108
Fish 8, 9, 30, 46, 59, 60, 227
Fits 22
Flesh 28, 47, 56, 60, 75, 78, 82, 83, 85, 107, 146, 160, 173, 177, 189, 190, 207, 225
Flies 107
Flock 212
Flood 96, 131, 203, 226
Followers 30, 34, 51, 93
Food 3, 8, 9, 20, 21, 46-48, 59, 60, 111, 123, 144, 148, 188
Force 125, 211
Forehead (see head)
Forget 182, 186
Forgiving 15, 105, 134, 150, 165, 182
Formed 204
Forsaken 169, 199
Fortitude 91
Fortress 131, 179, 206
Fountain 168, 190, 198
Fracture (see bones)
Freedom 9, 28, 49, 69, 70, 75, 83, 122
Fruits 74, 97, 115, 116, 122, 161, 180, 206, 212, 215
Functional (see fever, leprosy, disloca- tion, fatigue)
Furnace 218, 219
Fury 218, 219

G

Gabriel 26
Galatians 83
Gangrene 150
Gehazi 142, 143, 148
Genesis 101
Gentleness 132
Gibeon 133
Gifts 77, 84, 107
Girl 17
Gladness 89, 162, 172, 180, 181, 183, 195, 229
Glory 32, 37, 40, 42, 56, 82, 84, 87, 92, 111, 114, 118, 162, 166, 174, 177, 178, 198, 199, 203, 204
Goal 76, 86
Goliath 130
Goodness 9, 31, 113, 114, 124, 127, 150, 165, 168, 181-185, 196, 202, 208, 226, 228
Grace 63, 69, 80, 82-84, 88-90, 104, 114, 178, 184, 226
Grave 12, 45, 52, 53, 196, 197, 214, 225
Gravity 47
Grief 2, 150, 156 (see mourn, groaning)
Groaning 53, 75, 81, 159
Group healing 1, 5, 8, 15, 19, 20, 31, 34, 63
Guidance 76, 121, 164, 171, 177, 178, 203

H

Habakkuk 228
Habitation 179, 183
Hagar 102
Hair 5, 201, 220
Halt 44, 227, 230
Haman 154, 155
Hand 31, 40, 58, 59, 73, 106, 107, 135, 153, 156, 158, 159, 175, 192, 193, 198, 199, 229
Happy 188, 206
Hard 101, 139, 192, 206, 207
Hate 3, 27, 131, 167, 226
Head 5, 85, 142, 220
Headache 142
Healing prayer 2, 91, 92
Hearing 5, 20, 45, 51, 143, 181, 191, 194, 201, 202, 208
Heart 56, 60, 90, 94, 124, 134, 164, 165, 182, 189
Heat 96, 201
Heavy laden 5, 80, 81
Hebrews 89
Hebron 127
Heirs 75, 102
Help 170, 171, 186, 188, 198, 201
Hem of the garment 7, 18
Hemorrhage 18, 74
Heredity 49, 209
Heritage 162, 201
Herod 26
Hex 120
Hezekiah 149, 151, 152, 196
High tower 131, 179
Holiness 61, 113, 115, 154, 166, 195, 202
Holy Ghost 56, 63, 65
Honor 133, 180, 221
Help 170, 171, 186, 188, 198, 201
Hope 93, 157, 158, 163, 188, 208
Horeb 112, 124, 138
Hosea 224
Humble 2, 202
Hunger 2, 8, 11, 48, 96, 110, 111, 167, 183, 188, 201, 203

I

Image 76, 199
Impediment 20
Impossible 10, 206
Impotence 1, 3, 44, 68
Incense 118, 198, 200
Increase 30, 116, 122, 162, 190, 197, 212, 213
Incredulity 72
Indigestion 3
Indignant 204
Inferiority complex 106, 158
Infinite 188
Infirmity 3, 33, 36, 44, 76, 82
Influenza (see contagion)

Inheritance 87, 96, 114, 162, 164, 169, 170
Iniquity 89, 114, 121, 157, 158, 164, 182, 195, 209, 228
Insanity 1, 13, 16, 63, 69, 71, 220
Insomnia 158, 160, 162, 186, 189, 212
Inspiration 41
Instruction 35, 162, 189
Intercession 76
Invalid 19, 36, 44
Invasion 146
Inward man 74, 80, 84, 172, 191
Iron 183, 184
Isaac 102
Isaiah 149, 152, 192, 196
Israel 103, 120, 121, 146

J

Jacob 103, 104, 121
Jairus 17
James 18, 21, 34, 91
Jaws 224
Jehoshaphat 150, 151
Jeremiah 204
Jericho 139
Jeroboam 135
Jesus commands disciples to heal 4, 35
Jesus heals (see Four Gospels, Matthew, Mark, Luke and John)
Jezebel 138
Job 156, 159, 160, 161
Joel 225
John's epistles 93
John's gospel 18, 21, 34, 41, 57, 61, 62
John the Baptist 5, 26, 27, 28, 33, 46
Joints 85, 90, 103
Jonah 226
Jordan 139, 140, 145, 146
Joseph 12, 104, 105
Joseph of Arimathaea 24, 38
Joshua 126
Joy 12, 41, 61, 92, 95, 153, 154, 160, 162, 166, 179, 181, 183, 202, 229
Judas 56
Judges 127, 133, 195, 211, 227
Judgment 6, 19, 45, 108, 122, 123, 158, 168-170, 176, 179, 181, 188, 194, 209, 221, 226, 228, 229, 231
Julius 72
Justice 6, 83, 123, 154, 157, 158, 161, 179, 189, 209, 221, 226, 228, 229, 231

K

Kidneys (reins) 162
I Kings 133
Knees 84, 156, 182, 195, 200, 204, 215

L

Labor 5, 35
Lack 9, 30, 122, 164, 167
Lamb 96, 97
Lame 5, 8, 11, 44, 61, 68, 195, 230
Lamentations 208
Lamp 132, 186
Law 36, 40, 44, 74, 77, 79, 83, 90, 126, 153, 161, 170, 186, 189, 195, 209, 211, 227
Laying on of Hands 14, 18, 20, 21, 26, 36, 65, 74
Lazarus 52, 54
Lead 164, 171
Leaf 161, 215
Leaping 61, 68, 195
Learning 191
Leaves 97
Leg (see limbs)
Legion 17
Leprosy 4, 5, 14, 29, 33, 37, 106, 117, 145, 146
Leviticus 115
Liars 121, 125, 229
Liberty 29, 75, 83
Life 9, 47, 51-56, 72-76, 78-83, 91, 180, 189, 190
Lift 36, 43, 61
Light 3, 28, 41, 46, 49, 64, 160, 165, 168, 186, 189, 199, 203, 228
Limbs 1, 14, 61, 63, 230
Lips 160, 175, 190, 191
Liver (see inward man)
Living 115, 159, 165, 175, 185, 188, 196, 197, 209, 213, 224, 226
Locust 134, 149, 225
Loins 85
Longevity 125, 126, 133, 158, 189, 190
Lord's Prayer 2
Lost 146
Love 3, 55, 76, 77, 88, 93, 94, 180
Luke 26
Lunatic 1, 16, 63, 69, 71
Lungs (see breath)
Lust 83

M

Maimed (see cripple)
Malachi 230
Mammon 3
Man of God 137
Manifestation 75, 77
Manna 48, 110
Manoah 127
Marah 110
Mark 13, 67
Marrow 90, 191
Martha 52
Mary Magdalene 12, 24, 25, 38, 52, 57
Matthew 1
Measles (see contagion)
Meat 3, 9, 40, 59, 65, 7 184, 188, 224
Medicine 18, 191, 207, 214
Melita 73
Mental Health 1, 7, 1 16, 17, 19, 85, 90
Meribah 113
Messenger 127, 230
Messiah 28, 33
Micah 227
Midst 172, 225, 226, 229
Mighty 84, 123, 157, 179, 229
Mind 16, 76, 82, 86, 90 159
Ministry 29, 80, 81, 84
Miracles 7, 9, 11, 33, 4 46, 47, 71, 124, 146
Miriam 117
Misery 149, 158
Moab 124
Mordecai 155
Moses 21, 40, 43, 48, 5 106, 107, 109, 112, 113, 115, 117, 118, 119, 124, 125, 126
Mountain 1, 11, 13, 1 24, 28, 31, 47, 106, 1 127, 138, 147, 149, 157, 168, 171, 192, 198, 201, 202, 212, 22
Mourn 2, 157, 166, 20 204
Mouth 107, 120, 124, 126, 137, 175, 182, 191, 193, 203, 205
Moved 162, 172, 175, 186
Multiply 46, 122
Murmurings 111, 112 194
Muscles (see strength, flesh)

N

Naaman 145
Nahum 228
Name 60, 130, 163, 180, 181, 199, 231
Nathanael 59
Nature 227, 230, 231
Navel 189
Nebuchadnezzar 216, 217, 219, 220
Need 37, 77, 90
Nehemiah 153, 154
Nerves 22
New 96, 200, 208, 213, 215
New Testament 1
Name 60, 130, 134, 163, 167, 180, 181, 184, 185, 199, 231
Nobleman's son 43
Nose (see face, breath)
Nourish 105, 135
Numbers 116

O

Obedience 77, 125
Offend 186
Oil 89, 136, 141
Old 169, 225
Old Testament 99
Oneness 51, 159
Open 195, 208
Oppressed 193, 196, 203
Organic (see heart, kidney, eye, ear, etc.)
Outward man 80
Overcome 95, 173, 203

P

Pain 11, 22, 23, 68, 103, 118, 119, 142, 156, 173, 192
Palsy (Paralysis) 1 14, 15, 63, 66
Panic 151
Paralysis 1, 14, 15, 63, 66, 135
Pardon 114, 151
Parts 85
Passover 57, 108
Past 192
Pastors 84
Path 163, 164, 186, 189, 200, 203, 227
Patience 91, 169
Paul 64, 68, 69, 71, 72, 74, 86
Peace 56, 58, 75, 82, 83, 85, 86, 87, 91, 110, 116, 169, 170, 189, 202, 204, 205, 207, 212, 224, 228
Peniel 103
Perfect 1, 2, 10, 82, 84, 91, 93, 123, 132, 134, 170, 181, 182, 187, 189, 196
Perform 159, 160, 174, 214
Perish 33, 35, 43, 51, 80, 155, 160, 169, 186, 198
Persecution 64, 76, 82
Persistence 7, 23, 49
Pestilence 134, 149, 179
Peter 3, 9, 18, 21, 39, 40, 57, 59, 62, 63, 66, 67, 92
Petitions 94, 163, 222
Pharaoh 105, 106, 109, 124, 125
Pharisees 4, 5, 6, 15, 20, 30, 31, 36, 50
Philip 46, 55, 63
Philippians 86
Physicians 18, 29, 150
Pilate 24, 35
Pillar of Cloud 109, 117
Pillar of Fire 109
Pit 160, 166, 170, 197
Plagues 15, 19, 33, 107, 118, 134, 179, 225
Pneumonia (see con tagion)
Poison 26, 73, 140, 144
Polio (see contagion)
Pollution 110
Poor 1, 5, 29, 33, 157, 168
Possessed 17, 69
Potiphar 104
Power 4, 16, 19, 22, 28, 29, 30, 33, 34, 56, 61, 75, 76, 78, 82, 84, 85, 87, 88, 89, 90, 96, 157, 159, 161, 172, 175, 176, 177, 178, 197, 201, 206, 208, 220, 221
Praise 123, 131
Prayer 7, 11, 22-24, 26, 30, 31, 35, 64, 67, 69, 74, 91, 101, 119, 134, 137, 143, 149-152, 160, 163, 173, 178, 196, 222, 226
Pregnant (see birth)
Prepare 28, 113, 230
Presence 81, 114, 163, 171, 181, 187, 224
Preservation 102, 108, 138, 146, 158, 168, 170, 171, 184, 188, 201, 221
Priests 37, 113
Principalities 76, 85
Prison 5, 67-70, 188, 198, 199, 201, 207
Promise 27, 79, 90, 91, 93, 101, 102, 106, 127, 131, 134
Proofs 5, 12, 33, 34, 39, 40, 49, 54, 58, 60, 61, 62, 148
Prophecy 5, 28, 29, 77, 127, 225
Prophet 6, 21, 27-29, 32, 39, 40, 46, 50, 84, 90, 117, 123, 125, 137, 139, 141, 145, 147, 152, 196, 204, 205
Prosperity 95, 104, 124, 126, 153, 157 161, 169
Protection 56, 85, 107, 150, 221
Proverbs 189
Psalms 161
Psoriasis (see skin disease)
Publius 74
Pure 2, 93, 110, 132, 140, 146, 159, 228, 230
Purges 172, 230
Purpose 76, 192, 201

Q

Quails 110, 182
Quietness 194, 206

R

Rage 146, 172, 191, 218
Rain 92, 135, 136, 137, 141, 178, 202
Ransomed 195, 225
Rebellious 176, 183, 202
Rebukes 33, 227
Recompense 129, 195, 206
Reconciled 81, 104
Recovers 26, 29, 118, 146, 196, 197, 205
Red Sea 109, 118
Redemption 39, 76, 96, 157, 159, 167, 172, 182, 183, 195, 198, 199, 201, 203, 208, 225
Reflection 104, 115
Refuge 125, 129, 171, 172, 174, 179, 181, 206
Rejoice 149, 150, 162, 163, 166, 175, 184, 191, 195, 197, 204, 229
Relief 81, 188, 192
Remembrance 56, 137, 175, 192, 201

Remission 28, 41
Renewal 80, 182, 197
Repentance 19, 28, 35, 41, 121, 225
Rescued 83, 87
Resist 93
Resources 46
Rest 5, 90, 151, 158, 169, 173, 206
Restored 16, 17, 31, 32, 37, 135, 137, 148, 161, 164, 202, 203, 206, 208, 211, 225
Resurrection 4, 18, 24, 25, 32, 38, 52-54, 58, 60, 62, 63, 66, 71, 72, 137, 142, 148
Retaliation 34, 37
Revelation 95
Revive 17, 68, 137, 202, 224
Rewards 7, 23, 129, 132, 133, 179, 195
Rheumatism (see joints, pain, deformity)
Riches 9, 10, 20, 133, 182
Right 209, 211
Righteousness 3, 38, 85, 89, 90, 132, 133, 159, 160, 163, 164, 167-170, 180, 184, 188, 190, 192, 194, 198-200, 203, 209, 210, 231
River 97, 146, 161, 168, 172, 195, 198, 199, 204, 212, 214
Rock 112, 131, 132, 165, 170, 175, 178, 181, 183
Rod 106, 112
Romans 74
Run 189, 197, 229
Ruth 129

S

Sabbath 31, 36, 44, 45, 50
Safety 7, 29, 72, 73, 150, 151, 164, 211, 212, 217, 218, 221, 222
Salvation 60, 62, 70, 81-92, 96, 110, 123, 131, 132, 151, 161-188, 208, 226, 228
Samaritan 37
Samson 127
I Samuel 130
Sanctuary 116, 117, 214
Sarah 101, 102
Satan 6, 16, 156
Satisfy 163, 164, 168, 169, 175, 180, 182, 183, 188, 203, 225
Saul 64, 65, 130
Saviour 85, 86, 88, 193, 200, 225
Scales 65, 229
Scalp (see skin)
Science 216
Scripture 28, 29, 40, 57, 224
Sea 124, 137, 184
Sennacherib 149, 151, 152
Serpents 26, 43, 106, 119
Servant 31, 37, 167
Sheep 51, 108
Shepherd 164, 211
Shield 85, 125, 130, 131, 132, 165, 167, 178, 179
Shine 97, 114, 115, 158
Shipwreck 33, 72, 73
Shoe 124, 125
Shoulders 192
Shout 229
Shunammite 142, 143, 144, 148
Side 58, 59, 67
Sighing 156, 195
Sight 3, 4, 6, 10, 21, 23, 49-51, 64, 65, 80, 194
Signs 42, 43, 48, 62, 63, 107, 124, 125, 135, 193, 196, 202, 206, 210, 223
Silas 69
Silent 166, 181
Sin 14, 15, 28, 30, 35, 41, 44, 49, 50, 74, 83, 92, 114, 117, 119, 120, 165, 197, 208, 210
Sinews 158, 213
Sing 91, 162, 166, 180, 195, 229
Skeleton (see bones)
Skill 216, 217
Skin 4, 5, 14, 29, 33, 37, 114, 115, 145, 158, 159, 213
Slavery 104, 109, 113, 115, 122, 192
Sleep 71, 158, 160, 162, 186, 189, 212
Smallpox (see contagion)
Snake Bite 118
Snare 179, 190
Sneeze 143
Solitary 183, 195
Solomon 133
Son 22, 27, 32, 97, 101, 102, 127, 137, 142, 144, 148, 209
Son of David 3, 6, 8, 10, 23
Son of God 94
Son of Man 43
Song 166, 185
Sores 149, 156
Sorrow 2, 96, 154, 192, 195
Soul 60, 63, 78, 123, 163, 164, 186
Soundness 62, 88, 180
Source 20, 45, 54, 76, 107
Speak 120, 123, 190, 194, 204, 210, 229
Speech 4, 6, 20, 107, 120, 194, 204
Spine 36
Spirit 6, 28, 48, 75, 76, 77, 78, 80, 83, 84, 139, 140, 158, 160, 182, 187, 191, 213, 225
Spot 158
Spring 140, 198, 199, 200, 201, 203
Stammerers 194
Stand 151, 163, 192
Standard 203
Steps 170, 189
Sting 79
Stone 12, 24, 25, 52, 53, 54, 57, 68, 112, 130, 180
Storm 7, 33, 47, 72
Straight 28, 36, 199
Strength 84, 125, 126, 151, 153, 154, 159, 165, 171, 177-179, 194, 197, 198
Stripes 69, 70, 92
Strive 6, 148
Stroke 159, 194 (see also paralysis, heart)
Stronghold 227, 228
Strong Man 6
Stumble 165, 189
Substance 187
Success 126
Suck 204
Suffering 79, 93
Suicide 138
Sun 96, 97, 178, 201, 231
Sunstruck 142
Supply 8, 9, 20, 30, 46, 102, 103, 111, 112, 122, 136, 138, 141, 144, 164
Surgery, Mental 37
Survival 102
Sustenance 37, 113, 136, 162
Sweet 110, 189
Swim 146, 215
Swollen 73
Sword 76, 85, 90, 116, 119, 125, 130, 152, 157, 190, 225, 227
Syria 146

T

Tabitha 66
Taught 29, 30, 34
Taxes 9

Teaching 5, 107, 164, 185, 191
Teaching to Heal 16
Tears 95, 96, 185, 196
Teeth 22, 198, 209
Tempest 33, 72
Temptation 91, 124
Ten Commandments 114
Tender Mercies 182
Terror 40, 123, 179
Thanksgiving 37, 80, 87, 166, 180, 181, 184, 185, 222
Thessalonians 87
Thigh 103
Thinking 3, 76, 170, 180, 181, 187, 192
Thirst 2, 48, 96, 110, 112, 152, 183, 195, 198, 201
Thomas 52, 54, 58, 59
Thorn 82
Throne 96, 179
Time 21, 26, 36
Timothy 88
Titus 88, 89
Toes (see feet)
Tongue 6, 20, 23, 25, 26, 27, 107, 190, 191, 194, 195, 202
Torments 1, 16, 22, 63, 71, 94
Touch 15, 19, 20, 37, 58, 157
Tower in Siloam 35
Transfigured 21
Transform 76
Transgressions 209, 210
Translation 87, 139
Transportation 47
Treasure 113
Treatments 21
Tree 95, 97, 110, 161, 189, 191, 198, 212, 215
Trembling 64, 123, 173, 223
Tribulation 76, 79, 95
Tried 92, 132, 159
Triumph 154, 180
Troubled 80, 82, 92, 156, 157, 165, 170-172, 180, 183, 184, 228
True 96, 127
Trust 6, 80, 83, 131, 132, 152, 162, 163, 166, 167, 168, 170, 173, 177, 179, 189, 206, 220, 228
Truth 49, 54, 84, 85, 95, 133, 137, 164, 171, 172, 174, 179, 181, 188, 189, 196, 197, 207, 224
Tumor 142
Turn 208, 210, 226
Twelve 19, 34

U

Unbelief 23
Unchanging 230
Unclean 13, 15, 16, 19, 31, 63, 127, 128, 195, 213
Unconscious 22, 68, 71
Understanding 20, 40, 133, 153, 154, 158, 159, 186, 188, 189, 190, 191, 193, 194, 197, 199, 216, 217
Unfettered 230
Upright 132, 133, 163, 170

V

Vain 207
Vanity 75
Vessel 64, 141
Victory 79, 96
Vigilant 93
Violence 157
Viper sting 73
Vision 3, 50, 64
Voice 4, 6, 20, 26, 27, 51, 172, 176, 211
Vomited 227

W

Wait 169, 175
Walking 5, 6, 7, 44, 61, 68, 83, 84, 124, 133, 134, 174, 178, 182, 189, 197, 230
Wall 110, 119, 153
Want 46, 164, 167
War 150, 157, 165, 172, 198, 227
Wash 49, 96, 145, 146, 172
Waste 136, 179
Water 6, 41, 97, 103, 112, 131, 146, 164, 203, 214
Way 54, 64, 113, 114, 159, 164, 183, 189, 195, 199, 200, 206, 208, 211, 227, 230
Weakness 78, 82, 90, 156, 162, 195
Wealth 10
Weary 197, 202
Weather 33, 72, 92
Wedding 41
Weeping 18, 32, 53, 58, 66, 103, 154, 166, 196
Whirlwind 139, 140, 198
Whole 7, 8, 19, 20, 32, 37, 44, 191
Wickedness 85, 150, 158, 182
Widow 29, 32, 136, 141, 188, 231
Wilderness 102, 103, 109, 111, 112, 113, 119, 124, 135, 138, 177, 195, 198, 200, 212
Wind 7, 33, 47, 91, 110, 138, 141, 214
Wine 41, 127
Wings 113, 129, 168, 173, 174, 175, 179, 187, 197, 231
Wisdom 91, 157, 158, 172, 182, 189, 190, 217
Withered 11, 31, 44, 135
Witnesses 41, 45, 46, 193, 199, 200
Woman of Canaan 8
Womb 122, 201, 204
Women 12, 38, 39, 96
Wonders 69, 184, 225
Word 29, 30, 32, 41, 49, 55, 71, 77, 80, 85, 88, 90, 113, 117, 120, 123, 124, 132, 135-137, 156, 160, 173, 183-186, 189, 190, 200, 205, 227
Works 2, 5, 45, 47, **48**, 49, 54, 55, 84, 86, 88, 89, 91, 114, 122, 153, 170, 172, 177, 180, 182, 183, 184, 185, 187, 192, 193, 200, 206
Wounds 188, 194, 206, 225
Wrath 29, 145, 155, 169, 190
Wrestle 103
Wrist 31

Y

Yoke 192, 203, 224, 228
Young man 9, 71, 225

Z

Zacharias 26
Zebedee 12
Zechariah 230
Zephaniah 229